My Birding Big Year and Beyond

Jane Neskey

ISBN 978-1-63874-446-7 (paperback)
ISBN 978-1-68517-149-0 (hardcover)
ISBN 978-1-63874-447-4 (digital)

Christian Faith Publishing, Inc.
832 Park Avenue
Meadville, PA 16335
www.christianfaithpublishing.com

Printed in the United States of America

I want to dedicate this book in memory of my dear sweet sister Rebecca, who passed away in 2020 after a long and hard battle with cancer. She was my main supporter, and this book exists due to her support. Back in 2012, when I first began writing my birding stories and sharing them with family via emails, she told me, "Jane, these stories are great. You should put them together as a book!" She told me to be sure to save copies and that she would help me through the process of getting it published.

Family always came first to her, and she was always there to help any of us with anything we needed. She was always fun to be around and brought smiles to us all. My sister was a very caring person who volunteered to various organizations to protect our environment and nature's creatures. I am grateful to have so many wonderful memories of time spent together. She will be greatly missed by many. May she rest in peace.

Contents

Introduction

This book is a collection of short stories about my birding adventures across New England and further with family and friends. I am grateful that I inherited a small one-room cabin on a lake in the Great North Woods of New Hampshire—surely has been a location of many great adventures and memories. My stories are not just about the birds we saw but also about sharing time together out in nature, the lessons learned and memories made.

I come from a large family; I have five siblings. I was raised to enjoy the outdoors, to respect Mother Nature and all of God's creatures. When raising my own children, I strived to instill those same values in them. I am proud of the adults my son and daughter have become, the careers they chose, and the positive path through life they have taken. I tried to set a good example by volunteering my time to various organizations focused on protecting our environment and all its creatures. Hopefully by sharing my birding adventures with others, I can help inspire them to take time to enjoy and protect the world of nature around them.

Not uncommon for a large family as we each grew up some left our hometown. We each got married and started our own families. Some joined the military, and others followed that good job, spreading us all across the country. After my parents passed, we did start the tradition of a family reunion to gather once a year at the family cabin in the Great North Woods of New Hampshire. I always knew I was welcome to visit family any time but indeed my birding adventures inspired me to overcome my anxiety and get on a plane to visit family and new places and look for birds!

Enjoy reading about my adventures from 2012 to 2020; some are silly some are serious.

My Big Year

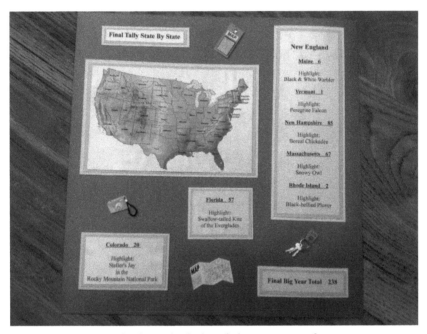

I made this, I had placed the majority of my
stories into a scrapbook I made.

This chapter is where all the craziness started, the year I decided to compete in a Birding Big Year competition! The adventures I had and the fun times spent with friends and family exploring nature. So many experiences I never would have had if it weren't for my hobby of birding. All while counting the birds I saw, hoping to rack my numbers up.

Stiff Competition

I just returned from a winter birding trip to the Parker River National Wildlife Refuge on Plum Island. I was there last weekend in the snow and cold but was rewarded with a sighting of the snowy owl. This weekend, the temperature was a good twenty-five degrees warmer, and I was hoping to get another look at the snowy owl, plus see more of the many migratory birds of the refuge.

When we arrived early, we were surprised to see the first parking lot almost full. We pulled in thinking there must be something interesting to see to draw all these people. It's kind of like mooseing in Pittsburg, New Hampshire, when you see cars pulled over you stop to see what everyone is looking at. Often, I feel kind of weird walking around with my binoculars hanging from my neck and my birding bag with bird book handy slung across my shoulder; I get some strange stares. But not today! Today, the parking lot was full of fellow birders with backpacks, bird books, binoculars, and spotting scopes. My husband John even mentioned all the different license plates; there were cars from Maine, Rhode Island, Connecticut, Pennsylvania, New York, Massachusetts, New Hampshire, and Vermont. I knew it was big news to hear that there were three snowy owls spending the winter on the refuge, but wow, some people are sure serious about adding to their life lists. People were jumping out of one car and piling in together in a single car then rushing off down the refuge roads. There sure was a strange vibe going on that I would understand later on.

We pulled over at a cleared area along the salt marsh, I could see a few birders set up with spotting scopes and walked up to see what was there. I said hello to a man set up with two pairs of binoculars around his neck, a spotting scope, and a video camera set up. I asked

14

him if he had seen anything interesting, he gave me a stare and then moved to in front of this equipment and says, "Everything is interesting to me." I didn't get it. Do I look threatening or something? Did he think I was going to steal his equipment? Usually, birders are such a friendly group his reaction to me didn't make sense.

I walked farther along the trail and came upon a man with a spotting scope talking on a cell phone. He was calling out coordinates. "I'm to the east...flock heading toward you at six o'clock... you got them? Great! Competition was incredible this year. There are teams from the whole northeast here...meet you at Hellcat Trail... Out."

I said "hi" and walked on. He says nothing back to me, and he gives me this deep stare. I'm getting confused. I climb the observation tower; there are four guys set up with spotting scopes, talking. It's a small platform; I can't help but listen. They are writing on a clipboard; the conversation I overhear goes like this: "How we doing? Not bad, I think we are catching up on the female team...I think we should get extra points for spotting rare species...yeah, but the rules don't go that way you only get one point for each different species we see...darn, here comes the biker team!" I turn and see four guys on mountain bikes pull up.

Okay, now I'm going to figure out what's up here; there was obviously a competition of some sort going on. There was a refuge ranger parked on the side of the trail. People are walking past him and showing him papers. I'm tempted to talk to him, but he was busy, so I move on. We stop at a few more sites, and this craziness continues. We hike out to a salt marsh blind and the "biker team" was also there. One of them has a spotting scope, and the others are looking through binoculars. The guy on the scope calls out, "Buffleheads at three o'clock...got it, the others call out...redhead in the reeds at seven o'clock...got it, they all call back."

I walk right up and say, "Hi, I'm not on any team. I'm just trying to enjoy the birds. What have you spotted out there." Finally, some friendly birders. Once they understood I was not any competition to their team, they shared their spotting scope, and I got to see a redhead and a northern pintail.

It was a great day of birding, the weather was unbelievable for January, temps in the high forties, and sunny. It was fun to be among so many enthusiastic birders. I admit I would have joined in on the bird count competition if I had known it was going on, but at least the strange behavior of my fellow birders made sense now. There certainly was some stiff competition on the island today. I myself added three more new species to my life list as well as another sighting of the snowy owl.

Let the Counting Begin!

February 12, 2012

After my exciting day on Plum Island, I did do some research and found out that the event going on that day was the Super Bowl of birding. It was a competition sponsored by a local Audubon Society group where at the end of the day, whichever team saw the most different species of birds on the refuge won a trophy, awarded at a dinner held at the end of the day. It sure looked like everyone competing was having a lot of fun.

The whole experience inspired me to make 2012 my Big Year. A Big Year is a birding competition where a birder counts all the different species they see in one calendar year. The current title holder has 748 sightings; his record has been held since 1998.

I realize I have little chance of getting anywhere close to those numbers; the average birder in the competition ranks in the five hundreds. My current life list count is only around 180, with this year's count at only 33, but what the heck, I'm going to try.

This may be the year for me to reach my personal best, with my annual trip to Florida to visit with family coming up soon. I began researching the birds of the Florida Everglades. I hope to add a few new birds to my life list. And I look forward to a trip to JN Ding Darling National Wildlife Refuge on Sanibell Island. I need to spot the Roseate spoonbill! Florida certainly does offer a lot of birding opportunities.

I have never really been much of a traveler; honestly, flying on a plane makes me very nervous. I am lucky to have so many great places to visit here in New England on a day trip. But I am a bit of a competitive person, and the challenge to see more birds and rack up my count was an incentive to get on a plane! So my birding adventures have opened my eyes to many new life experiences, more than just about counting birds.

Covert Operation

February 16, 2012

I have worked at our local school as a lunch lady since my children were young. I'm an empty nester now but still enjoy working in the school. The great hours offer me plenty of off time to enjoy my hobby of birding. One day, it was such a mild day, coming home from work that I rode with my window down. As I was driving along, I heard the excited chatter of a familiar bird. Although it was acceptable to count a bird you have heard but not seen as a species in your Big Year count, I felt I had to at least try to spot the birds. So I decided to turn around and try to spot the birds. I pulled over and got out my binoculars and leaned over to try and see the birds out the passenger side window.

But as I was on the right side of the road and so wasn't the yard the birds were in; I couldn't see them high in the tree. I backed up a bit and tried again to see them through the front window, but this time, I was looking straight up into the sun. I decided to drive forward and turn around in the next driveway then head back in the direction I started. I pulled over to the side of the road and leaned out my window with my binoculars. It was a whole flock of European starlings; they were squawking and tweeting and hopping among the bare tree branches. The sun was hitting their feathers and their iridescent colors were shimmering in the sun. I was enjoying watching them, but when I lowered my binoculars, I noticed that the home-owner was standing on her porch with her arms folded staring at me. Oops!

I pointed up toward the noisy flock and quickly drove away. Perhaps it was only a coincidence but only a short distance up the road a police cruiser was heading toward me, lights flashing! I looked straight ahead and drove on. I got one more species to add to my list! Thinking about the homeowner's reaction, I realized I certainly did look suspicious. Lesson learned: next time, I guess I will have to conduct a more covert urban birding operation. Or I could become a jailbird!

Wanderlust

February 20, 2012

Saturday was a great birding day! Thanks to my brother-in-law Mark for passing along the Boston Globe article on the rare bird spotted on Cape Cod. A lazuli bunting had been seen at Wellfleet Bay Wildlife Sanctuary. This bird lives in Mexico and the southwestern US, so to spot one in New England was big news. My sister Chris and my friend Beth agreed to travel to Cape Cod with me in search of this rare bird.

I called the sanctuary to be sure the bird was still there and where would be the best place to find it. The bird was there, and they said it was a regular visitor to the feeders in the courtyard. Now this was Chris's kind of birding. We didn't even have to leave the building; we just had to wait by the windows till it arrived to feed. After the cold sandblasted wind, I made her trek through in search of the snowy owl on Plum Island she deserved an easy find.

We arrived midmorning and staked out a good viewing spot by the large windows. As time went by, the crowd grew. There were old and young, men and women some with high-powered cameras and others with binoculars, all with high hopes of seeing this rare bird. We waited a least forty-five minutes, but nothing. I moved about the crowd listening to the theories of how and why this bird got to be on the cape. Some thought it might have arrived on a boat by mistake and flew off at the first sight of land. Others thought maybe someone was in the black-market trade of exotic birds, and this one got away. Still, another man was going on about it being global warming and the earth being off its axis, and well, he was getting kind of out there, so I moved away from him.

Without realizing it, I had gotten to the back of the crowd, which had now become three deep at the window. Then it happened.

A man called out, "There it is!" The crowd surged to the window binoculars raised. I heard oohs and ahhs, but I can't see. I jumped up and down, trying to see above the crowd. I found myself saying, "I can't see! I can't see!" A nice man backed up and let me get up closer; pointing, he told me the bird is on the ground to the right of the feeder. I strained to see it; I turned and asked the man, "You mean that little tan bird on the ground? I was expecting it to be blue?"

I was disappointed. I was expecting the bird to be brilliant blue, white breast with a blue and rust bib. This was a scruffy tan bird. I mean I got up at the crack of dawn on my day off, dragged my sister and friend on a three-hour drive to see this? The man tells me it was a first year male (aka teenage bird) to look as it moves into the sun, and I'll see the blue. He was right now I could see the blue tail feathers, the dusty blue and tan bib and some tufts of blue on his head. Gee, after all, this little guy made one heck of a long trip from home, so he deserved to look scruffy.

I came up with my own theory of how he got on to Cape Cod. I think it was time for him to leave his parents' nest. He didn't know what he wanted to do with his life. The wind was blowing northeast, and he let wanderlust carry him forward. I hope he makes it.

We walked a beautiful trail along the salt marsh, saw twenty-seven species of birds! It was a great day of birding. Great weather. Great company. My Big Year total was now forty-six and counting.

Needle in a Haystack

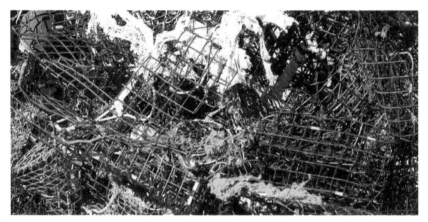

This is a Cape May Warbler.

The NH Rare Bird hotline *(yes, there is a hotline, I have it on my speed dial)* said there was a sighting of a Cape May warbler along Rye Beach, so I thought I'd drive up and look for it. I live in southern New Hampshire and having easy access to the ocean or the mountains is one of my favorite perks of my state. The New Hampshire coastline is not very long; I enjoyed the drive along the rocky coast watching the waves crashing on the rocks sending spray high into the air. I arrived at the location the Hotline said to park and sure enough it was packed with vehicles. Luckily, I found a spot to park and unpacked my binos and birding backpack and headed off along the trail to reach the open coastline and search for this rare bird.

I didn't get far along the trail when I noticed a group of four coming toward me—a man, a woman, and two children. They all had backpacks on and the adults both had binoculars hanging around their necks, that told me they were defiantly fellow birders. They politely stopped and moved to the side of the trail to let me pass them. I thanked them and asked the children, "You see anything interesting?" The little girl excitingly jumped up and down, flapping her arms, and was whistling a melodious tune. Then she told me, "I saw the bird and heard it singing!" The young boy stepped in front of her and told me loudly, "I saw it first!"

The woman (presumably their mom) told them to calm down. She then asked me, "I see you have binoculars are you looking for birds?" I tell her yes, that I was hoping to see the Cape May warbler. The man then tells me, "Good luck, it's going to be a needle in a haystack!" He explains to me how to find the bird. He said the tide was getting high and that the bird was among a pile of busted up lobster traps and washed-up debris along the shoreline. He tells me to focus on the contents of the lobster traps and watch for movement, again he tells me, "It's hard to see!" We talked for a little while; it was nice to see a family out on a cold February day enjoying nature. Then I continued on, as I walked away the young boy yells to me, "Good luck finding the needle!"

I soon reached the end of the trail and came upon the open shoreline. No surprise with the parking area being so full there were a number of people lined up along the beach. Many of them were setup with fancy cameras on tripods and focused on the sand dunes and scrub brush along the shoreline. I considered going over to see what they were all looking at, but I remembered the advice the man I had met on the trail had given me. He told me to go right when I got to the end of the trail, toward the rocks and look for the washed-up lobster traps.

So that's the direction I went. Sure enough, only a few yards up the shoreline, I saw hidden among the rocks two battered-up lobster traps and a pile of seaweed. Certainly wasn't a spot I would have gone to look for a bird. But *bingo*! I suddenly saw movement and focused my binoculars on the debris pile.

There it was—a Cape May warbler! I watched for a while as the little bird flew in and out of the debris pile and snatched up the brine flies. At one point, it even sat on top of one of the lobster traps and sang his beautiful song loud and clear. What a great sighting thanks to a fellow birder, I got to add another new bird to my Big Year list.

When I got back to the head of the trail, I went toward the group of people I had seen earlier.

I wave and yell, "Hello, what are you all looking at?"

One of the men tells me, "We are looking for a rare bird that is supposed to be here somewhere." I ask him if the bird he is trying to find happens to be the Cape May warbler. Yup, that's the bird they were all searching for. I tell them I just saw it and direct them to the area among the rocks. They thank me, gather all their gear, and head toward the rocks.

I told them, "Good luck finding that needle in a haystack!"

Florida State Bird

March 5, 2012

Well, I just returned from a great birding trip to Florida! Since my job at a school gives me February vacation week off, I have been escaping the cold New England winters for a few years now. My trips are made possible by the generous hospitality of my oldest sister Sissy and brother-in-law Bill. So I guess you can call me a snowbird?

We returned to Oscar Scherer State Park, which is one of the last areas in the state to find the Florida scrub jay. I saw them last year but needed to see them again to count them for this year. It was very hot and humid, eighty-eight and blaring sun. We took off on the green trail, about a two-mile loop through the scrub pines and grasslands. As we entered the trail, I noticed a large black vulture sitting on a dead tree branch, I swear it was watching us as we passed by. Sissy joked, "Don't fall down, or he'll get ya."

The heat and sun were scorching, we would stand in the meager shade of one scrub pine then make a run for it through the blazing sun to the next bit of shade. Meanwhile, that vulture also moved from tree to tree following us. Very creepy, it was so hot, so still, not a sound at all, except for the shrill call of a red-shouldered hawk circling high on the thermals above us. And that vulture never stopped staring at us silently.

We were out on the trail about an hour, the sweat dripping down my face into my eyes. I could barely see in my binoculars because my eyes were stinging from the sweat. But Sissy was being so patient helping me search for that bird. At one point, we could hear them calling and just make out a blur of movement in the dense bushes. I was ready to venture into the bulrushes to search for them, but Sissy said, "No way! There's all sorts of snakes and biting creepy crawlies in those bushes. Stay on the trail!"

Now it is in the rules that you can count a bird if you only hear it but don't see if you have a witness. Sissy agreed to vouch for me that I had seen the bird before and that we heard it this year, so I could count it. Since that vulture was still following us with his eyes, and I swear licking his chops (well, if he had chops to lick, I think he would; maybe it was just the heat waves) I agreed with Sissy, and we headed back. When we recounted the day's events to Bill and about the black vulture eyeing us, Bills straight faced remark was, "Well, you know that's the Florida State bird they are everywhere waiting!" Believe me his sense of humor is as sharp as ever. For the record the Florida State bird is the mockingbird.

I may not have seen the Florida scrub jay, but I did see an amazing amount of beautiful birds. Including the delicate magnolia warbler that visited us during our picnic lunch, the frantic Ruddy Turnstones that darted about on the beach and the graceful swallow-tailed kite we saw in the everglades. My grand total for my Big Year count was now up to 101! Thank you so much, Sissy and Bill, for a wonderful vacation.

Epic Fail

March 11, 2012

After having time to decompress from my wonderful birding vacation to Florida, I came upon the answer to why we didn't see the Florida scrub jay. Now I know most (well, maybe all) of you really don't care, but I thought I would offer myself up to ridicule and laughter for my mistake.

A little background info for you, the Florida scrub jay is a threatened species that has only a few areas in Florida left to live. Like most jays, they are noisy, curious and smart but humans are destroying their habitat. So picture this: Sissy and I travel to one of the last safe havens for the Florida scrub jay. It was a very hot and humid day; the sun was blazing. In the parking lot, I asked a fellow birder if they had seen the Florida scrub jay and was told they had seen a family with a young one on the green trail. So off Sissy and I go, what great news to know there was pair with a young jay, offering hope for their future.

John gave me a Nook for Christmas, and I am still getting used to it. I downloaded a great Audubon Birding App that I love, it has multiple pictures and range maps and best of all sounds. Now it's not considered fair game to use the sound app to call in birds, the experts say it confuses the birds and can stress them out. But hey it's crunch time here, these birds are on the decline, I'm only here for the day I'm gonna use every trick I can.

We get out on the trail away from anyone else. Sissy holds out her hand with peanuts in it as an offering to the jays, this worked like a charm last year. I hold my Nook high over my head and repeatedly press the sound button for the Florida scrub jay hoping to draw one into view. But we struck out. The birds were there, in the bush but never came into view. *Now* I know why!

In my haste to lure the jays into view, I had been repeatedly pushing the wrong call sound. I was pressing over and over again the "alarm call," not the mating call. It worked perfectly, I was screaming to the jays, "Danger, danger! Take cover and hide!" which they did very well. And I had been calling to the vulture that had been eying us, "Dinner, dinner come and get it!" it's any wonder that vulture was following us.

So I blew it; I may not get another chance to see the beautiful Florida scrub jay whose numbers are dwindling. Another lesson learned: Haste makes waste. Go ahead laugh at me I deserve it. *Epic fail!*

Current Big Year bird count was now at 108.

Blaze Orange

I just returned from a great weekend birding at my cabin in Pittsburg, New Hampshire. The old cabin made it through another winter in one piece. Sad to say, though, that the mounted grouse we had hanging up on the wall didn't. It seems the flying squirrel picked all the breast feathers off the poor thing to use for its nest. Well, at least the flying squirrel was warm for the winter.

The first day we got there it was damp and cool, but I wasn't going to let that get in my way of birding. I headed out down the trail; the snow was about midcalf, not to bad but still tuff to walk through. So I started to follow a deer trail that was more packed down. The snow was crunchy and made noise as I walked, so I would stop now and then to listen for birds. I noticed some coyote tracks in the snow; they had a little rain collecting in them, so I was confident they were old.

I stopped a few times and could hear a flock of pine siskins in the bush. But I also thought I heard something crunching in the snow off to my right, umm, perhaps the coyote? Suddenly the flock of birds flew across the trail into a group of dense spruce trees. I followed them, breaking through the deep snow. I got up under the spruce boughs that were being held down by the snow and entered a little area free from snow. There in the branches above me was a flock of about twenty-four pine siskins, and they were flitting about and singing. I felt like I was in a birdcage; it was a magical feeling. But wait…there was definitely something crunching in the snow coming toward me.

At first, I thought it might be a coyote but the crunching in the snow was too loud for a small coyote. Maybe it was a deer, but no the sound was loud, something heavy…maybe a moose? No, the stride of whatever was making the noise was too short to be a large long-legged moose. OMG…OMG…it must be a bear!

Okay, so I calmed down and weighed my options. There was no way I can out run a bear in this deep snow. So I decided I'll climb the tree. I know bears can climb, so I figured I'll use my binoculars to swing and bop him in the nose. My heart was racing. I'm reaching for the branches, ready to climb. I can see something coming toward me…the branches are moving… It's got blue legs…and a blaze orange body…and a gun? It's a pair of hunters! They enter my little cage under the tree, and he says, "Aya…lost are ya?" I could tell by his thick French Canadian accent that he was a local. I explain that I'm not lost I was just birding and had followed the pine siskins into the spruce trees. I tell him I didn't realize it was still hunting season.

He tells me, "Rabbit till the end of the month." I apologize for not wearing my blaze orange and thank them for not firing at me, he replies, "You're a mite big for a rabbit, eh?"

The other hunter tells me, "Weathers a changing might wanna take cover, eh?" I thank them for their advice and start back down the deer trail toward the cabin. The two hunters head off in the opposite direction; as they walk away, I look back and see one of them shaking his head. I don't need to hear him to know what he was saying…"flatlanders." That's what the locals call anyone who lives below the notches.

All in all, it was a great weekend. I saw some new birds including the fantastic white-winged crossbill! You have got to look this bird up to appreciate my sighting. So let's recap what have we learned from my birding adventures so far. That I have to be careful where I point my binoculars or I might get arrested. That I need to learn how to correctly use my Nook before I try to fool Mother Nature. And when in the Great North Woods always wear blaze orange! Oh, and I did encounter the coyote late the next day. But he took one look at me and hightailed it in the other direction…ya see, I'm a mite bigger than a rabbit.

Current Big Year total: 112.

Fowl Mood

Well, another weekend means another birding excursion. I listened to the rare bird alert hotline, and checked out the Audubon website, and decided to take a trip to Plum Island in Massachusetts to catch some of the migrating ducks. I studied the bird book, so I would be able to quickly identify any of the new ducks I might see. I got up early Saturday morning to head for the shore.

But as I sat with my morning coffee patting the cat in my lap I wondered, why am I doing this? I mean with the high cost of gas and all the errands and housework I should be doing why am I spending the day traipsing around Plum Island in search of birds? I mean who cares? What difference am I making? This Big Year competition, am I just a joke?

Young or old we have all been there, hit that wall, doubted our efforts, like studying for that test or dieting. You get in a mood where you wonder, "Is it worth it?" Who cares. I was in deed in a very "fowl" mood. Missy bit me, growled and jumped off my lap, so much for improving my mood. I had prepared for the trip and gotten up early, heck the housework can wait till Sunday, I headed for the shore.

I arrived and stopped at the first overlook pool to scan for ducks. An elderly couple pulled up at about the same time. The man gets out of his car and scans the pool and yells to the women, "Northern pintails! Quick, come see!" He does the birders happy dance and gets out his note pad and writes down his sighting. There are a couple of versions of the "birders' happy dance"; the male version usually involves chuckling like Daddy used to and saying something like "Gosh, will ya look at that" in an excited voice. The female version, no surprise, is more animated and usually involves a little jump up and down. I just looked at the flock of Pintails…eh seen them before nothing new. My fowl mood hadn't improved. I move on.

There are a few cars pulled over to the side of the trail, this usually indicates something good has been sighted. I pull over and get out. There are about eight people gathered around with scopes set up and mega camera set ups. There not one hundred yards off the road is a snowy owl sitting atop a small pine tree! A car from Rhode Island pulls up and three twenty somethings jump out, a girl and two guys. They are all excited to see the owl, the girl does the birders happy dance and punches the guy in the arm, saying, "Told ya it would be worth the trip! Now you can add the snowy to your list!" Eh…seen it; my fowl mood hasn't improved I move on.

I spend some time at the bird blind watching a mixed flock of black ducks, mallards, and a lone redhead. Eh…seen them, I decide to move on. As I get to the parking area, a woman from Connecticut pulls in and as she is getting out asks me if there was anything interesting at the blind. I tell her there is a redhead mixed in with some blacks and mallards. She does the birders happy dance and says, "Wow, a redhead! That's a life listers for me how exciting!" She fumbles to get her scope out of the back seat of her car and thanks me as she rushes up the trail. My fowl mood hasn't improved. I move on.

I stop to eat my lunch in the car and wonder why I can't seem to shake this fowl mood. I mean have I become so jaded that I can't enjoy what nature has to share? The day hasn't been a total bore I've seen some new birds: a group of northern shovelers and some horned grebes. But I wanted that thrill of an unexpected sighting, something to take my breath away. I wanted a birders' happy dance sighting.

After lunch, I begin to head back off the preserve. I enjoy talking with other birders and watching a northern harrier eat his lunch of some prey he has torn apart. I decide to stop at Hellcat trails before leaving the island and take a walk along the wetlands boardwalk. I head to the observation tower and then it happens. Yes, I do the birders happy dance! There in the pond is a pair of mute swans gliding across the water. Their magnificent beauty takes my breath away. I've seen swans before but not in the wild. I thought that swans, like flamingos were an ornamental captive breed. But here before me was a grand pair, in the wild, these birds are not small, they're quite impressive.

I head home with my mood much improved. As I drive the hour ride home, memories of all the birders' happy dance moments with family and friends run through my mind. I relive the time when Chris, Beth, and I were in Cape Neddick Maine at my sister's camper on the ocean one September weekend. It was dusk, a beautiful clear night with the full moon shining. We decided to take a walk to the rocky shoreline and enjoy the view when suddenly a large flock of birds fly across the sky in front of us highlighted as they pass in front of the moon! They turn and circle above us, and we identify them as nighthawks. Believe me the three of us excitingly do the birders' happy dance, as do other campers who also saw the majestic sight of nature across the sky. Another moment that came to mind was the time I was visiting Sissy in Florida, and we were sitting on her lanai enjoying the calming view of the lake when suddenly a bald eagle swooped down and grabbed a fish right in front of us! Then it flew straight toward us with the fish in its talons, so close we could see the water dripping off the fish. My sister jumps up and down yelling, "Did you see that?!" For sure her birders' happy dance that time was the best I've ever seen. Remembering that day still made me smile as I drove home along the highway after a spirit lifting day enjoying nature that erased my fowl mood.

Come on now; we all need a birders' happy dance moment now and then.

Current Big Year total: 119.

Slow and Steady

April 2, 2012

Here is a weekly update on my Big Year count. It has been a quiet week of birding, but I was still able to add a few new birds to my list. I spent a very nice day at my youngest sister Becky's new house in Merrimack, New Hampshire, doing some birding. Their new place has really diverse habitats with lots of possibilities for interesting birds. With the pond across the street, the stream running through their property and the old growth wood lot in their backyard attracts many different species. Add to all that natural bounty the welcoming buffet they put out for the birds, and it sure adds up to lots of bird visitors.

I saw mallards in the pond, robins on the lawn, a hairy wood-pecker, downy woodpecker, white-breasted nuthatch, and red-bellied woodpecker at the suet feeder. A pair of northern cardinals, chicka-dees, tufted titmouse, goldfinches, and dark-eyed juncos at the seed feeders. And an eastern phoebe hovering over the stream, catching little flies for lunch.

Becky and my brother-in-law Christopher had seen a mystery bird in the pond a couple of times, but it wasn't there when I was so its identity remains a mystery. Maybe I'll catch sight of it on my next visit. Becky and I also heard a very musical song-tress in the wood lot. Between the two of us and our bird apps we decided it was a winter wren. I won't count that in my Big Year totals till I get to see it. So a return visit to Becky's Park (my nickname for her yard) is indeed needed.

The only bird I saw at Becky's Park that was new that I can count for my Big Year total was the Eastern Phoebe. Though, I did see a pair of eastern bluebirds on a fence in Hudson as I was heading home. And today on my way home from work I saw a northern goshawk perched on a fence post at a Brentwood farm.

Now I know I'm not the only one counting species out there. I may be the most vocal about my intentions but come on, fess up; we all have lists going. Sissy has quite a list going on her Kindle, and Becky showed me her list on her iPad. And I know Beth made a trip out west and has a good list going as well. So what's your number? Me, I'm going at it slow and steady, enjoying every sighting and the bonus of visiting with fellow birders.

Current Big Year total: 122.

Housing Boom

April 16, 2012

Well, spring has sprung in the Great North Woods!

All the birds are busy preparing for a new brood. I watched as the red-breasted nuthatch excavated his nesting cavity in the side of an old pine tree. Do you know that as they are digging into the pine, they smear the sap all around the opening of the hole to keep bugs away from the nest? Pretty ingenious uh. I watched as a golden-crowned kinglet pulled lichen off an oak tree and flew off with a beak full to build his nest. And I watched as a crow made a couple of trips across the lake carrying large sticks in his talons, to build his nest with.

Do you know that you can help out our feathered friends by supplying them with some building materials? Birds love hair to line their nest with, when you clean out your hair brush don't throw the hair away, instead put it on a branch out side for the birds to find. If you groom your cat or dog do the same with their hair. In fact, the chipping sparrow is so dependent on hair to line its nest it has been seen pulling tuffs of hair off a sleeping dog. After all, it's not like the birds can go to the local Home Depot for their building supplies. I always put stuff out for them, even a few cotton balls stuck on a tree branch. You can even buy a nesting ball at bird stores that you can fill with fluff and hang on a tree for the birds to pick at.

I saw a few interesting birds to add to my list like the yellow-bellied sapsucker and the common redpoll, but by far, the best sighting was the boreal chickadee. I have been searching for this little bird for years, way before I was counting for my Big Year. The boreal chickadee lives in the far north and rarely cross the border from Canada to visit the US. I knew if I was to ever get a chance to see this bird it would be in Pittsburg, New Hampshire, at my cabin. So I have always been on the lookout for him. He looks a lot like our favorite black-capped chickadee but has a rusty brown head instead of black and rusty coloring along his sides. He is a fascinating little bird of the north, they store food away like a squirrel would to survive through the long northern winters. Believe me, I was doing the birders' happy dance when I spotted him!

Current Big Year total: 134.

No Woodie for Me

April 23, 2012

Well, I have had a couple of interesting birding days. On Saturday, Beth invited me to join her on a morning bird walk in Nashua. It's a nice walk along the railroad tracks by the river, we were in search of the wood duck that she has seen there. They are an interesting duck, they nest in tree cavities, and you don't expect to see a duck sitting in a tree. Unfortunately, we didn't see the wood duck, so no woodie for me. But I did get to see a yellow-rumped warbler! Spring is here! The warbler migration has begun!

Saturday evening, I was sitting on my deck listening for the barred owl that lives in the woods when a pair of birds flew over my head and into the woods. It was dusk, but I still got a good look at them as they flew over. They were a bit smaller than a dove and thinner, they were dark brown and one had white on its tail feathers. I knew there were only a few choices as to what they could be. I knew they weren't mourning doves, perhaps a nighthawk, but they didn't have the white wing bars nighthawks have. As I was looking through the bird book to identify them, the unmistakable song came from the very area they had just landed.

The clear sound…*whip-poor-will*…*whip-poor-will*…*whip-poor-will*. After all these years of hearing them in the woods, I finally saw them! I remember listening to the Whip-poor-will call as a child in Rhode Island. Together with the description and the song there was no denying I had just seen my first whip-poor-will. Yeah!

Awoke Sunday morning to gray skies, a Nor'easter was due in by afternoon. I figured what the heck I would make a quick run to Plum Island to catch some birds. A storm always brings in the birds. The duck migration is in full swing, and I knew there would be some good sightings there. More than half of the island is closed because of the nesting piping plover, so I was limited on where I could go looking for birds. It was windy and gray but the rain was holding off. Birders on the island were a buzz about snowy owl sightings. I was surprised to hear the owl was still there, I would have thought they would be making the long trek back to the Arctic tundra by now. Everyone was asking me if I had seen the snowy. I never did see the owl, but I did see over three dozen beautiful green-winged Teal and a couple dozen ruddy ducks!

I stopped at the Hell Cat trail and a fellow birder told me there were some purple finches a bit up the trail. I was carefully listening for their song but new bird sounds drew my attention. I never did see the purple finch, but I did get to see the magnolia warbler and palm warbler!

I have had a very productive couple of birding days. I got to see some new birds and plenty of old favorites to add to my Big Year totals. It seems like what I didn't see helped me see what I did see. So I never did see the purple finch or the snowy owl or the wood duck, but the birds that I did see sure made up for it.

As usual on the hour drive home from Plum Island, my mind was racing, thinking about birds and putting together plans for my next birding adventure, who should I visit next? What might I see? As soon as I got home, I sent out a flurry of emails to family and friends to set up dates and times to go birding.

My first email was to my older sister, Sissy and older brother, Dougie, to try to get the answer to an old bird question. I asked them, "Do you remember what kind of bird used to make its nest under the porch in Rhode Island, by the cellar door? I remember when we tried to go into the cellar it would fly out at me. I remember I was fascinated by the nest but boy did that bird scare me every time."

My brother responded, "It was a Robin." Certainly, a common well-known bird to me now but not as a five-year-old.

But it was fun to relive the old times with my family.

Next emails were sent to my younger siblings Chris and Eric, while on the childhood memory tour I asked them, "Do either of you remember when we tried to 'save' the baby blue jay we 'found' out by the summerhouse? Do you remember how the parents dive bombed us trying to protect their baby? We thought we were helping the poor thing, but it died anyways. Of course, now we know the parents would have fed it, and it would have been fine had we just left it alone." They both replied with fun childhood memories we shared.

Next email to my youngest sister, Becky, asked her, "Have you seen or heard the winter wren again? Someone recorded a sighting of a winter wren on the NH Rare Bird Alert hotline. I'd still like to see one, it would be a life lister for me. The pond across the street must be coming more active by now. I think a return trip to Becky's Park is in order! Yup, she replied and plans were made to get together.

Okay, emails sent to siblings now time to widen the circle and reach out to my nieces.

Katie and Shawn, I'm pretty sure the raptor we were hearing at the party was a red-shouldered hawk. I wanted so badly to take off into the woods in search of it, but I didn't want to embarrass your sister in front of her friends. I didn't want them to think I was some anti-social crazy old bird lady, and I really did want to visit with all of you. Look forward to visiting you at your new home soon and explore the birds in your yard!

Liz and Justin, great party! I love your new place, what a nice yard for Ella to grow up in. I see many birding adventures in her future. I look forward to my next visit, but warning this time there will be no holding me back from exploring your back woods.

Jesse, did you ever identify the raptor that you saw and heard in your yard? I'd be glad to come visit and help you identify the birds in your yard!

Tammi, thanks for the info on Nevens Bird Sanctuary. Would you possibly be able to take me there? I don't know Methuen at all. We could meet somewhere. Maybe Saturday? The article said that there was a great horned owl nesting in the great blue heron's rookery. Now this would be a major sighting for me! To see a great horned owl and it's young!

Reaching out to all worked! Arranged multiple dates to get together to do some birding, stories will follow.

Current Big Year total: 140.

Latest Tally

May 1, 2012

Just got back from the cabin, we were up there last week since it was school vacation for the school I work at. Most of the snow was melted, and we were able to drive right up to the cabin. That was a plus at least we didn't have to hike in that last mile. Though, the melting snow did make the old dirt road very slippery mud. Threw the truck into four-wheel mode and made it up the hill! It was nice and sunny temps in the sixties on Thursday, and then wind, cold temps in the twenties and snow on Friday. Very typical weather conditions for Pittsburg in April.

Thankfully we arrived to power on! No trees had fallen and taken down the wires, it is something that happens often at the cabin. It is understandable why since the cabin is nestled in the deep woods on an unmaintained dirt road. No cable, no internet, no TV. One time, the kids did get a weak TV signal, but it was based out of Quebec, Canada, and in French. Interesting to watch but none of us speak French. That is one of the main reasons we love being there, on a lake in the Great North Woods of New Hampshire. Great fishing, hunting, hiking and birding! So many great memories of time spent with family and friends.

The cabin made it through another winter with no major damage. We opened up the cabin turned on the water and luckily there were no broken pipes! Yet another common problem considering the extreme cold and heavy snow that is typical for the area. Unfortunately, there was some damage to the wood siding where a critter of some sort had chewed on the wood leaving gnaw marks. John checked the crawl space under the cabin and sadly he found a dead porcupine. Poor little critter.

Fishing was good for John. The first day there I did put out some cotton balls on a bare tree branch for the nesting birds. Wasn't long before a chickadee flew onto the branch and began pulling at the cotton balls and flew away with one. By the next day, all the cotton balls were gone. That will make for a very comfortable nest lining for them. Birding was good for me, though, the cold weather hampered any new sightings. Just too cold for the warblers that had just migrated back, everybody was hunkered downed against the wind and cold. I did see a Nashville warbler that landed on a branch right outside the cabin window. The wind was ruffling his feathers he looked so cold I felt bad sitting there with a hot cup of coffee, he looked like he wanted in out of the cold.

Current Big Year total: 148.

Haunting Memories

May 4, 2012

Well, this isn't my usual bird story but something I need to share. Some recent events have brought back old haunting memories. I apologize for sharing the depressing events. But sometimes you need to go back in time to understand the future.

In the nineties, I was very involved in town and state politics. I served on my town conservation committee, I was the town representative on the Exeter River Local Advisory Committee (ERLAC) my work to educate and clean up the river earned an award from the governor. I served as my town's representative on the states Rivers Council. I was a citizen observer/volunteer for the NH Audubon Society, the Loon Protection Society and the NH Fish and Game Department, some of my work helped develop legislation to protect birds, turtles, and salamanders in New Hampshire.

I don't share all this to make myself seem important, I'm not. I followed the example of my parents; they were strong believers in helping out community and volunteering. They both were very involved in town affairs and were well respected by their peers. I share all this to make you understand how much I cared about my town and state, of volunteering my time to help people understand the importance of our environment and the creatures we share our lives with. But there was something that was way more important to me that caused me to walk away from all public involvement to protect nature.

As is the case in many towns, there was a very large tract of land owned by one family. It was a jewel, an old farm house and fields, acres along the Exeter River, old growth upland forest and expansive wetlands. Land that was uninhabited by humans and loved by many birds and animals. When the last living homesteader died, it left the land in the hands of distant, out-of-state owners who had no interest in the land only the money it could provide.

I worked tirelessly on applying for state grants to help the town purchase the land. We worked on warrant articles to try and get the towns voters to approve appropriating funds to buy the land for conservation. I made presentations to voters showing the studies made of this property, that it contained vernal pools that offered important breeding habitat for endangered salamanders. That the wetlands contained an important rookery for the great blue heron and other species. All to no avail. Even when the town did approve some funds for the land, an out-of-state developer offered the owner more than double what we could. The town lost a precious piece of land.

The out-of-state developer had grand ideas for the property, including dozens of new houses and roads through the property and along the river. All this involved multiple meetings before the conservation board where the developer was seeking variances and permits to do work that was going to impact sensitive areas and wetlands. The developer was not used to the New Hampshire rules, and some meetings became very heated, threats were made against committee members. It shook me up. Even though the police assured us they would keep an eye on us, I didn't feel very safe.

My job meant site walks to inspect the work being done to ensure that the proper procedures were being followed. There were six of us on the board, and we took turns pairing up on site walks. This was one of the largest projects in my town, and the developer planned stages of work each year. So unfortunately, the committee members had more contact with this man than we wanted. But I and the others, we were following the rules the town and state set. Also, unfortunately, the developer's complaints of being "picked on" by the committee continued. One member quit because of his personal threats; the town hired a lawyer to deal with him.

Each spring, I would hike out to a large wetlands, which abutted the wetlands on the developer's property; I had been doing this since before he owned the property. I was mindful to not trespass; I stayed on the side owned by the state. I had been recording the activity at a large great blue heron rookery that was in the swamp for years. Great blue herons need wetlands to nest. They build their nests in colonies (called a rookery) for protection. They build nests in the dead trees standing in the water. There was a dozen or more nests, and I would record the activity of each nest till the fledglings left in early summer. I would send my reports to the state biologist in Concord. The state biologist had visited the site with me, taken pictures and map coordinates to document this area of "special interest" for environmental protection.

One day as usual, I headed out to the rookery to record the latest happenings. I packed up my tripod, spotting scope, binoculars and backpack with my notebook. As I came to the top of the hill overlooking the swamp, I stood still in utter shock. The water was gone! The swamp was nothing but a black stinky mess of slime! The herons were not on their nests, some of the nests were torn apart. There were crows in some of the nests, picking at the remains of the heron young. It was the worst thing I have ever seen; it haunts me even now. Without the water to protect the nests the raccoons could attack the young. Without the water there was no food source for the parents to feed the young, frogs and small fish. What was happening!

I reported my findings to the authorities. The town police investigated, Concord sent down the state biologist and Fish and Game send down a ranger. Turned out what happened was that the developer had removed a large beaver dam that was at the far end of the wetlands and on his land. He put in a culvert and pushed a road over it. All done illegally. When confronted, he denied that he did anything. He insisted that there never was a beaver dam there, that it was always a culvert and road there, that he just improved the old road so he could access the far lots for development. He didn't see what all the fuss was about, so a couple of birds died.

Well, he didn't count on me being involved. I cared! I had all those years' worth of records showing that there was indeed a beaver dam holding back the water in the wetlands. That the great blue heron rookery had been there for years and was listed as a state area of special interest. His actions started a whole chain reaction of environmental problems. As the wetlands drained, they also drained a small local pond. Neighbors complained of the water disappearing, there was nothing left but dead smelly fish. This developer caused the biggest environmental disaster chain reaction that our town had seen since the 1800s when the train derailed and sank in the mud of the great swamp in the center of town.

The developer was cited for many violations, he was fined and given a "cease and desist" order. There were court dates, testimony, and legal red tape back and forth. I had to face this man more than I was comfortable doing. His threats became personal; he blamed me for his financial problems. But I had to stand up for what I knew was right. He was told by the state that he had to remove the culvert and any fill he dumped into the wetlands and restore the area to its original condition. He was also to compensate the town's people for the environmental mess he had caused to the neighborhood. The lawyers agreed that their client would provide a recreation center building on the site for the town's people to use.

The bottom of the construction industry fell out. The developer did none of the environmental corrections, he basically walked away. The whole thing has been languishing in the courts for years. I felt so helpless; I felt I had failed. His threats against my kids were more than I could stand. I didn't care to press charges I just wanted out. I stepped away from all involvement. I didn't quit but when I was up for reelection a few months later I asked to be taken off the ballot. I asked to be taken off all volunteer lists. I went invisible to the political world in town.

About a month ago, a big deal was made of the dedication of the new town recreation center donated by said developer. It turned my stomach; the sight of those baby birds being eaten still haunts me. I was asked by an old friend if I was going to go to the ceremony. I had no interest in attending. I said there was no cinder block building in the world that would ever make up for the loss of the rookery and all those birds.

I've been asked to rejoin the conservation committee. The current chairman said they could use my knowledge. That there were a couple big projects coming up before the board. I don't know if I can reenter the political scene. The sight of those baby birds being eaten by the crows still haunts me. Or is that exactly why I do need to get involved again? To banish those haunting memories? To this day, I'm still struggling to make the right decision.

Velocity Raptor

May 7, 2012

It's been a good birding weekend. Thanks to Tammi and Dennis I got to see a wood duck!

Birders' happy dance! Birders' happy dance!

Can't ya just see me doing a little jig? A couple of weeks ago, Tammi saw an article in the local paper about the work being done to the Methuen rail trail, which runs along the Nevins Bird Sanctuary. The article mentioned that a large great blue heron rookery was along the trail. It reported that a great horned owl had been seen nesting in one of the heron's nest. So of course, Tammi thought of me, and I'm sure glad she did. It was nice of Tammi and Dennis to give up their Saturday morning to take me out there.

Boy I tell you I've never been treated so good. Dennis carried my tri-pod and the scope, Tammi took care of me so lovingly. I fractured my wrist, I'm fine, no big deal, I'm on the mend. Any ways Tammi was so sweet to me, she carried my raincoat when the sun came out. She picked up and carried my sweatshirt that I removed when it got warmer, I didn't realize it, but I guess I was dragging it in the dirt when I thought it was draped over my field bag. She tied my sneaker when my lace came undone; though, Tammi, you double-knotted it so good I couldn't get it untied once I got home. Since John was at the cabin in Pittsburg fishing, I was home alone and darn that knot was tuff to undo with one hand. She even put out her arm for me to steady myself when we had to hop over a fence to get to the best viewing spot. Dennis picked a tick off me and Tammi checked my hair for bugs. I felt like a kid again! I felt so special!

They took me to the rookery, and it was so soothing to see a large healthy heron rookery again. It helped begin to banish those awful memories of the destroyed rookery in my town. There was a good dozen active nests. We watched the activity as they went about their daily routine, flying on and off the nests taking care of their young. Unfortunately, the owl had already fledged its young and the family had moved on early in April. But it didn't matter that I didn't get to see the owl. I got my woodie!

There in the quiet back water of the Spickit River among the thick green algae covering the surface of the water was a wood duck. It was a magical moment. The duck didn't even look real, he slowly moved across the water without even disturbing the green algae film. It was as if he was a toy or decoy, but he was real! Dennis was so nice, he offered to try and find a path through the thick brush and see if we could get a better view, but I was so enjoying the surreal moment that I didn't dare move away. I just wanted to stand there and watch that beautiful duck.

I tell ya I think I may have hooked Tammi and Dennis on birding. Dennis has a good eye for it. He was able to help locate and identify a yellow warbler and a warbling vireo (or as Tammi called it a velociraptor, no idea how she came up with that name). The vireo is difficult to identify because they generally stay high in the trees, so you're always looking up at their belly, and they are a small plain olive gray bird with no strong markings. The best way to identify them is their eye color and their song. They have one of the prettiest songs you'll ever hear.

Sunday was such a nice day I decided to make a trip to my "go-to" birding spot, Plum Island and saw more great birds. That combined with some new birds I saw at home and those I saw in Methuen added to my total. Thank you again, Tammi and Dennis, for a great Saturday!

Current Big Year total: 157.

Noah's Oak

May 13, 2012

Sometimes nature can provide us with some very valuable lessons. All we have to do is take the time to listen. We are all familiar with the story of Noah's Ark, and some of us may wonder how all those different species of animals could all be in that ark together and not fight or kill each other. Well, I have a modern-day answer to that question.

Last week, after days of rain, the sun finally came out and the temperature soared to seventy. As I got home from work, the yard was full of bird song, and I suited up to head out in search of the songsters. By suiting up, I mean my ritual to protect myself from the ticks in the woods before I go out in search of birds. This involves tucking pant legs into my socks, tucking shirt into pants, wearing a hoody to cover my hair, a hat to keep the ticks from my face and then spraying myself with bug spray, it's quite an ordeal. Just as I was ready to leave my brother-in-law Stanley stopped by to pick up his mail. He mentions all the birds singing and asks me if I knew what this one particular bird singer was that he didn't recognize.

He helps me find the bird high in the oak tree, I recognized the song right away, it was a prairie warbler. We have a very tall old gnarly oak tree that has seen its share of ice/wind storms and has a number of bare branches on its lower half. As we were standing in the yard, the weather began to change, the sky got threatening the wind came up and the temperature dropped.

Stanley says, "Hey, isn't that a scarlet tanager in the oak?" There on the branch was a vivid red scarlet tanager. And just above it on a branch was a deep blue indigo bunting, and above that was a vibrant orange Baltimore oriole. Then a group of lemon-yellow American goldfinch fly into the old oak. Farther up in the oak, a trio of blue with orange/yellow throats, northern parula's fly into the tree. At the

JANE NESKEY

tippy top is the yellow-breasted prairie warbler. All these colorful birds in one tree! Even Stanley mentions he's never seen anything like it. He can't believe they are all in the same tree at the same time next to each other and not fighting. I'm glad he saw it with me, so I had a witness to such a rare sight.

My theory is that our gnarly old oak tree is a Noah's oak. That all the birds knew it was a safe haven from the approaching storm. That they all understood that to survive they had to tolerate each other and make peace. I feel privileged to have seen it. A lesson we all can benefit from.

I had a good birding weekend at the cabin and saw a number of new birds. My favorites were the Canada warbler, the blue-headed vireo and the black-throated green warbler. Those of you with birding apps enjoy the songs, the vireo is quite the songster. :)

Current Big Year total: 164.

Product of His Environment

May 28, 2012

I think we all are familiar with the northern mockingbird, how he can mimic various other birds and sounds. Some find them a very annoying bird, but I rather admire their talents.

Each morning when I arrive at the high school, I work at I am greeted by a mockingbird that sits atop the lamp pole in the parking lot by the athletic fields. Now this bird has some unusual calls that just have to make you laugh. Mixed in with the usual mimic of bird calls this little guy throws in some more modern sounds.

One day as I was walking across the parking lot the bird calls out the sound of a car alarm going off. I had to laugh when two teenage boys who were walking just ahead of me stop. One boy hits the other in the arm and says, "Dude, is that your car?" They both stop and look back at their car.

Another day, there was a group of students running laps in the field and the bird calls out the sound of a whistle. All the students stopped. The coach yells out, "Keep going, that's the bird not me," they all burst out in laughter. You have to wonder if this is an advantage or disadvantage during home games.

A different day, there was a Coke salesman (no, our school can't sell Coke; we buy water and juice from him) walking into the building just ahead of me when the bird calls out the sound of a ringing phone. The salesman pulls his phone from his shirt pocket, turns and looks at me laughing and says, "Did you hear that? I thought that bird was my phone!"

I have really enjoyed listening to the many calls this mockingbird belts out each morning. He has brightened my day and made me laugh, I marvel at his talents to mimic. The other morning just before I entered the employee entrance near the loading dock, I heard the familiar sound of a trucks back up beeps. Part of my job is to check in deliveries, I turn wondering what is being delivered today. Yup, you guessed it, that mockingbird got me! He added the sound of back up beeps to his repertoire.

I guess he is just a product of his environment. Just as we all are. But he sure has brightened my mornings.

I hope everyone had a nice Memorial Day. We just returned from the cabin; weather was great, but the black flies were horrid. I got to see some interesting birds including a colony of cliff swallows and a Swainson's thrush. Also there is a nesting pair of loons along the trail to the river; let's hope the water level doesn't raise suddenly swamping their nest, and I hope their eggs hatch this year.

Current Big Year total: 172.

Attention Hikers and Climbers

This is a Peregrine Falcon nest on the walls of a quarry in Vermont.

June 2012

My son called to ask if I might be interested in coming out to Vermont for a visit. He said that he had been rock climbing in Bolton Quarry when he saw an unusual warning sign, it said, "Attention Hikers and Climbers Cliff Access Closed Beyond This Sign Sensitive Species—Nesting Peregrine Falcons." He asked me if I had seen a peregrine falcon yet to add to my Big Year count, would I be interested in seeing one? *Yes*, I would! We arranged a time and date to meet up. Jeremy and Crystal took me out to the old quarry, what a beautiful area. Jeremy explained that we would have to climb up the opposite side of the quarry to see the nest and stay far enough away from the nest so as not to disturb them. He told me he had found a way to get there safely, but it would be steep. Was I ready to try it? It was tough! Jeremy scrambled up to the top like a mountain goat in a blink of an eye! Crystal stayed by me and reached out her hand to me to help pull me along. We got to a clearing and sure enough we could see the nest across the quarry on a rocky ledge! What a great day spent climbing in an old quarry with Jeremy and Crystal, a day's events that likely never would have happened if it weren't for my search for birds. One more new bird to add to my list!

Baked Potato on Stilts

June 25, 2012

After graduating from the University of Vermont with her bachelor's degree, my daughter moved to Colorado to attend Colorado State University to attain her master's degree. I will admit it was very difficult to wave goodbye as she drove away with her belongings in a trailer to travel from New Hampshire to Colorado. No fear of flying was ever going to keep me from visiting her!

My sisters Sissy, Chris and Becky agreed to join me on a trip west. We had a wonderful time visiting Jeanine in Colorado! I saw some amazing new birds like the Steller's jay, black-billed magpie, and mountain bluebird in the Rocky's. There will be plenty of stories of our adventure to share around the campfire at the family reunion.

We left Fort Collins on Saturday to head to Denver because Becky needed to fly out early Sunday morning and Sissy was leaving Sunday afternoon. Chris and I were staying till Monday morning. Jeanine drove to Denver to spend the day with us, and we all had a nice day at the Denver Zoo. After, Becky left us three sisters decided to rent a car and explore a nature refuge that was close to our hotel.

The Rocky Mountain Arsenal, National Wildlife Refuge was a war-time chemical manufacturing site that has been transformed into a wildlife sanctuary. We stop at the visitor's center and are told that there are a number of burrowing owls on the refuge. This is exciting news! The park ranger tells us to look among the prairie dog towns for the owls who take over the prairie dog burrows. She tells us to look for baked potatoes on stilts that the fledgling owls will be popping in and out of the burrow waiting for the parents to return with a meal. There is one main road that leads to a couple of small lakes with trails around them. Most of the roads have signs warning Authorized Vehicles Only or Active Military Site. We excitedly head for the lakes trail watching all the prairie dogs along the side of the road hoping to see baked potatoes on stilts.

We walked a beautiful trail around one of the smaller lakes. We saw a mule deer, violet-green swallows and the vibrant bullock's oriole but sadly no burrowing owls. The heat was intense, we sat under the shade of some tall trees and ate lunch. It was time to get Sissy back to catch the shuttle for the airport, as we drove back, we watched carefully all the prairie dogs' burrows for baked potatoes on stilts…none. There were plenty of those cute little prairie dogs, they were popping in and out of their burrows just like whack-a-mole at the arcade.

After Chris and I had dinner, we decided since we still had the rental car let's take one more drive through the park in search of those baked potatoes on stilts. The park closed at 6:00 p.m., it was only a little after five, so we figured we had some time. When we were at the visitors' center, the ranger had given us a map where she circled the areas, most likely to see burrowing owls, we decide to check out one of the shorter trails circled.

The heat was scorching, in the high nineties even late in the day. We park and Chris suggest that I try to climb up the rocky hillside rather than take the longer switch back trail to the top of the plateau. She only had on sandals and wouldn't be able to make it up, she suggested that if I see any baked potatoes on stilts when I get up there to wave and she'll come up the long way. Ummm, sounded like a good idea…*not*!

The rocky hillside was a jumbled bunch of lose rocks, and they moved as I was climbing sending dirt and gravel into the pile. Each time the rocks shifted I would hear chattering and screeching coming from the rock pile. There were critters living in there that did not appreciate me disturbing their homes. I decide to jump off the rocks onto the brushy hillside…not such a good idea. The prairie grass cuts like razors! My ankles and hands were getting slashed! Ouch! But at this point, I was closer to the top than the bottom, so I kept going.

When I get to the top, my head is bounding. I'm sweating profusely; it's darn hot on this prairie. What am I doing? This is crazy…

all in the search of baked potatoes on stilts. The high altitude combined with the heat has my brain in a fog. But wait. There ahead is a prairie dog town, the little fellows are running and chattering popping in and out of their burrows. The ranger circled this area as good viewing, I'm here, might as well take a look. I scan the area with my binoculars, the heat waves distort the images, but then it happens. Yup, there is a baked potato on stilts. Ummm, well, no, it doesn't really look like the burrowing owl...or maybe it does...the heat is baking me, and I can't think straight.

I look a couple more times. I'm pretty sure that I see an owl. What I see is *not* a prairie dog that I'm sure of. It is much darker and round, and the wind is ruffling the feathers on its head. Prairie dogs don't have anything on their heads to ruffle. I look away to wipe the sweat from my eyes, when I look back it's gone. I scan the prairie and see it again, and then it is gone just as fast. I decide to motion to Chris to come up, she has to come up here and help me identify my sighting...as she likes to say to "confer and confirm."

She hurries up the switch back trail and gets to where I am standing, but alias she doesn't get to see what I saw. There are no dark brown rounded little bodies popping up and down the burrows. It is hot, hot, hot! I ask Chris if she thinks we can make it to a bench that is closer to the prairie dog town, so we can get a better look. She says we could make it there but then we have to make it back and that it's getting late the park will be closing soon. I notice something troubling; I'm no longer sweating, and I don't have any more water; the heat is too much. So we head back to the car.

When we get to the main gate, we see that it's closed! Oh no! Now what do we do? I'll be honest, I was getting nervous. I was worried we were going to have to call 911 and explain why we were on the wrong side of the gate. Chris remains cool, she tries another exit, but it only brings us back to the main gate. We backtrack to another side road, but the signs warn "UXO (unexploded ordinance) Authorized Vehicles Only." Chris is ready to take the road to see if it leads out, but I caution against it.

Chris remembered that there was a small sign on the main gate, that maybe it has a phone number we can call to have someone let us out. So we head back to the main gate; she slowly drives up close and tells me to read the sign. It says, "Caution moving gate"; as the car gets close enough, it triggers the gate to open. We never were locked in! We head back to the hotel and jump into the pool to cool off.

As I lay in bed that night, I went over our folly. My younger sister is a real trooper, she was willing to brake laws and risked injury just to help me realize a goal and see the burrowing owl. Well, after going over my bird guides and the great pictures in my Nook I realize what I saw was juvenile burrowing owls, they are darker and rounder than the adults. So they didn't actually look like baked potatoes on stilts; they looked more like a small meat loaf popping in and out of their burrows.

Great memories for sure.

Current Big Year total: 198.

Family Time

It has been a hectic couple of weeks for me, I just returned from some relaxing alone time at the cabin. Since June 11, I have only slept in my own bed four nights, between our great Colorado trip, time with Chris in Maine and time at the cabin I haven't been home much. But hey I put up with a low paying job to get the summer time off that's what it's all about, I'm not complaining.

While at the cabin I was privy to a special event. There is a short window of time when young birds leave the nest but are still in need of their parents to feed them. As these young fledglings are learning the ropes of life in the wild, they noisily follow their parents constantly squawking and flapping their wings begging for food. All parents out there know the behavior I'm talking about.

Early one special morning as I sat on the porch with my coffee, I hear a tweeting and see a family of yellow-rumped warblers hopping among the branches of the pine tree by the porch. The young ones flapping their wings with mouth open waiting for breakfast. Next my attention is drawn to the loud "*pep, pep, pep*" of four hairy woodpeckers as they land on a dead stump and the parents drill for bugs which they feed to the young ones.

Next, a large flock of grackles noisily invade the quiet as they hop along the ground, overturning leaves in search of food. All the while the young ones flap and squawk waiting to be fed. Next a group of blue jays join the grackles as if to say, "Hey, I want some of that too!" the young jays call out to be fed, I don't envy those parents geez.

The best was the hummingbird family. As the female and a slightly smaller and paler-colored young hummer alight onto the hummingbird feeder by the window to drink, the male lands on a tree branch sitting still briefly. Suddenly the male hummer buzzes toward the feeder and fends off another male that was trying to land on the feeder. The male defended the feeder multiple times to ensure his mate and his young had sole access to the nectar. It was so touching to see how fiercely he guarded his family.

All the time I spend trekking the woods in search of birds and here I am witness to a special time in nature, all while still in my PJs sipping my morning coffee. If that doesn't calm your soul and reenergize your thoughts nothing will.

Current Big Year total: 200.

Watchful Eyes

July 21, 2012

Well, here it is the end of July the summer is just flying by. Birding has been slow; I've pretty much reached the saturation point for bird sightings. I've seen about all there is out there at this time. Don't get me wrong I see plenty of birds daily just not any *new* birds. For example, of the possible twenty or so species of herons I've now seen all but two, the American and least bittern.

So I figured it's time to switch things up and try some new birding areas. I hadn't been out to Plum Island for over a month, so I headed out to try and find the piping plover last week. The whole beach on the nature reserve is closed due to the nesting piping plover, so I knew it was going to be tuff to spot one. I had to drive to the far end of the island and access the beach just off the reserve. They have huge signs and a fence warning you not to proceed any farther, that the beach is *closed* due to the nesting birds. But there were other birders there, we all gathered at the fence with binoculars and spotting scopes searching for those little shore birds. Also there was the official "plover warden"—yup, there is such a title. This guy would set up his chair with umbrella and cooler at the fence with his walkie talkie (to call in back-up if any of us break the line?) and sit there all day guarding the fence to make sure no one disturbs the plovers. Now come on that is one dedicated bird lover!

I asked the guy if he got paid for sitting on the beach all day, and he just laughed. But ya know what he was a really nice man. He scanned the beach and helped me locate a piping plover as well as a red-throated loon. He told us about how the nesting was going, the history of past efforts and the outlook for the bird's future. It was nice talking to him, I thanked him for volunteering his time to protect the Plovers. It was a good feeling to be with other likeminded birders, sharing sightings and news of rare birds. It refreshed my drive to add to my Big Year count. So I head into August, reenergized, ready to search out far corners of woods and water for bird sightings to add to my count.

Current Big Year count: 208.

Bittersweet Reality

August 22, 2012

Well, here it is the end of the summer, school will be starting soon, and I'll be back to work. I was working on a report of the Lake Francis loon family. Loons mate for life and this particular pair has been trying to nest in our cove for the last few years, unfortunately they have not been very successful. The water level in Lake Francis is controlled by Murphy Dam, so it is constantly changing. For some reason, the loons had picked one of the worst places on the lake to try and build a nest, right by the mouth of the Connecticut River where it flows into the lake. Loons are very awkward on land and rarely leave the water, they will build a nest on a small island or clump of greenery close to shore. Because of this location, the nest has flooded and the eggs have been destroyed the last few years. Finally this year, they were successful in hatching an egg. It was uncertain for a while the water level rose suddenly and nearly swamped the nest in June.

Also, this year the loons have had some human help, I am a Society for Loon Protection volunteer and have been keeping records and sending updates to the State Biologist. Thankfully there was funding available, and I was able to have a floating sign placed near the nest warning boaters to stay clear. I was also able to get a floating nest platform that will be installed after the loons leave for the winter. Hopefully they will use it next year, thus solving the problem of their nest flooding out.

Because the loon population has been decreasing on our New Hampshire lakes, the state has been working to eliminate the use of lead fishing weights because the loons ingest them and die of lead poisoning. The Loon Society banded the loons, so they could be followed and offer more insight to their protection needs. I wasn't so keen on them banding the loons, I was worried it would be too stressful on them or hurt them. But they did it at night, they quietly floated up to the sleeping loons in a kayak (loons don't sleep on land) netted them, placed a band on their leg and released them, all in a matter of minutes. They are now officially known as the Lake Francis State Park loons. I'm still not sure how I feel about them being banded, it means they aren't so wild any more. But in the long run if it will help save our loons I think they would be okay with it.

The egg hatched in mid-June to much fanfare by the adult loons who yodeled loudly throughout the night and kept close guard on the nest till the chick completely emerged from the egg. Once the chick hatched it took to the water, riding on the back of its parents. The baby is about the size of a tennis ball and spends its first few weeks riding on a parent's back; it never touches land. The parents take turns carrying the chick and fishing for food, they never leave it alone. At about three weeks old, the chick begins to swim alongside of its parents but is still never left alone. I have watched the chick grow throughout the summer.

There was one very frightening encounter when I feared the chick was done for. I was in the cabin when I heard a lot of noise on the lake, the loons were calling loudly, and I could also hear the call of a bald eagle. I ran down to the lakes edge and watched as the two loon parents fought off a bald eagle that was diving for the baby loon. I could see the eagle with its talons stretched out reaching for the baby loon. The baby loon can't dive underwater to escape like the adults can, so it is in danger from predators from above. The parents both backed up to the baby loon keeping it close between them but the eagle wasn't giving up easy. It was one of those situations when you want to turn away but can't stop yourself from watching. The parents flapped their wings and lunged at the eagle each time it swooped down trying to get the baby. They battled on the water for a while, I could see feathers flying, but in the end, the parents drove the bald eagle away. Their baby was safe.

The young loon is now the same size as its parents; though, it won't have its adult plumage till next year. The loon family will be heading south soon. The loons of New Hampshire winter in Great

Bay, there the water never completely freezes, so they can still fish for food. Next spring the parents will return and nest again in our cove, but I won't see the young loon again. The young loon will return to our lake but not our cove. The young loon will seek out a mate and start its own family somewhere else along Lake Francis. It is a bittersweet reality. The parents have risked their own lives to raise their young, and then they send it out to fend for itself. But so goes the cycle of nature, over and over again.

Current Big Year total: 209.

Searching the Salt Marsh

August 26, 2012

Well, the time has come, the lazy days of summer are over, and school starts tomorrow. It has been a great summer for birding the weather has been fantastic, the best it's been for a long time. To end these last couple of days of freedom, I thought I would head to the ocean and explore the salt marshes for migrating water fowl.

I went to Plum Island on Friday and scored a couple of new birds. I was walking along Hellcat trail when I saw a group of people at a clearing. It doesn't take much to figure out that when you see a group of people with telephoto lenses and spotting scopes that there must be something interesting to look at. There along the edge of the marsh was a pair of Whimbels, they belong to the Sandpiper family but are one of the largest with a long downward curved bill. What is most interesting is that they don't live in New England, they are just passing through on their migration from their breeding grounds in Canada to their winter home on the Gulf Coast.

To escape the heat and get out of the sun I headed for the bird blind to cool off. I was rewarded with another new sighting. Again, there were fellow birders set up with scopes, and I was able to see a small flock of Wilson's Phalarope resting in the marsh. These birds are also in the Sandpiper family just passing through to their southern winter homes. I sort of felt like I was cheating, I didn't really find either of these new birds, I just came upon fellow birders who shared their findings.

Saturday was another beautiful day, so I decided to head to Cape Neddick to do some more salt marsh birding. The tide was dead low and I knew I could hang out at Chris's trailer for the day and have plenty of time for birding. I sat on a stone wall at the edge of the marsh for nearly an hour, there was all sorts of bird activity to watch.

Because the tide was so low, the marsh was down to a thin trough of water teaming with fish. It was easy pickings for many birds.

I watched as a Belted Kingfisher made repeated dives into the water for small fish. There were ring-billed gulls and herring gulls fighting over fish and small crabs. There were flocks of Semipalmated Plovers flying back and forth in formation feeding on small fish. There were tree swallows swooping low over the mud flats for small bugs and a common nighthawk chasing the tree swallows.

But the best sighting of the day was the most unexpected. As I sat and watched the activity on the mud flats of the salt marsh just out of the corner of my eye, I spotted movement along the marsh edge. There emerging from the cover of the reeds was a least bittern. The least bittern is a very secretive member of the heron family, and I have been trying to find one all summer. He lingered in the open for about five minutes then just as suddenly disappeared back into the thick reeds.

I still have until December 31 to add new birds to my Big Year list, but now that the summer is over, I won't have as much time for birding. But I'm always scanning the woods and sky for new birds.

Current Big Year total: 215.

Why, People? Why?

September 9, 2012

There was a news report of an injured loon found on Back Lake in Pittsburg. The loon was found sickly and taken to an animal hospital for care. X-rays showed that the bird had been shot over a dozen times with pellets. Unfortunately, the loon had to be euthanized. The loon is a protected bird, what possible reason would anyone have to harm a loon? No one can say they didn't know it was a loon, that they thought it was a duck, hunting season for ducks isn't open. Come on, people. Why? Why?

Why do these things happen?

Yesterday a small flock of five turkeys came through our yard. This is not unusual we often have wild turkeys in our yard, I put out cracked corn for them and enjoy seeing them. Unfortunately, there was one of the turkeys that had an arrow protruding from its hind quarters. Someone had shot it with an arrow but not killed it. It walked slower than the others and was shaking its feathers as if to dislodge the arrow.

I called wild life control to report the injured bird. There isn't much anyone can do, they suggested that if I was able to catch it by throwing a blanket over it, and then perhaps, they could remove the arrow and save it. I have a blanket ready by the door but I'm not so sure I can chase down a turkey and wrangle it to the ground, but if I can I will!

The reality is that I am more likely to find it dead in the woods. If I do, I will remove the arrow; hunters are required by law to write their name and address on each arrow. But of the most concern is that this is *not* hunting season for turkey right now. So whomever shot the turkey is a poacher, so I kinda doubt that they put their name and address on the arrow. Come on, people. Why? Why?

I spent Sunday at Plum Island searching for birds but all I could think about was how cruel some people can be. I never did see the poor injured turkey again. Why people? Why?

Current Big Year total: 216.

Lucky Dogs

September 16, 2012

This past Sunday, John and I traveled to Misquamicut State Beach in Westerly Rhode Island; this was the first time I have been back to Rhode Island since I left in 1964 as a child. Our daughter-in-law Crystal was running in the Surftown Half Marathon; we went to cheer her on and hang out with our son Jeremy. Running isn't always a spectator friendly sport, but this race had a great course: on the seaside road. The weather was great, sunny with a nice breeze. At the starters gun, thousands of runners took off; we couldn't find Crystal among the throng, but luckily, the runners looped back to pass right by us. So we got to cheer her on as she ran by and then as she came across the finish line. Great job, Crystal!

When the runners were out of sight, we were able to stroll along the beach. I would listen, and when we heard clapping and cheering, we knew runners were coming; and we headed back to the road side. While walking along the beach, I was lucky enough to see some new birds. There was a small group of mixed peeps sunning themselves in the seaweed at the high tide mark. Most of the smallest shorebirds, those five inches to seven inches are called peeps as a general term. Jeremy helped me confirm their Ids, and we were able to quietly walk all most right up to them as they were sunning and preening.

The new birds I was lucky enough to see were the western sandpiper and the black-bellied plover. But the real lucky ones are the dogs of Vermont. The charity that Crystal raised money for by running the marathon is Vermont Rescue Dogs. So thanks to Crystal, there are some very lucky dogs in Vermont!

Fall migration is in full swing, get out there and do some birding. Current Big Year total: 218.

Dinner for Three

September 23, 2012

I just returned from a beautiful fall weekend at the cabin, the foliage is always breathtaking. Just before I drive away, I always go down to the water's edge to say "goodbye" to the lake. As I did that this morning, I saw an incredible sight. Across the lake there is a tall birch tree and sitting in the tree were three bald eagles, such a beautiful sight, the white birch with golden yellow leaves and three magnificent bald eagles perched on its branches. I couldn't believe it, three bald eagles together in one tree! As I was watching them through my binoculars, two flew off, I followed one as it landed in a tall spruce not far from the birch, the other landed on the ground near the water's edge. Even without binoculars there is no mistaking these majestic birds with their white head and tail and huge thirty-inch wingspan.

Then as if seeing three eagles together in a tree wasn't cool enough, I watched as the eagle in the birch flew to the edge of the water and landed on a dead deer. I hadn't noticed the deer carcass before but now I could understand why the three eagles were there. The other two eagles joined the first and patiently waited on a large rock for the alpha bird to feast first. I watched as the eagle torn bits of meat off the carcass while sitting on the protruding rib cage. It was gross but fascinating at the same time.

John was watching as well, and we considered trying to get a picture. But we had everything loaded in the car to leave and the cabin was all locked up. It would have taken an hour or so to unpack the suitcase to get the camera, open the cabin back up, drag the kayak down to the water, and paddle over to the opposite side of the lake and attempt to take the eagle's picture. Even if I did try to paddle over to get closer for a picture, there was no guarantee I wouldn't end up scaring them away in the process. I didn't want to take that chance and cause the eagles to lose out on a good meal.

As I drove the four hours home, I regretted that decision. I wish I had taken the time and paddled over to try and get a picture. When will I ever see such an incredible sight again? As driving, I fantasied about getting that one unbelievable fantastic shot and entering it in a nature photo contest and winning first place. Then I could afford to buy the very expensive equipment to take up the hobby of digiscoping. Then I could have taken a picture while standing on shore in front of the cabin across the lake of that incredible sight of three bald eagles at nature's table, enjoying dinner for three.

Fall is a special time at the cabin. I saw two new birds that were migrating through from Canada to their winter homes far south. A flock of yellow-breasted chats and a pair of mourning warblers.

Current Big Year total: 220.

Shades of Gray

September, 30 2012

I know that some of us are old enough to remember the days of black-and-white TV; yes, youngsters, there really was a time when there was no such thing as color TV. Well, I feel as if I just had a black and white weekend as if I were in an old TV show. We can call it *The Many Adventures of Jane.*

Chris had invited her friend Beth and myself to join her in Cape Neddick, Maine. We were hoping to be able to see the common nighthawks during their migration. The conditions were the same as last year's fantastic sighting, a full moon just after a storm at sea. Unfortunately, the weather did not cooperate, we had strong winds, rain and gray skies. But fortunately, there were those that found safe harbor in the campground cove. We were able to watch a pair of seals feeding in the cove. They looked like gray dogs bobbing in the rough surf. This was the first time I have gotten to see seals in the cove.

The rain simmered down to a cold mist but the winds stayed strong. We were able to see quite a few sea birds that had taken cover in the cove. There was a great black-backed gull walking around the campground dragging one wing, looking for food. Have to wonder if the storm beat him up or if he had a run in with one of those seals. Hopefully he will survive the winter. We saw many black, white and gray herring gulls and ring-billed gulls riding out the storm in the cove. We saw an arctic red-throated loon, who spends the winter along the Atlantic coast but is only black and white in his nonbreeding plumage. It was indeed a gray day. About the only shot of color in the cove was one lone red-breasted merganser feeding along the shore in the surf.

The rain let up so we decided to head up Mt. Agamenticus…(I can hardly say the name never mind spelling it). There is an observation platform at the top, and it is a well-known migration route for hawks heading south for the winter. We were hoping to get to see some hawks, but alas as we climbed the mountain in the car we also climbed into the clouds and mist. It was windy, cold, gray and wet at the top. Not a bird it sight.

It was still early in the day, so we decided to take a walk along the trails at Rachel Carson Nature Reserve. The sky was gray but the rain finally stopped though the wind was still steady and the temperature was cool, not really the best bird watching day. As we walked along, I was telling Beth how I had seen almost every warbler that lived in New England except for two. The cerulean warbler, which is very rare and may soon be listed as endangered and the black and white warbler, which is considered one of the most common warblers yet I have spent all summer looking for one. Not thirty seconds later, there is a flock of little birds that are above us. It is hard to see any details as they dart in and out of the trees and then Beth gets a good look and calls out, "Black and white warblers!" I swear it happened that fast; I finally get to see my elusive warblers and add another species to my list. Thank you, Beth!

So I had a gray weekend in more ways than one. My birding adventures were black and white and shades of gray. Gray has such a negative vibe, represents the unknown or confusion. But that's how life goes now and then: the storm clouds will part, and the sun will come out. So let's all embrace the many shades of gray life has to offer.

Current Big Year total: 221.

Slow Boat to China

October 14, 2012

Just returned from the cabin; spent the weekend buttoning up the place for the winter. It's always sad to close the place up and drive away. We had snow squalls then sun and temps near forty then snow again pretty typical Pittsburg weather for this time of year. The job of closing the place up was made a bit more difficult because a Skunk has decided to hibernate under the cabin. He did not take lightly to being disturbed when John tried to get under there to turn off the water.

I did take the kayak over to the spot where I had seen the eagles. When John pulled the kayak out from under the cabin was the first time he saw the skunk, so we had to store the kayak inside the cabin; wasn't going to take the chance of making Mr. Skunk angry. I was pretty sure I knew the location of the carcass the eagles were eating but the water level was much higher than before, and I couldn't find it. Perhaps it sank into the deeper water or maybe the coyotes dragged it away. In any case, there was no evidence of it to be found.

The young loon is still on the lake, the parents have left. It was so sad to hear the young loon call during the night. I sure hope his instincts kick in, and he heads south soon. There were a lot of hunters in the woods, so I had to be very careful about my birding walks. But luckily, I was able to get one new exciting sighting. A black-backed woodpecker! Those of you with birding apps check him out. I heard him before I saw him, and it took quite a bit of work to find him in the dense woods. Especially when there were hunters' guns going off around me. Don't worry I wear my blaze orange, remember I'm a might bigger than a rabbit, eh.

An interesting news story some of you may have read about, the osprey project. They fitted three NH osprey with tracking devices to learn more about their migration. Here in New Hampshire, they are protected, and we have made great progress in their protection, but we are a global world and the areas birds migrate to needs protection as well. The world is losing important natural areas fast and these studies hope to educate people and countries of the importance of the rainforest and coastal flyways.

You can follow the ospreys journey at www.nhnature.org/osprey_project/maps.html.

One male, Art, has made it to South America safely. Unfortunately, it seems that the female Jill has died somewhere in Brazil. The other male Chip has everyone puzzled, it seems he has gone way off course and become lost at sea. His locater signal has him on a cargo ship far out to sea. His survival is unlikely. It appears the poor young osprey is on a slow boat to China.

Current Big Year total: 227.

Saw a Sora

October 21, 2012

Had another great day of birding on Plum Island Saturday, it sure has been my "go-to" spot for birding. Beth and I tallied up forty-five different species for the day. Chris was recovering from a nasty cold and couldn't join us, so sorry she missed out. We were on the island a bit over four hours, the day started out gray but soon cleared and the temps rocketed to the seventies! Yup, seventy in October, can't beat that.

We both added new birds to our life lists. We weren't on the island but minutes when we spotted a large flock of Eurasian Wigeon bobbing up and down in search of food in the marsh pool. Just as its name implies, these birds breed in Eurasia and only occasionally visit the Atlantic coast. We were lucky to be in the right place at the right time to see such a large flock during their migration. If you look these up in a bird guide, I can tell you they were much more hansom in person, with their rusty brown head and golden mohawk.

We stopped at a spot where we saw a couple of men with elaborate camera/scope equipment to see what they were watching. They sell their nature pictures and were telling us the cost of their equipment ran into the thousands! Yikes I guess I'm gonna give up the idea of taking up digiscoping after all. They were waiting to capture pictures of the Northern Harrier that was hunting in the fields. We spotted one later, the bird did not disappoint those watching as he flew and hovered close to the road in search of prey. A magnificent bird indeed. We spent time watching the mixed flocks of sparrows trying to ID them all. Which can get difficult because they all have very similar markings. Beth was able to add a new species to her life list.

As we sat in the car and had our lunch before heading out to the bird blind, we watched as a small flock of birds flew into the scrub pines. We made note of where they landed and decided to look for them as we walked the trail to the bird blind. And sure enough, we spotted the birds, they were red crossbills! I have seen them before, but they were a first for Beth. We enjoyed watching them hang upside down and pick apart the pine cones. Those with birding apps look these up, the female is an olive yellow and the male a deep red, very pretty birds with a weird crossed bill.

We walked out to the back marsh pools carrying the scope and then out to the platform overlooking the ocean hoping to finds something good. But alas just the usual suspects, lots of greater and lesser yellow legs, gulls, common eiders, and cormorants. Nothing new or exciting. It was getting late, time to begin the drive off the island. But we had one last place to stop before leaving, Hellcat Trails to check out the observation tower and trails.

Those of you who are not familiar with the area let me set the scene for you. There is a narrow board walk that weaves through the tall marsh reeds for about one mile or so, you can't step off the boardwalk and depending on the tide the water can be very high. It can be quite peaceful as you walk among the reeds gently swaying in the breeze. As Beth and I walked along, I tell her I rarely see any birds along this trail because those that inhabit the reedy marsh are all too secretive, and hide deep in the reeds.

By now, the sun is shining and the temperature has risen, there are many people enjoying the board walk. Couples and families, children run and laugh along the boardwalk. Beth and I figure with all this activity the chances are slim that we will get to see any shy marsh birds. I ask her if she has ever seen a Sora, she replies that she has heard them but never seen one. I mention that I'd really like to see a Sora, which would be an exciting sighting.

Then suddenly from behind us we hear this loud *swarrrkkk* it stops me in my tracks. I tell Beth that is a new sound to me, let's turn around and find where that sound came from! We follow the sound and Beth notices movement in the reeds. She calls out, "SORA!" I can't believe it; I search where she is looking but can't find the bird. Then I just catch a glimpse of a small chicken like shorebird, with yellow beak, black smudge on its face turning into gray neck, and then dark back. "SORA!" Just as suddenly as it appeared it disappears back into the thick reeds.

So all this time, I've been quietly tiptoeing along that trail trying to sneak up on this shy marsh bird when all along, it was the loud clickity clack of many feet along the boardwalk that finally pushed the shy little bird into view. Beth is indeed my birding good luck charm, for the second time she has seen a bird I'd just mentioned to her that I wish I could see. Thank you, Beth. Finally, I saw a sora!

Current Big year total: 229.

Rumors

November 3, 2012

I haven't been out birding for a couple of weeks since last weekend we were preparing for Hurricane Sandy. Thankfully we had very little damage here, lost power for a couple of days nothing we weren't prepared for. So I was anxious to get out and do some birding; Chris and I headed to Parker River National Wildlife Refuge (Plum Island) to see what we could find. The island was evacuated during the storm and had been closed to visitors but was open this weekend.

The weather wasn't the best, cloudy, cool and windy, but hey it's November in New England. I had heard rumors that the storm had blown in birds from far away, so we stopped at the Audubon center before entering the refuge to see what had been sighted. They had a printed list with some pretty interesting sightings, I was excited to get out there and see what I could find. The Audubon volunteer told us she had heard that there were some white pelicans on the island. What?! White pelicans belong in Florida not New England!

As we stopped along the trails in search of birds, I would ask fellow birders if they had seen any good sightings. I asked one woman if she had seen the short-eared owl listed as a sighting on the list I had. She told me she had heard rumors that someone saw one but that she hadn't. At another stop, I asked a man and women with fancy camera gear if they had seen any snow buntings that I had heard there were some on the island. They said they had also heard that rumor, but so far, they had not seen any.

When we came upon the parking area for the dunes trail that leads out to the ocean viewing platform, we were excited to see about eight cars there. I knew that had to mean there was something good sighted out there to draw so many fellow birders. As Chris and I walked along the boardwalk across the sand dunes, we decided to see if Chris had the good luck touch that Beth had for bird sightings. Each time I mentioned a particular bird to Beth that I was hoping to see wouldn't you know it would be the very next bird we would see. So I told Chris I was hoping to see a razorbill that was listed on the bird sightings list and Chris said she was hoping to see a dolphin.

When we got up to the viewing platform, there were about a dozen people there many set up with spotting scopes others with binoculars. People were calling out sightings: "I got a horned grebe in the swells off the rocks," and everyone would turn and focus their equipment in that direction. Someone else calls out, "Red-throated loon off to the far right." Again, the group would turn in unison. They were happy to share their scopes so we could get an up-close look. But these were all birds I've already seen, nothing new. I asked one woman if she had seen any razorbills, she said she had heard a rumor there were some on the island, but she hadn't seen any. I was disappointed.

This was the first time I had been birding on the island when I didn't see any new birds. Don't get me wrong we had a nice day, we saw flocks of one hundred or so of northern pintails and flocks of American wigeons. Chris enjoyed watching the wild swans, and we watched a red-tailed hawk sitting in a low branch with in arms reach. Chris didn't get to see any dolphins, but she did get to see a seal bobbing in the surf. Not a dolphin but close, does that count? So I had spent the day chasing rumors of rare sightings on the island. Oh well. Better luck next time.

The only new bird I have seen in a couple of weeks was a Carolina wren blown in by Hurricane Sandy. Literally, it was blown in by the storm. I was sitting by the window watching the storm when a strong gust blew the small wren right into the side of the bird feeder. Whack! I feared it was dead, but it held on with its tiny claws as the wind blew it sideways ruffling its feathers backward. When the gust let up, the bird quickly took a couple of bites of suet then the next gust blew it off the feeder, and it was gone. I haven't seen it since. I sure hope it made it through the storm safely.

Current Big year total: 230.

Red Team? Blue Team?

November 12, 2012

Last Wednesday, the day after the election I made an observation at the feeder that got me thinking. I had just gotten home from work and was unwinding while sitting watching the birds at the feeder. There were goldfinches, pine siskins, chickadees, titmouse, doves, woodpeckers, and juncos all busy feeding. Suddenly they all scattered when they heard the high-pitched scream of a hawk. I picked up my binoculars and followed the sound to see the hawk, but it wasn't a hawk at all. It was a blue jay that has learned to mimic the sound of a hawk and in doing so scares all the other birds away from the feeder.

I have seen this bird do this before, and you have to marvel at his smarts. The blue jay jumps onto the platform feeder and begins to use his beak to shovel seed out onto the ground. Blue jays have a hard time feeding from tube feeders because of their size, they much prefer to eat from the ground. The blue jay jumps to the top of the feeder pole and bounces up and down while making his *jay, jay, jay* call. Soon a whole group of blue jays fly in and begin to feed. Meanwhile, the first blue jay chases away any other birds that try to land and eat. Not sure who made him boss, but he makes sure his team is taken care of first.

The blue team monopolized the feeder until a red-bellied woodpecker flew onto the feeder and scared away the dominant blue jay, and then the rest of the blue team scattered. The woodpecker went about his business enjoying the suet and slowly the other birds returned. Starting with one red cardinal then two more red cardinals. Next the doves landed on the ground and began to eat, followed quickly by the Juncos. The thistle feeder was soon full of goldfinches and pine siskins, again the sunflower feeder was full of Titmouse and chickadees. In my observation, the red team seemed much more inclusive and willing to work together. But then, if you were on the blue team, I guess you could say the same thing.

In their world, blue team or red team, what's it really matter? They're all just trying to survive.

I enjoyed Monday off in honor of Veteran's Day and decided to head to Plum Island for some birding. The weather was unbelievable for November, sunny and near seventy! The island was busy, lots of people out enjoying the good weather and many birders too. I saw some new birds, a group of Surf Scoters, some black guillemots, a pair of American coots and a fox sparrow.

In honor of Veterans Day, I want to thank all the men and women of our military for their service. For if it weren't for brave Americans like them to ensure our country's freedoms, I may not have been able to enjoy a beautiful day walking the trails of a bird sanctuary enjoying my freedom. Blue team? Red team? What's it really matter? We are all Americans just trying to survive.

Current Big Year total: 235.

Trust Yourself

December 9, 2012

Well, it has been a while since I had a chance to get out and do some birding. We, for some crazy reason decided to take on the job of repainting the whole inside of the house and that has taken up every spare minute for nearly a month. This past Saturday we finally put away all the painting tools and called the job done! So I was anxious to get out to Plum Island and do some birding, even though I know this time of year there is little out there to see. My Big Year ends December 31, so I'm really scrambling to add to my totals. The day was clear, temps near forty, not too windy.

As usual, there were other birders on the island and plenty of interesting birds to see. But not anything new to me so far. Like mooseing in Pittsburg, I always watch for cars pulled over or groups of people as a hint that someone has spotted something good. I often eaves drop on others conversations about their sightings or outright ask them what they're looking at. I don't always trust myself to identify sea birds, they still confuse me. Birders are more than happy to share their spotting scope with me or help me locate a good sighting.

There was a group of birders with scopes set up watching some birds on the rocks. I could see them with my binos but not really well. I asked one of the guys what kind of birds were those sitting out on the rocks of the jetty. He told me rock sandpipers. I was amazed! These birds belong in Alaska and winter along the western coast what were they doing here? I thanked him for the info but was just not sure, I strained to pick out any good field marks on the small flock sitting on the rocks. I walked away ready to count them as a very rare sighting. I figured with the nice fancy equipment that guy had he must know what he was talking about.

Farther along the beach, I came upon a group of birders gathered on the viewing platform with scopes set up and everyone was very excited. I asked one person what was sighted, and he told me a small group of western grebes were just off shore feeding. What!? Western grebes here in New England? I just wasn't sure about what I was looking at through my binoculars, a man offered his scope for me to get a closer look. They sure did look like western grebes, even if it didn't make sense for them to be here. I walked away ready to count them as a new sighting.

I thought about it all the way home, I was pretty confident that those were western grebes, but I wasn't so sure about the rock sandpipers. I always doubt myself, especially when I don't have anyone to "confer and confirm" my sightings with. I looked through all my field guides, and it made more sense that they could have been purple sandpipers (which are not purple) not rock sandpipers. But I just didn't trust myself to make the call. So I'm not counting the sighting; I know none of you would challenge my sighting, but it's like cheating at solitaire. Why bother?

I need to learn to trust my own abilities to identify the birds I see instead of looking for outside confirmation. There's not much time left to add to my list but I'll be more confident with my sightings and continue to add to my final Big Year total!

Current Big Year total: 236.

The End

Well, here it is the end of 2012 and the end of my Big Year birding competition. When my daughter Jeanine was home from college for the holiday, I was excited to be able to spend time with her at Plum Island to do some birding. I wanted to show her where I had been doing all the birding I had been writing about. I was hoping we could spot some new and exciting bird for me to add to my count. Jeanine hasn't been to Plum Island since she was a child. I wanted to make it a perfect day, so I packed us a nice lunch, made sure Jeanine had her hat, gloves and layers on for warmth. I packed all my bird guides and my Nook was all powered up ready to "confer and confirm" any new sightings.

It was a cold and blustery day on the island. But Jeanine was looking forward to seeing the ocean, and I was anxious to find a new bird. We stopped at the first salt marsh pool on the island, I reached into the back seat for my field bag, and I couldn't believe it. No, it couldn't be true. I packed so carefully. Or so I thought. For the very first time ever I forgot to pack my binoculars! NOOO! But in the end, it didn't matter. I had a great day spending time with Jeanine. We walked the Hellcat trail through the sand dunes and along the ocean. It was cold and windy, and I didn't see any new birds, but I didn't care.

Because, this whole year has been about more than just finding new birds. It's been about sharing and spending time with family and friends. It's been about me stepping out of my comfort zone and doing things I never thought I would. I have traveled to New Hampshire, Maine, Vermont, Massachusetts, Rhode Island, Florida, and Colorado in search of birds. I have gone places I never thought I would, done things I never thought I would, and seen things I never thought I would.

I have scaled the side of an old quarry in cold rain in Vermont in search of the peregrine falcon. Of course, my son Jeremy scrambled up the sides like a mountain goat, while I slipped on the wet rocks, I'm not so fond of heights and felt a bit queasy when I looked back down. But I knew I was safe with Jeremy by my side. But I wanted to see a new bird. I have endured the extreme heat of the plains in Colorado in search of the burrowing owl. Chris and I took some chances out on the plains, I hate the extreme heat, we were out there alone. But I wanted to see a new bird. I have ridden an air boat in the everglades of Florida to search for new birds. I'm not so fond of swamps—all those bugs, spiders and snakes…ewww. But I wanted to see some new birds.

This past Big Year hasn't just been about the places I've gone, it's been about the people I shared those experiences with. It's the impromptu trip to Cape Cod with Chris and Beth in search of the rare lazuli bunting from Mexico. It's sitting with Sissy on her lanai in Port Charlotte, Florida, with our morning coffee watching the majestic great egret fish for its breakfast. It's a morning walk along the Methuen Rail Trail with Tammi and Dennis where I got to see my first wood duck. It's being in Colorado with my sisters and Jeanine and seeing the brilliant Steller's jay in the Rocky Mountains. Every bird sighting is a memory, a memory I'll carry forever.

So I ended my Big Year bird count as I began it. I started at Plum Island sighting the beautiful snowy owl visiting from the Arctic tundra. On December 31, the last day of the year, I returned to Plum Island in search of a new bird. So it was only fitting that the last new bird to be added to my list was a large flock of noisy snow buntings visiting from the Arctic tundra. I'll still be out there looking for birds. But for now, it is the end of my Big Year competition. The count doesn't matter *I won!*

Final Big Year total: 238.

Final Tally State by State

Maine: 6 species
    Highlight:
    Black and white warbler
Vermont: 1 species
    Highlight:
    Peregrine falcon
New Hampshire: 85 species
    Highlight:
    Boreal chickadee
Massachusetts: 67 species
    Highlight:
    Snowy owl
Rhode Island: 2 species
    Highlight:
    Black-bellied plover
Florida: 57 species
    Highlight:
    Swallow-tailed kite of the Everglades
Colorado: 20 species
    Highlight:
    Steller's jay in the Rocky Mountain National Park
Final Big Year total: 238

Birding Across New England

Plum Island Massachusetts

Cape Ann Massachusetts

Cape Neddick Maine

Mt. Agamenticus Maine

Northern Vermont

Southern New Hampshire

Merrimack New Hampshire

Nashua NH

Hudson NH

Newmarket NH

The stories in this chapter are about my birding adventures in New Hampshire, Massachusetts, Maine, and Vermont, with family and friends old and new. I have lived in New England since I was born in 1953. But my hobby of birding inspired me to travel to areas I had not been to before even places close to home. That's one of the best benefits of birding, you can enjoy what's in your backyard or local park. Sure, traveling farther can offer more sightings and adventures.

It's all about getting out and enjoying nature!

The Saga Continues

March 31, 2012

A couple of days after my grand adventure with Katie in search of the great horned owl my brother-in-law Stanley found a dead owl. He was checking out the back fairways on the golf course he works at in preparation of opening day when he spotted the owl laying in the snow at the base of a large pine tree. Of course, he thought of me and brought it home in a plastic bag. It was a beautiful specimen, what a shame it had to die. I called NH Fish and Game to ask if I could have it stuffed and was told that the great horned owl is a federally protected owl and that it was against the law for me to possess one, either dead or alive.

I asked Fish and Game if they would like the body to have stuffed for their education centers. They said that due to budget cuts they didn't have any money in their budget for taxidermy projects. I asked them if I could donate the cost to have it stuffed. Over the years, I have enjoyed stopping at the Twin Mountain nature center and other state-run nature centers, and I thought I could "pay back" by funding the taxidermy. They were very interested; I was told that the enforcement officer assigned to my area would contact me.

After a day or so of phone tag, the conservation officer finally contacted me. The first thing he asks me is where I have the owl body. I tell him it is wrapped in plastic and buried in a snow bank in the yard. He informs me that the great horned owl is a federally protected species and that I am in violation of the law by owning said owl. He tells me that if I have it in my house, garage, shed or any man-made structure that I can be arrested. He tells me to be sure to keep it out side. Jeepers this guy is serious he's beginning to scare me. He tells me that he will come to the house between 8:00 and 9:00 a.m. the next morning to retrieve the owl.

The officer explains that he has a list of state approved educational centers licensed to possess federal mounts. That he appreciates my offer to donate the cost for the taxidermy, but that the areas waiting for an owl will handle the cost. Sure enough, the officer arrives the next morning, luckily it was Good Friday and John had the day off, I had to work. The officer said the owl was in great shape and would make a fine mount. It turns out that the Concord Audubon Center will get the owl, they will mount it and put it on display for all to enjoy.

The officer checked over the poor owl; his opinion was that it seems to have broken his neck. Most likely in the hot pursuit of a squirrel or other prey he misjudged the distance between the branches and ran into the tree. But at least he will live on in spirit on display in our state's capital for the enjoyment of all the visitors young and old.

And so the saga continues as I search to see the great horned owl. A few days after our adventure Katie was able to make it back to the rail trail, and she got to see an owl fly over her head. My brother-in-law finds one on the ground by his feet. A newspaper article talks about the many sightings of the great horned owl on Plum Island, that the park rangers have had to close down the area to protect the nesting owls. I still search for my sighting. I contact Tammi to ask if she had made it back out to the rail trail near her to see if the great horned owl is nesting in the heron rookery. I am even more determined than ever to find one!

Still Counting!

February 2013

My Big Year competition might be over, but I'm still out there birding! So this year instead of trying to see as many different species of birds that I can I strive to see some of the rare/elusive birds I haven't yet seen to add to my life list.

I had read an article in a magazine about the great winter birding opportunity on Cape Ann, Massachusetts. The article mentioned specific areas to stop and look for sea birds that spend the winter along the coast. Some of the birds I was very interested in getting a chance to see were, the king eider, the razorbill and the harlequin duck, all life listers for me. So on Saturday Chris, Beth, and I headed to Cape Ann for a day of winter birding.

Our first stop was at the Fisherman's Memorial in Gloucester harbor. There were lots of gulls, a few black ducks and a pair of diving birds that neither of us could identify. No king eider, razorbill, or harlequin duck. But it sure was *cold*, even though we had on multiply layers and thought we were dressed for the cold it was finger and toe numbing cold. The sun was nice and bright but the temperature was barely thirty, and there was a strong sea breeze.

We got back into the car and continued to follow the route for winter birding that the article suggested for best results. Our next stop was at the elks club along the ocean. The article suggests parking in their lot and across the street overlooking the ocean is a viewing spot to look for birds. We were excited when we first arrived to see that there were a few birders set up with spotting scopes scanning the ocean. We were hopeful that meant they had spotted the king eider that the article said could be found here.

We hurried over and asked the other birders if anyone had seen the king eider, only to be told that yes, they had but at eight thirty that morning and not since. We were disappointed but enjoyed taking with the other birders and there were plenty of birds to see there. We enjoyed watching a large flock of Buffleheads as they in unison would dive and then all pop back up out of the water. We saw some common goldeneyes, red-breasted mergansers, common eiders, black ducks, and a couple of grebes. But no king eider, razorbills, or harlequin ducks. We stayed as long as the cold would allow us then headed back to the car to warm up and continue our quest.

The next stop the article suggested was Eastern Point. The article mentions a wildlife preserve and an ocean breakwater where we can park and search for the king eider, razorbill, and harlequin ducks. Thank goodness we had a GPS because we traveled through narrow zig-zagging streets along the old seaport and out onto a private peninsular with grand old seaport homes. When we arrive at the lighthouse, we are a bit disappointed to find the "wildlife preserve" is a gravel parking lot on the beach with slat marsh around us.

We scan the ocean for birds but see only the usual species. We eat lunch in the warmth of the car then head out to the Dog Bar Breakwater, where the article suggests to look for king eiders, razorbills, and harlequin ducks. We make our way across the rocky beach and climb over boulders to make it out onto the rocky jetty. Umm, I guess the king eider, razorbill, and harlequin duck didn't read the article because there were none of them there, just the usual species. But darn it was *cold*! White caps licked at the rocky jetty and the cold wind cut right through to the core.

We make our way back to the car defeated. We joke about if the birds had read the article and knew they were supposed to be here. There is one more spot to try. The article suggests traveling to some rocky ledges over the ocean called Rockport headlands. To quote the article, "Perhaps the spot on the entire East Coast for close views of harlequin ducks." Now the last couple of times I've been birding with Beth she has been my good luck charm, each time I would mention to her a particular bird that I hoped to see, wham sure enough that would be the next bird we would see. But this time it wasn't working so well, I was joking with her that maybe I had to rub her like a genies bottle and ask for my wish to see a harlequin duck be granted.

We turn a tight corner and find ourselves high above the ocean, and we can see a group of birds on the water. We spot a small pull off but the sign says "parking by permit only," there are six or eight cars already there. I want to check out the birds we saw on the water and figure, "What the heck? If I can't park here, they can ask me to leave," and I pull in. We notice everyone is in wet suits, strange indeed. I figure no one will notice me as I set up my scope on the cliffs edge. Chris has had it with the cold and decides to stay in the car, she tells Beth and me to come back and get her if we spot anything good.

Yup, you guessed it: I break into my "birders' happy dance"! We don't even get the spotting scope set up before we both see on the water below us five Harlequin ducks! Magnificent ducks, diving and jumping in and out of the surf. Those of you with bird apps check this species out. My birding good luck charm came through again!

We enjoy watching the ducks we had spent the day searching for and as we head back to the car I stop and speak to one of the men in a wet suit. He explains that they are all here for testing to earn their diving certification. He tells me the cove has a large reef and strong currents and is an interesting place to dive. Then it makes sense why this is such a special place to find the harlequin duck. These ducks live in the high Arctic and spend their lives on rough fast-moving rivers. In the winter, they migrate to rocky New England coasts where they can find mussels and crustaceans among the rocks and underwater reefs.

We never did get to see a king eider or the razorbill, but I bagged a new bird for my life list! So this is Jane's birding adventures part 2. I'm on the hunt to track down new, rare or elusive birds to add to my life list. Still counting birds!

Mother Nature's Rules

March 2013

The Rare Bird Alert, Audubon website and Ebird were all a buzz about the sightings of a great horned owl on Plum Island. The reports stated that there was a nesting pair in the small pine grove at the Bill Forward Bird Blind. Wow this could not be an easier find, I knew exactly where that was. So I set out early Saturday to find this owl.

We have had a couple of really nasty Nor'easters the last couple of weekends, and I had seen the news reports of extensive damage done to homes along the coast line on Plum Island. Nearly a dozen homes had fallen or were in danger of falling into the ocean as the high tide and extreme waves had lashed at the coast line. The National Guard was patrolling the area and the island had been evacuated and closed off. I work with a woman who has family on the island, their home was spared, and she said that the refuge was not damaged. I checked their website, and it didn't say the refuge was closed, so I decided to head out in search of the owl.

Along the road, just before the bridge crossing onto the island, there were large flashing signs saying, "ALL BEACHES CLOSED," "AREA PATROLLED," "VIOLATORS WILL BE ARRESTED." Ummm…I decided to pull over just before crossing the bridge, I got out and scanned across the water to the island. My friend had told me that the only road on the island was blocked off just after the small restaurant on the corner as you cross the bridge. The road to the refuge was the first right hand turn after crossing the bridge, before the intersection where the restaurant was. Sure enough, as I scanned with my binoculars, I could see a military jeep in the road and wooden sawhorses set up.

I decided to give it a try and cross onto the island, I figured the worst that would happen was that they would turn me around; surely, they wouldn't arrest a gray-haired bird lady?

Phew…I made it onto the refuge with no problems! As is usual, I stopped at the first lot to check things out. (Well, let's be honest any of you that have been on the refuge with me knows that the first lot is the only place on the refuge where you can relieve yourself without having to hold your breath *and* has flush toilets.) I see a birder with a scope set up scanning the salt marsh at the edge of the lot, he looks familiar, I decide to walk over and ask what he has spotted. It was an island regular, Tom, he runs a website about bird sightings on Plum Island. Picture Santa Claus in camouflage and khakis instead of a red suit and with a spotting scope over his shoulder instead of a sack of toys, and that's Tom.

He was watching a pair of bald eagles sitting atop a nesting platform. No matter how many times I see an eagle it still impresses me, their beauty and size. We talk about birds a bit. I tell him I am on the island to see the nesting great horned owl. Unfortunately, he tells me that the park service has closed off the area where the owls are nesting. It seems the owls had become too popular; the paparazzi were becoming a problem. People with large camera set-ups were literally camping out for the day, setting up with chairs, and coolers snapping away, all hoping to get that once in a lifetime moneymaker shot of an elusive owl. The park service had no choice but to restrict access to protect the owls. I was disappointed but supported their decision.

Tom tells me that if I go to the edge of the fence at the far side of the parking area by the boardwalk, I might get a sighting of a horned lark. He said there had been a small flock in the field to the left there earlier that morning. I haven't seen a horned lark, so I walked over to see what I could see. Of course, the boardwalk to the beach was taped off with yellow caution tape and a sign warning "NO ACCESS: Violators will be punished."

I have heard many pleasant bird songs in my search for birds, and it sure calms your soul listening to Mother Nature's little jewels communicate. But the "bird" I was now hearing was anything but pleasant. A helicopter had swooped in and was hovering overhead to my left. As I turned, I could see the arm of a large yellow excavator above the dunes and hear the distinctive sound of a bull-dowser. I could hear the sound of wood crunching and see dust rising above the dunes. I'm sure the helicopter was another news crew taking pictures of the demise of someone's home. It felt wrong to be watching as Mother Nature reclaimed her territory. I decided to move on.

Even though I knew the area where the owls were was closed, I figured I would drive by and maybe I could see something from the road. As I drove along the dirt road as expected, every parking lot with access to the beach was tapped off and signs warning "NO ACCESS: Violators will be punished." The island felt sad and lonely, the sky was gray, and it was cold. Sure enough, as I approached the bird blind, I could see the yellow caution tape and more signs "NO ACCESS: Violators will be punished." I pulled over the best I could and put on my flashers, I got out and stood along the edge of the caution tape scanning the pine grove hoping to see the owls.

Nothing, I couldn't see a thing, no owls. A young couple I had passed walking along the dirt road came up, they asked if I was able to spot the owls, I told them sadly no. Like me they had also come onto the island in the hope of seeing the nesting great horned owl. They said they had parked at the Hellcat trail and walked the half mile to this spot to try and see the owls. We talked birds for a bit then they both immersed themselves in scrolling through their iPhones, I got the hint, I wished them good luck and drove away. As I looked in my rearview mirror through the dust my car was kicking up, I could see them lifting the yellow tape and running for cover of the pine grove. We birders can be intense; honestly, I had thought about it as well, but I was too afraid of being caught to take the chance.

The island was sad; I could still hear the helicopter hovering overhead. As I drove over the bridge, I looked in my rearview mirror and could see the dust clouds and smoke of the demolition of people's homes and dreams as Mother Nature reclaimed her territory. Man can try to tame her, but in the end, man must learn to live by Mother Nature's rules.

I haven't given up in my search for the great horned owl. I checked out Ebird, and I found that there have been multiple sightings in the area where my niece Katie lives. A nesting pair in the backwoods of Hampshire College, a pair along the Station Rd rail trail and at Haydenville Loop. I contacted Katie ASAP, and we made plans for me to come out to visit, and she agreed to help me find the owls!

BVD

June 2013

I had quite an adventure recently hiking the trails on Mt. Agamenticus in Maine. Chris had a client in Maine on a Tuesday and decided to take off the Monday and spend the time at her camper on the ocean in Cape Neddick, and she invited me to stay with her. It was good timing because it was an awful heat wave and the ocean offered cooling breezes and fun in the surf. We enjoyed Monday just sitting in our sand chairs with our feet in the ocean cool as cucumbers. When Chris needed to go to work on Tuesday, I thought I would explore the trails on the mountain to search for new birds. The mountain was a short drive from the camper, Chris expected to be back from work around three, so I had plenty of time to explore.

Mt. Agamenticus is famous as a hawk-watching site. During their migration, thousands of hawks can be seen passing by. There is a mountain access road to the summit and a nice lodge and great views. I took one of the trail maps and planned out my route. I was trying to be conservative in my expectations and ability, I was alone, and it was hot and humid. I decided the two-mile turtle trail that made a ring around the summit sounded doable. I needed to take a shorter access trail from the summit to connect with the turtle trail and decided to take the shortest straight line trail to connect.

I got my binoculars, my bird bag, water bottle and molasses cookies, I set off on the straight-line sweet fern trail from the summit. Just as I enter the tree line the trail drops suddenly along sheer smooth rocks. I pass the remains of some sort of tower all rusty as the trail gets steeper and slipperier. I consider turning around but when I look back the climb is steep, and I figure I've committed to going down, so I proceed. My heart is pounding, I'm sweating profusely, and suddenly I slip and fall onto my butt and begin to slide down the rock face. I tell ya that was one heck of a ride down the rest of the trail on my butt!

As I catch my breath, I yell at myself, I know better than that, I know how to read a map. Do you see my mistake? Umm, did I mention Mt. Agamenticus used to be a ski area? A straight line on a map from the summit of a mountain down is just that *straight down*! The trail followed the ski lift, the rusty towers were what was left of the ski lift minus the chairs. Well, that got the adrenalin going! I push onward along the trail into the cooler dense pine forest.

I was glad to be off the bare summit and out of the blaring sun but the forest cover didn't offer much relief, it was so humid I felt like I was breathing cotton candy the air was so thick. I was hearing birds but nothing new, got a good look at a nice black-throated green warbler. I could hear a thrush singing in the trees but couldn't see him. I needed to pee, which kinda surprised me since I was sweating so heavy, I didn't think I had any moisture left in me. No was else was on the trail, I decided to go down the embankment into the spruce trees to be under cover as I relieved myself. Hey any port in a storm will do.

The pine needles and leaf litter were slick and don't ya know I fall onto my butt yet again and slide down the embankment. Just that kinda day, I guess. After my pit stop, I was left with the quandary of what to do with the used tissue. I often carry a small plastic baggie for such occasions but Chris didn't have any at the camper so what to do. Umm, I know I'll just lift this loose rock sticking up and put it under there, I don't want to leave it out in the open where anyone could see it. As I lift the rock to dispose of my spent tissue, something small and black slithers quickly away. Yikes, *snake*! Believe me I made it back up the embankment faster than I did down. (Well, maybe it wasn't a snake, not really the right habitat, it was more likely a large salamander, but at first glance, my mind yelled *snake*!)

Okay then, I'm back on the trail and continue on. There is that thrush singing again. I search the treetops and finally get a brief glance at him as he flies away. I quickly leaf through my bird book trying to identify which thrush he might be. I narrow the possibilities down to either a Swainson's thrush or the Bicknell's thrush, I mark the pages of the bird book and push onward. I've been hiking for a bit more than an hour, and I come to the intersection with a trail back up to the summit. This time I choose the trail with lots of squiggly lines, which I know means there are a lot of switch-backs to the top making the climb easier.

I break out of the tree line and back onto the bare summit and the heat hits like a blast furnace in the face. Darn it's hot out today! I find some shade and sit on a rock out-cropping for a rest. I'm sweating heavy, my heart is pounding, and I feel a little shaky. I sit and have a swig of water and a molasses cookie and turn on my Nook to try and identify that thrush. I watch as turkey vultures make slow circles riding the thermals overhead. Umm, gee, Sissy, do you think their eyeing me?

The more I look over my bird guides the more confused I become, is it a Swainson's or Bicknells's thrush? The Bicknell's would be a new bird for me; they are rather rare, and they only live in Maine and Nova Scotia. I need to get another look to be sure, my molasses cookie break has bolstered my strength, so I decide to head back down the trail to the intersection where I saw the bird. I look down to tie my loose shoe lace and pick a tick off my ankle, it's time to move out of here.

I never did find the thrush again, so I have to list it as a BVD (in birders' lingo that means "better view desired"). I had an adventurous day and when I shared my day with Chris when she got back from work, she was not happy with me. She made me promise not to go off by myself and do something like that again. Yeah, maybe she is right, but we will see if I learned that life lesson or not.

Island Airshow

November 2013

This past Saturday was forecast to be one of the last warm and sunny days we would see here in New England for a while. A strong cold front was moving in bringing frigid arctic winds and temperatures. So I thought it would be a good day to head to Plum Island to do some last birding before winter really took hold.

Stopped at the first beach access area, and I scanned the ocean waters for sea birds. The wind was picking up and my eyes were watering, but I managed to spot a white-winged scooter, a common loon in winter plumage and a horned grebe. Something alarmed the grebe, and it began to "run" across the surface of the water flapping its wings trying to take off like a large heavy plane. This dance across the water is what the grebe is known for, and I was excited to get to witness the display. Not a bad start to the day.

At the next stop, the Overlook Pool, I saw a pair of northern pintails, dozens of black ducks, and mallards. They were all butts in the air as they bobbed for food below the surface. As I was watching the antics of the ducks, a large flock of Canada geese came from behind me and landed on the water. It was a strange sensation to suddenly have a flock of geese fly low over my head, they surprised me, I could hear the wind across their feathers as they flew over my head. They stretched out their webbed feet like landing gear and glided across the water to a stop.

Next stop, was at the wardens shed, I could see that there was a large flock of some kind of small birds flying low across the salt marsh. I lost sight of the flock by the time I got out of the car and started to walk behind the buildings. There was a man standing in the field with a camera aimed at the ground. I walked very slowly toward the man, not wanting to disturb whatever he was taking a picture of, I scanned the field with my binoculars trying to see what he was looking at. He motioned to me to stop, which I did, and then he pointed to his right. I could see the grasses moving but still couldn't see what was making the grasses move. The man motioned for me to move toward him, I slowly began to walk through the tall grass.

Then suddenly in an explosion of feathers and tweeting a large flock of snow bunting burst out of the tall grass and surrounded me! It was fantastic! I felt like I was in a Disney movie, all these small tweeting birds surrounding me. I was certain I could reach out and touch one, but I was to transfixed to try. The flock made a tight circle around me then in unison they zigged and zagged over the marsh. One of nature's best aerial acrobats they could make any stunt flier jealous. Then they swooped back low over the marsh and settled into the tall grasses again, completely hidden.

The sunny weather was starting to change, the winds were picking up and the sky was clouding over. It was getting cold fast. Stopped next at Hellcat Trails as I drove along the refuge dirt road. On top of the ridge at Hellcat Dike, there was a mature bald eagle. He was on the ground, he had something he had just killed in his claws and was tearing it apart to eat. Interesting to watch, but I decided to move on and let him enjoy his lunch in peace. Also, there was the strange sight of one lone white egret standing in the beaver pool at Hellcat, fellow birders there were all speculating why this one bird was here and not heading south to Florida where it belongs.

Next stop on the island was the bird blind. The pool at the blind was void of any birds, but I was finally able to find the great horned owl nest. Yeah, I had to kinda sort of break the rules, and I went off the trail into the scrub pine grove to find the nest tree. But I tried all summer to see the owl and never did, at least I found his nest, so I'll be a step ahead of him next season. I had been on the island for an hour by now, the wind was blowing the dirt from the refuge road into little dust tornadoes, my fingers were frozen even in my gloves, and my cheeks hurt from the cold. I guess it was time to head home.

As I head back along the dirt road to exit the refuge, there was a group of cars stopped along the side of the road near Hellcat Dike. There was an elderly man standing in front of me holding up his hands for me to stop. I got out and went to see why all these people were standing in the road with cameras and binoculars. A sure sign that something really interesting was going on! The elderly man tells me of the incredible sight that just took place.

He tells me the bald eagle I had seen earlier was joined by a second adult on the dike and a fight began over the food. Then even more exciting a pair of immature bald eagles swooped in to try and claim the kill. He explains that then all four eagles took to the sky and were fighting and dive bombing each other. He said the birds flew so low across the road that one car was nearly hit, that was why he had stopped traffic. He says it was an airshow like he had never seen before!

I missed the airshow put on by the eagles, but I enjoyed my own private airshow put on by the snow buntings and the surprise airshow put on by the flock of geese and the comical airshow performed by the horned grebe. I was glad I had decided to make the trip to the island. As the holiday season progresses, the pressures mount and time moves to fast everyone should try and take time to enjoy the simple pleasures nature can provide us. I know that I sure enjoyed my island airshow. I think of those snow buntings swirling around me, and I smile. Snow buntings live in the Arctic, they only come south to New England for a short time in the winter. So it is a real treat to see them.

Second Chances

January 2014

I think it is safe to say we have all had one of those days/weeks where we wish we could have a do-over. Stop time and go back and do things differently. Yuck, I had just such a week. This extreme cold gripping New England was making me crazy. I was spending too much time staring at the computer screen, in a virtual world I don't fully understand. I had to get out of this house and into nature!

The weather forecast for Saturday was for a New England heat wave! Temperature to climb up near thirty and sunny, though the caveat was the very windy conditions. But no matter I decided I needed to head to Plum Island to clear my head, or freeze it off in the process. I needed to see some birds!

I checked out the Rare Bird website and E-Bird to see what was out there to be found, I went through my bird guide and marked the pages of some of the birds I hoped to get to see. There were reports of flocks of horned larks and Lapland Longspurs being seen in the salt plains. And reports of as many as fifty razorbills seen in the ocean just off shore and in the open waters under the bridge. As I drove over the metal bridge onto the island, I saw in the water below what I thought looked like a flock of razorbills bobbing in the icy waters. I have been trying to see these birds for two years, but they were on the opposite side, and I couldn't stop on the bridge to get a better look, oh well.

Well, the weather man wasn't quite right about the forecast. The island was windy, cloudy, cold and gloomy. I stopped at all the usual spots scanning the ocean and salt marshes for birds. Nothing, hey the birds knew better than me, it was not a day to be out in the elements. I did get to see a northern harrier soar over the marsh and hover low in search of a meal. The wind was fierce, but he held his own, but finally gave up and settled on a barren branch to rest. My mood wasn't improving—heck, why bother; I decided to call it a day and head home.

I decided to stop at the new visitor/ranger station to pick up a program guide for 2014. I was determined to get out at least once each weekend, I wasn't going to get sucked into that virtual world, spending my time staring at a screen. As I entered the building, there was a large sign; it said, "Owl Release Today at 3:00 p.m.!" Umm, that sounded interesting, I asked the woman behind the desk what it was about. She told me that a snowy owl had been rescued from Logan Airport earlier in the morning and that they were going to release it on the refuge. That we could watch the release if we parked at lot #1.

I told her I had just come off the refuge, I've seen the snowy owl before, that I had been out for a couple of hours already, I was cold and heading home. She wouldn't accept that, she tells me when am I ever going to get to witness such an event again, be able to get up close to such a magnificent bird again? Yeah, she was right, but I told her I really didn't feel like paying to get back onto the refuge, I was cold. Truth was I felt gloomy I just didn't care. She offers me a cup of coffee and tells me she will call the ranger at the refuge entrance and ask if since I just left could I show my ticket and get back onto the island to watch the release. The ranger tells her that the ticket is good for the whole day just show it at the gate on my way back in.

I sat in the car deciding what to do. Do I really want to go back onto the island? Heck the woman was right, what a chance, could I really pass it up? I turned around and went back, parked at lot #1 and waited for the owl to arrive. I had about half hour before the release, I began to rethink this again, this was stupid, I turned on the car to leave. Suddenly I see a large flock of birds, land in the dune grasses at the edge of the parking area. My birding brain took over, I grabbed my binos, jumped out of the car and crept up to the flock. They were horned larks! A life list species for me!

A crowd was starting to gather, all in anticipation of the owl's arrival. The rangers drive up and establish a perimeter keeping the crowd back. A small blue hatch back drives in, a man lifts a wooden box out of the back and pushes back the cover, and he lifts out with his bare hands a snowy owl. He holds the owl up while walking around for all to see. He tells us it is okay to take pictures that we don't have to be quiet. He wants the owl to fear us, he wants the owl to learn to stay away from the two-legged creatures surrounding him. He tells us how he trapped the owl and then examined it, tagged it, and gave him a meal of live rodents. Now it was time to release him to his new environment and hope for the best.

The man asks if there are any questions. He talks about how he became a raptor rehabilitator that he has saved five hundred owls, hawks and falcons in his lifetime. People ask why does the owl seem so calm right now, he explains that he has a full belly and doesn't know to fear humans. The owl is so beautiful, constantly scanning the crowd. As he walked by, holding the owl, I could look right into the owl's eyes, see the texture of each feather. Such an amazing bird.

A man from the crowd asks why did he get involved, why did he feel he had to remove the owl from Logan Airport. Why not just leave the owl alone? Let what happens happen. Why did he feel he knew what was best for the owl and not that the owl knew what was best? The man says he thinks everyone made a big deal out of nothing; it wasn't his business to remove the owl. Others in the crowd express the same sentiment.

The rehabilitator stands still, holds up the owl over his head, and says, "Do you see how large this bird is? Do you have any idea what would happen if he was to be sucked into the jet engines of an airplane? Do you want to be the one to not do anything and take a chance in many dying because one bird caused an accident?"

The man from the crowd steps forward, he says, "I apologize, I applaud the work you do, I am thankful for caring people like you."

The man holds the owl high and tells the crowd to count to three. He is going to release the owl. We all count 1...2...3...! The owl rises up, circles the crowd tips his wing toward us and soars off into the scrub brush of the dunes. The crowd cheers! The man yells, "Don't we all deserve a second chance!"

"Thank you all for being a part of this special event." Profound… very profound. Was he talking to me?

As I head back over the bridge, leaving the island, I slow down, look over the edge, and there in the icy waters below are razorbills! Wow, I got a second chance, I got to see two new species to add to my life list. In my book, we all deserve a second, third, fourth…to infinity chances. I can only hope to earn a second chance.

Puzzle Pieces

I love the challenge of a good puzzle. Keeps the mind humming. We had to attend "personality workshops" for work to help make us more understanding employees. I'm sure it's no surprise that my main personality traits are "problem solver and analytical." For years I have suffered from bouts of insomnia. I've tried all sorts of techniques to fall asleep, most to no avail. I've tried sister Chris's technique, to put the problem keeping you awake in a mental box, close it and put the box away on a shelf. Well, that didn't work out very good for me. I first had to mentally design the box, what color should it be, a lock or no lock? Then I needed to build the shelf, how many shelves would I need, how many troubles do I have? Should I paint the shelves or stain them? Any ways you get the idea sleep still eluded me, sorry I do digress. As I said, I do enjoy solving a good puzzle.

I had a woodland puzzle in my backyard that needed to be solved. One night when I let the cat out, I heard an unusual sound coming from the back woods. It was loud, it wasn't a frog but didn't really sound like a bird either, I wasn't quite sure what it was. I asked John to step outside and listen to it, he wasn't sure what it was either. And so began my quest to identify the strange noise in the woods. There are only a few birds that are active in the evening so that narrowed the possibilities. I knew it wasn't an owl or the whip-poor-will, I suspected it might be either a nighthawk or the woodcock.

The next night I again stood on the back deck at dusk and sure enough the sound was coming loud and clear from the woods. I played the song of the nighthawk on my bird app on my nook. But got no response, the woods went quiet. Then I tried the song of the American Woodcock, and got an immediate response. This was exciting the Woodcock was a Life List bird for me! The pieces of the puzzle were beginning to fall in place. But I needed visual confirmation. I had to get out into the woods and see who was making the strange sounds I was hearing.

The next night I went to the edge of the woods with a flashlight waiting to hear the sound again. There it was, it sounded so close. I decided to try to creep into the woods and locate it. Unfortunately, it wasn't that easy, there is still snow in the woods, and I got tangled up in the dense raspberry vines. The vines pulled at my pants and scratched my legs, my hair got caught on the low branches of the trees. Finally, I made it to the area the sound was coming from—a small clearing in the woods made by a fallen tree. The sound was right there, sounded like it was right at my feet, but I couldn't see anything! I scanned the area with the flashlight but nothing. I tried to walk farther into the clearing but fell over a rock and dropped the flashlight. The sound stopped. I fought my way back through the picker bushes to the house.

The next day, I decided to follow my foot prints in the snow back to the area I had heard the sound. When I did that, I saw a much easier way to get there than I had taken the night before. I searched the area carefully, used a stick to poke at the piles of fallen leaves and rustled the bushes to see if I could flush the Woodcock out into the open. All the puzzle pieces pointed to the sound as being from a Woodcock, but I still needed that last piece to be sure.

That evening I was ready. I stood outside waiting to hear the sound and right on time at seven forty-five he began to call *preeent... preeent...preent...* Flashlight ready, I headed into the woods. Straight back to the leaning tree, take a right and go through the two tall spruce trees then turn left, follow the deer trail till I get to the rock jutting up. This time I didn't fall over the rock. I stood very still and waited. All was quiet. Then it happened the bird began his song and in the light of the flashlight I see the final piece to the puzzle!

An American Woodcock sitting on the ground performing his mating dance! He would call *preent...*bob up and down, and then turn call *preent...*bob up and down, and then turn call Preent...bob up and down, and then turn till he had made a full circle. Then he reversed direction and repeated the steps. I was able to take a couple of pictures in the light of the flashlight of the bird as he danced. As if that wonderful sight wasn't enough, a second bird came flying overhead in answer to his calls. I could just make out its silhouette against the evening sky. They joined in a circle and spiraled upward then seemed to fall straight back down softly tweeting the whole time. I felt so privileged to be a witness to their dance.

Sometimes I wonder if maybe some of the puzzle pieces in my brain got misplaced after the fractured skull I suffered as a kid. I can't solve all the problems of life. I don't have the answers to the endless questions. I can't always find the missing pieces to put things in order. But that night I didn't need to pretend to put my worries in a box and place it on a shelf. As I lay my head on the pillow, I could still hear the funny song of the Woodcock and as I closed my eyes, I could see him doing the dance nature taught him to perform. That night I solved at least one puzzle.

It is 7:51 p.m. now, and I just stood on the back deck; the little Woodcock is indeed still singing in the woods. I hope to sleep well again tonight.

Are We There Yet?

September 2014

Fall migration is in full swing here in New England. Resident birds are making their way to warmer wintering spots and birds from the Arctic are making their way to our coastlines. I haven't been to Plum Island to do some birding in a few months, so I thought it was time to make a trip and experience the excitement of migration. Every season brings new discoveries, new bird sightings to add to my life list.

Migration is certainly one of the marvels of nature. To think that the ruby-throated hummingbird I see visiting the feeders at the cabin in the summer will fly all the way to Central America for the winter season is unbelievable. The fact that these tiny little birds can make such an amazing flight there and then turn around and come back just blows my mind! Can you imagine taking that kind of family trip every year after year? How many times do you think you'd hear, "Are we there yet?" from the back seat.

It was a nice fall day on the island, I found an empty colony of nesting tunnels in the side of a sand dune made by the bank swallows. Now that I know where they nest, in the spring I can go back to that spot and watch them. What an amazing migration the bank swallow makes, they travel from that nesting colony on Plum Island all the way to South America.

I saw many flocks of great egrets and snowy egrets roaming through the slat marshes searching for food to fuel up for their trip to the Gulf Coast of Florida and beyond for the winter. These might be some of the original "snowbirds" from New England heading south to bother Sissy and Bill along the beautiful coastal beaches of Charlotte County. Are we there yet? Get ready, sister and brother-in-law, I will be there in February before you know it looking for new birds. Do you count me as a snowbird?

But the rock star of migration on Plum Island at this time was a Hudsonian godwit. This is a very uncommon and rare sighting that I was lucky enough to be in the right place at the right time to witness. These large shorebirds are part of the sandpiper family, they have a long-curved bill. They live in Northern Alaska and British Columbia and usually travel nonstop from James Bay Canada to their wintering grounds in South America. But for some reason, this one juvenile bird stopped on Plum Island. It was hanging out with a flock of mallards seemingly in no hurry to fly any farther south.

This bird was drawing a lot of attention. There were a couple of volunteers from Audubon set up on the viewing platform overlooking the salt marsh with bird guides open to the Hudsonian godwit showing people the details to look for. They also had two spotting scopes set up and were letting birders get a close up look at the rare shorebird. There was a ranger there directing traffic and keeping the paparazzi under control. It was quite a scene in deed.

I think I know why that Hudsonian godwit stopped on Plum Island. I think that young bird while flying in formation with the rest of its flock asked its dad that nagging question one to many times. That shorebird's dad probably told him if he asked one more time "Are we there yet?" that he was gonna pull over and let him out on the side of the road. And that's just what he did. Time will tell if that young shorebird catches a ride with another passing flock or spends the winter on Plum Island. But I bet next time it won't be asking, "Are we there yet?"

Why Did the Chicken Cross the Road?

September 2014

This past Sunday, John and I had a chance to visit with Jeremy and Crystal in Vermont. From our home in southern New Hampshire to theirs it is a three-hour drive but Route 89 is a very scenic drive. It was so nice to see them, it was a beautiful fall day in Vermont. They are both doing well, their garden has been fruitful this season, and they are busy with canning. The house smelled so delicious when we arrived, they had just made over a dozen zucchini loafs and apple butter was cooking as well. We got to meet the newest additions to their homestead, Ms. Claire Cat and Mr. Archer Cat, sweet little kitties. Yes, the dogs, Bella and Dexter, get along fine with the cats. Those of us who are owned by cats know who really rules the household, Ms. Claire Cat keeps the dogs in line.

Looking out over their garden, I could see the chickens roaming through the tall grass when it occurred to me that I spend a lot of time talking about the virtues of birds in the wild and don't give domesticated birds their proper credit. Chickens have a bad rap, jokes are made at their expense, but they are pretty smart birds. Crystal's chickens behave very well, they come when she calls them and will follow her around the yard. And they certainly do provide them with plenty of fresh eggs.

Though Crystal said that one morning when she was checking the coop for eggs there weren't any. She was baffled at first as to why the hens hadn't laid any eggs, and then she noticed a hen sitting in the tall grass in the yard. When she pushed back the grass, she saw that the hen had made a nest in the grass and laid her eggs there not in the coop. She said that chickens tend to keep flying out of their

116

enclosure, I guess the lure of the wild grasses is just too much for them. These ladies are smart they know where the nice sunny spots are, can't blame them if they "fly the coop" now and then.

Crystal said that because the hens have been escaping their enclosure, she worried that they were at risk from predators from the sky and woods. But the hens don't seem "chicken" at all. They strut about the yard enjoying the multitudes of seeds and bugs. Every now and then, they will stop and lift their heads and look around for danger. Unfortunately, one day, Crystal said that a large hawk did swooped in and carry one of the ladies away. But still the others seem undeterred, they sure don't seem afraid so why do people call each other "chicken" if we are timid or won't accept a dare?

So let's give these hardworking ladies the credit they deserve for all they do for us. Why did the chicken cross the road? Hey who cares why, give the chick a break, can't a girl take a walk about now and then without all the questions.

Golden Acres

October 2014

My youngest sister Becky has served on the Merrimack Conservation Committee for a couple of years now. As I once also served on my town's conservation committee, we often discuss conservation issues. Becky has told me about the volunteer work she has been doing, that she helped blaze a new trail and build a bridge along the trail in the Wildcat Falls Conservation Area. It occurred to me that it was about time I visited this special wild area to see the fruits of her labor.

So my sister and I made plans for a light hike on a beautiful fall day. Nothing can soothe your soul or brighten your mood like getting out in the fresh air and surrounding yourself with nature. Especially during fall as the leaves are all turning a golden hue with splashes of red and orange. We hadn't walked very far along the trail when I nearly stepped on a garter snake sunning itself in the warmth of the morning sun. I was a bit surprised to see a snake so late in the season.

We soon cut off the main trail onto the side trail that Becky had been working on. We entered into a forest of towering oak trees, the golden rays of sun shone through the canopy, it was like we were in Mother Nature's cathedral. I stood still for a minute just looking at the golden glow surrounding me. And don't ya know there was another Garter Snake laying across the trail! Yikes that's two snakes I almost stepped on in less than an hour. The trail made its way down to the edge of the Souhegan River and ran along the banks through a small pine grove before climbing back up the ridge.

This area was a woodpeckers paradise, we came upon numerous standing dead trees with nesting holes excavated. As we walked along, we could hear the nasal *yank-yank…yank-yank…yank* call of the red-breasted nuthatch. There was the sharp peek-peek-peek call of the hairy woodpecker. The unmistakable loud call *cuk...cuk... cuk...cuk...cuk* of the pileated woodpecker rang through the woods. At seventeen inches, this bird is North America's largest woodpecker, always impressive to see drilling into a fallen log for bugs. The most unusual call was the red-bellied woodpecker, with its soft musical *churrrr...churrrr...churrr* coming from the woods.

As we made our way along the trail, we climbed a set of granite steps (aka the knee busters) that had been set into the steep ridge to access the top of Wildcat Falls. Becky said the river was low so the falls were not as impressive as they usually are, but I wasn't disappointed. I thought the view was stunning. We sat on some rocks at the top of the falls and enjoyed a picnic lunch. It was so peaceful listening to the sound of the rushing water this was indeed a very special wild place worth every effort to preserve.

I'm very proud of the volunteer work my little sister has been doing. I look forward to a return visit to the Golden Acres of Wildcat Falls (minus the snakes).

Down the Drain

October 2014

Well, birding has been kind of slow now that the weather is getting colder and the bulk of traveling birds have migrated through. Still, every now and then, a little surprise visitor shows up. Recently I had a Carolina wren show up in my yard, it had been hanging around for a week or so. It's a bit unusual for them to visit this late in the season I hadn't seen one all summer and speculate this one was most likely just passing through.

For some reason, it took over the squirrel feeder as its home. I gave up trying to keep the squirrels away from the bird feeders years ago and just gave them their own feeder. It sort of looks like a squirrel-sized dog house on a pole with a deck to place bread scraps, etc., on. I have been seeing the little wren going in and out of the squirrel house and often sitting on top of it. I was worried the poor little bird was going to starve as it gets colder and the bugs die off. The wrens main diet is bugs and that's why it is unusual for them to be this far north this time of year.

So I decided I needed to get some meal worms for the little bird. I made the thirty-mile drive to the feed store just to buy the little wren some dried meal worms for dinner. Geez for dried up bugs they aren't cheap. An eight-ounce bag cost twelve bucks! I placed some of the gross looking little worms in the squirrel feeder and watched for the wren to fly in and enjoy them. It didn't take long before the wren was feasting on the worms, at times it had three or four in its mouth as it flew off. I almost wondered if it was sharing them with more wrens that were maybe off in the trees somewhere.

I store all my bird seeds in the bathroom closet. I have multiple containers that fit nicely on the shelf and are easy to carry back and forth to the feeders. But I didn't have any containers available to put the meal worms in. It grossed me out each time I opened the closet and had to look at those worms in the plastic bag, so I stashed the bag out of sight on the top shelf. At the time, it seemed like a good plan.

One evening after my shower, as I pulled back the shower curtain, I realized that I had forgotten to get fresh towels. Haven't we all done that at one time or another? So dripping wet, I open the bathroom closet to get a towel to dry off with. I reach for my favorite fluffy towel, and as I pull it off the shelf, I inadvertently pull the plastic bag of meal worms out too.

The meal worms spill out of the bag and shower down on me sticking to my wet body and spilling out across the tile at my feet. At this point, I'm screaming! I'm jumping around trying not to step on the gross bugs strewn across the floor and at the same time trying to brush the worms off me. Needless to say, I jumped back into the shower and feverishly rewashed myself. Watching the expensive bugs floating in the water and circle down the drain. *Gross!*

I sure hope that little Carolina wren enjoys his ghoulish dinner of disgusting dried meal worms, I nearly lost my dinner as those worms rained down on me. Good luck if any of you can enjoy dinner now that I have painted that gross mental picture of me wet and covered with meal worms, try getting that image out of your mind.

Happy Halloween!

The Naked Birder

November 14

This past Saturday Beth, Chris, Becky, and myself spent the day on Plum Island. This was the first time Becky had joined us on the island for some birding. She was a little hesitant about spending a chilly windy November day on the Atlantic Ocean. But she was a real trooper, she came prepared for the weather with sweater, down vest, ski jacket, scarf, hat, gloves and snow pants. Truth is it wasn't really that cold on the island, temps were around forty. Though the wind was cold coming off the ocean, it was still better to have it and not need it than need it and not have it, right?

I was excited to show Becky all my favorite places to bird on the island and share the experience with her. I did my research ahead of time to see where the birds we were hoping to see might be. Beth was hoping to see a Brant, I was hoping to see an American Pipit, Chris had no expectations, she just enjoys seeing something interesting or different. So we headed out across the boardwalk over the dunes to the ocean, wondering what we might spot.

Beth and I are ahead of Chris and Becky, as we are walking, I hear this faint *whiit…whiit…whiit*. You see I am an ear birder, I usually hear the bird before I see it. Beth and I stop, I cupped my ears in the direction the sound seemed to be coming from, but it had stopped. We walk along a little more when I hear the sound again whiit…whiit…whiit. The sound seems to be coming from behind me, I turn and bring my hands to my ears to zero in on the sound. I see Becky walking toward me, with each step I hear *whiit…whiit… whiit…* Duh, it's the sound her snow pants are making as she is walking.

We scrambled across the rocks at the end of the island to get a better view of a large flock of Surf Scooters feeding just off shore. We see an assortment of gulls and a loon in its winter plumage. The sun is warm but the wind is cold, it's time to head back, time for lunch. As we are driving along the dirt road of the refuge, we see a group of cars pulled over at a trail head. There are people with large camera outfits and scopes gathered. This is a sure sign that something good has been spotted!

We stop, and I ask Becky to roll down her window and ask them what's been sighted. It's the snowy owl! Wow it's on the island early this year. It was the same trail that we saw the owl on with Emily. I ask the girls if it's worth stopping and walking out to see it. Beth, Chris, and I have seen the snowy before, but I didn't think Becky had. But Becky says, "Nah, I've seen them before I'm not interested."

I'm really surprised; as we drive on, I question her further. I ask her when did she ever get the chance to see an Arctic snowy owl before.

"Uh," my little sister answers, "Oh, I've seen plenty of pictures of snowy owls." What?! I'm flabbergasted! I can't believe someone would give up the chance to see a live snowy owl. But my little sister redeemed herself at our next stop.

We had one last stop to make before leaving the island, Hellcat Trails. I knew we didn't have the time to take the trail, but we wanted to make a quick check of the observation tower overlooking the salt marsh since there had been reports of Brants being sighted there. We get to the edge of the dike, and I'm scanning the marsh with my binoculars when Becky points out a tall bird she sees at the edge of the marsh quite a ways away. Becky didn't bring binoculars, she birds freestyle. I zoom in on where she is pointing, and it is an American Bittern lurking in the tall reeds! Wow! I can't believe she was able to spot that bird camouflaged among the reeds with her naked eye! Very impressive!

Family always gets a laugh out of this, I was birding in my ninja birder outfit, and it's my way of trying to hide from the birds as I sneak up on them. I had my long black scarf wrapped over my head and around my face with only my eyes showing. I was trying to get my binoculars off to pass them to Becky so she could get an up-close look at the Bittern, but in the process, I got the strap all wound up in my scarf. I couldn't get them off and didn't want her to miss the bird, so I hugged her to get close enough so she could look through my binoculars while I still had them around my neck. I think I might have embarrassed my sister a bit, but she got a good look at a life list bird.

As we are leaving Hellcat Trails, two medium-sized birds fly by at top speed in front of us. All I see are two dark blurs, Beth says all she can make out is that it was two of something that sped by. Becky again impresses us with her naked birding skills. She describes what she saw, two medium-sized birds, blue bodies, white belly, and rusty neck. After checking a field guide, she decides they were eastern blue-birds; yup, that description fits. Kudos to Becky on another great ID.

I do here by bestow upon my sister Rebecca the title of "The Naked Birder." Rest assured, this is a very honorable title; in birders lingo, a naked birder is someone who can spot and ID birds by the naked eye without the use of any binoculars, scope, or camera. A very special talent, indeed.

Beach Buddies

July 2014

Since I work at a school and have the summer off, I was looking for ideas to spend my days. Chris and Mark were gracious enough to offer me use of the camper at Cape Neddick during the week day when it is not being used. I knew that my sister Becky's mother-in-law Carle enjoyed the area so we made plans to meet for a day at the beach. As any birder will tell you, half of the fun in birding is sharing it with others. So we made plans to go to Mt. Agamenticus in the morning for a picnic lunch and hopefully get a chance to see the hawks as they climb the thermals into the sky.

When we arrived, we noticed a number of cars and a couple of school buses, obviously there was some sort of summer program happening. The summit area was a bit crowded with students, and it did limit our access to some of the viewing platforms, but it was nice to see the kids enjoying nature. I took Carle out to the rocky overlook so we could get a good view of the valley below. The biggest surprise was as we approached the area a group of kids were gathered and suddenly one of the kids yells to me. "Hey, are you Jeanine's mother?" I stop in my tracks. I say, "Hello yes I am." He tells me his name and explains that he went to school with my daughter and that they were on the X-Country Track team together. And that he remembered me always being at the meets, clapping and ringing a bell as each runner from the school ran by. He tells me he is the leader of the group of kids for a summer nature program. When he told me his name, I did remember him, but he surely had changed a lot since high school.

When we got to the overlook platform, I could hear plenty of birds but not a lot of them were venturing out from cover. I was able to spot a male Scarlet Tanager sitting in a tree. I passed my binoculars to Carle, and she got to see her first Scarlet Tanager! Nothing makes a birder happier than helping a new birder find that first life list bird. She described it; it looks florescent in the sun!

After walking around the summit, enjoying the views and a picnic lunch, we knew it was time to get off the mountain and hit the beach as the temperature was climbing. The tide was going out, and we planted our chairs in the sand at the water's edge and relaxed watching the sea birds. There were plenty of herring gulls just calmly bobbing in the waves. We enjoyed watching a small flock of common terns fishing in the surf.

We watched as the terns would dive into the surf from above and grab a small fish over and over. Carle counted eight times that it took one tern to dive forcefully into the surf before he was successful at getting a fish. Terns are such graceful seabirds to watch, with their forked tails and black cap. They hover above the water searching for fish then tuck their wings in and dive into the water with a splash. Carle brought up a good point; she wondered how do they get the "lift" to get back into the air after diving into the water?

We had a very relaxing afternoon. I didn't see a lot of birds, I didn't see any new birds, but it didn't matter. Carle got to see a new bird, and I learned to slow down a bit and really study the behavior of the birds I am seeing rather than rushing around to add to my count. I know sometimes I get a little frantic about finding that next bird. Best part of the day, I made a beach buddy to share a lazy afternoon with, to plant our chairs in the sand and stick our feet in the cold Atlantic water and just relax. Believe me we met up in Maine many more times. Another life lesson learned. Slow down, relax and enjoy what is around you even simple things can bring smiles.

Can We Chat?

December 2014

A couple of weeks ago, John was in the living room, and he called upstairs to me to come down quickly that there was a different looking bird in the bushes outside the window. I rushed down but the bird had flown off by the time I got to the window. I asked him to describe the bird, he said it was sparrow-sized (aren't they all?) had a bright yellow throat and greenish body. Ummm? I got my bird guide out and started to flip through the pages to try and find out what he might have seen. He is partially color blind so it can be difficult for him to really tell the colors of anything. I asked him to flip through the book and see if he spotted the bird he saw, but he couldn't find it.

I couple of days later he was out getting wood when he came back in and said he just saw that little bird again. That it was out behind the wood shed in the raspberry brambles. As it was a little after four and nearly dark, I strained to see any movement in the bushes. I saw nothing, I had missed it again. With his difficulty in distinguishing colors, I honestly began to doubt what he might have seen.

The following weekend was one of those rare New England days in the winter—the weather was sunny and near sixty. We decided to take a trip to Plum Island to enjoy the good weather, the snowy owl was back on the island and it's always worth the trip to see him. In the area of the S curves along the refuge road, we had stopped to see what the crowd that had gathered was about. People were lined up along the road with scopes and cameras and all pointing into the bushes. You know what that means, something good was spotted! It was a large barred owl just calmly sitting on a low branch resting.

As we are walking back toward the car, John almost steps on a dead bird laying on the ground. Poor thing :(He picks it up to show me, yeah gross but that's a guy for ya. I cringe and tell him to put it down! He says, "But this is the bird I saw in the yard." I look at it, and it is a dead yellow-breasted chat. What? He shouldn't be here, they are rarely seen this far north, but it *is* a yellow-breasted chat! The colors were prefect, have to say that even dead he was prettier than his picture in the book. It was still limp so it hadn't been dead for too long, kinda wonder if that was the owls kill and that was why the owl was being so patient about hanging around for pictures.

The next day, I checked out Tom's birding page (a webpage about bird sightings on the island) to see what had been spotted on the island, and I saw that the yellow-breasted chat had been seen at the S curves section of the road for three days prior to when we were there. And that the barred owl was also seen in the same area. As the crow flies, we aren't that far from Plum Island, it is very possible that the little Chat had been passing through our yard. So even though I didn't see it, it seems that we may have had a yellow-breasted chat visiting our yard.

Just goes to show you, you never know what may end up outside your window, so always keep your eyes open!

A Buck and Some Bones

December 2014

After a week of a Nor'easter slamming the coast and dumping rain on New Hampshire off and on all week, the sun finally reappeared on Sunday. John had been stuck in New Jersey all week for his company's regional sales meeting, one long boring blah blah blah meeting after another. So between the two of us suffering from cabin fever we were anxious to get out and enjoy the nice day. What better way to do that than to go birding on Plum Island.

When we arrived at the gate of the wildlife refuge, we noticed a large hand written sign, in bold letters saying, "ATTENTION ALL ACCESS TO THE BEACH AND ALL OCEAN SIDE BOARDWALKS ARE CLOSED." What? Geez. We just drove an hour to get here only to find out we can't walk along the beach. Crap. Well, we are here, so I guess I'll have to do some inland birding; it's still good to be outside, and the temperature was almost forty, and it was nice and sunny.

As we pass each trail leading to the ocean, we see that there is yellow caution tape across the path and even trash barrels blocking the path. Weird. I enjoy a good mystery so my mind was starting to turn…what was going on? Why the ocean side trails all were closed? Yet at a couple of the lots, even though the trail was blocked by caution tape and trash barrels, there were still cars parked in the lot? Where were the people who were in those cars? John speculates that maybe people parked there and walked along the road for exercise, ummm, maybe, we did pass a few people walking but not that many. The island is actually strangely quiet, no people anywhere.

We drive to the very end of the island and find that the trail there is not blocked so we park and make our way to the ocean. Just as we break out of the dunes, we see a large pile of debris pushed up against the entrance to the beach. The storm sure did make a mess of the shoreline, there are lobster pots and all sorts of bits and pieces of stuff littering the beach. Everyone knows that the best time to go beach combing is right after a big storm. Ahh so maybe this is why the beach was closed? Because of all the debris littering the area, maybe they closed it for safety reasons.

As we walk along the shore, there are shells everywhere and dozens of sand dollars. Not any birds but tons of "stuff" washed up. I notice that farther up the beach there is a group of people. I ask John, "Hey, if the beach access is closed, how did all those people get onto the beach?" He agrees it seems strange. I look at the group with my binoculars, even stranger is that they all appear to be dressed the same. I can't make out any wording on their clothes, but they are all dressed in black. They seem to be walking in a row, and they are all bent down looking at the sand. One person is crouched down taking pictures of the sand. Weird. We speculate that it might be a group doing a clean-up of the beach.

We decide to cut our losses and head home, John wanted to catch the football game on TV, there weren't any birds around so we headed off the island. Of course, I did see some birds, there were large flocks of Canada geese, assorted ducks and some black-backed gulls but nothing of any real interest. As we were driving along the refuge road, we came upon a man pulled over with big camera equipment scanning the marsh. Since he was the only person we had seen so far, I pulled over to see what he was looking at.

He was watching a northern harrier hunting over the marsh. As I followed the ridge of small trees that the bird was flying over, suddenly in my view, is a large eight-point buck! A magnificent animal indeed! I know that there is a small herd of deer on the island, but I haven't seen a deer on the island is more than twenty years. I didn't get to see many interesting birds on this trip but to see that grand buck made up for it.

Just before driving off the refuge, we noticed that one of the areas that was closed when we first went by it is now open. We decide to walk out to the ocean and see if we can figure out why it was closed before. As we are walking, I notice dog paw prints in the sand. This is strange because dogs are not allowed on the refuge. John speculates that maybe it was just a dog that got loose from one of the few houses on the north side of the island.

Once we get to the edge of the dunes and can see the shore, we notice tire tracks up and down the beach. And the whole beach has been raked, you can see the marks back and forth across the sands. Wow I guess it was a clean-up project, and they did one heck of a scrubbing of the sands, there wasn't even a blade of grass left behind. We drive home thinking we had figured out what had happened on the island that day.

Later that evening, as we are watching the news a report comes on that shocks us both. The headline is "Plum Island closed as police investigate human remains found on the beach." Yikes! The report goes on to tell the story that a man walking the beach found pieces of bones washed up. They report that the bones appear to be leg bones and have been sent out for testing. Wow! Now we can put the pieces together; now it makes sense why there was such a strange vibe on the island. That group of people all in black were probably cops, and the dog was probably a cadaver dog, it's any wonder the sand was raked in a grid pattern. I was searching for birds but inadvertently walked into a crime scene in progress. Creepy for sure.

Nonfiction

The January Blizzard of 2015 dropped a good thirty inches of snow in our area. The morning after the storm I was sitting at the kitchen table in my PJs having breakfast watching the flocks of birds at the feeders. This has been an irruptive year for pine siskens, and I've been lucky enough to have a small flock visiting my feeders. These little birds live in the boreal forests of the north but will travel south in years their food source is poor. Beth had asked if I could possibly get a picture of them as she had never seen pine siskens and wanted to get a better idea of what to look for. They are very similar to winter plumage American goldfinch and often mixed in with them in flocks. So I had the camera on the table waiting for the opportunity to get a good picture.

I have three different style feeders and two suet holders on a pole to accommodate different birds and their preferred style of feeding. It was a mob scene out there. I had a flock of eight goldfinch, six pine sisken, two downy woodpeckers, two hairy woodpeckers, one red-bellied woodpecker, two white-breasted nuthatch, eight chickadees, six tufted titmouse, two cardinals, and on the ground feeding were about two dozen dark-eyed juncos, two blue jays, and four mourning doves. Birds were flying in and out and swarming the ground below the feeders. It was a feeding frenzy out there!

I was eating my breakfast watching the birds when suddenly a large black blur flies in and lands on the feeder pole. It was a raven looking to scoop up a piece of old bread or two. Immediately the flocks of small birds exploded into a mass exodus of color and feathers in every direction! Even I found myself startled and jumped back in my seat. Unfortunately, one small bird flew into the window in its haste to escape. I do put special window clings on the glass to help keep the birds from flying against the glass. But in the frenzy of birds, one did still hit the window. I heard it clunk against the window and saw it drop down to the ground. I hurriedly opened the window and looked down to check on the little bird. All I could see was a small hole straight down into the deep snow. Oh no! The poor little bird is going to suffocate it can't get out of the deep snow!

Without thinking, I run out the back door and grab the snow shovel on the deck. Now I'm in my PJs and slippers, the snow is up to my thigh, it's windy and fifteen degrees out. Maybe not the best decision but all I thought about was saving that little bird. After the initial shock of plunging into the deep snow, I thought what the heck I'm cold and wet now might as well finish what I started. I made my way to under the window and using the shovel scooped up some snow with the small bird in it. Right away, as I lifted it out of the snow, it was as if it gasped for air, I brushed the snow away, and it gave out a little chirp.

I trudged through the snow back to the deck and put the shovel down with the bird still sitting on it. I could see that it was a pine sisken, I went back into the kitchen and got my camera and took a picture of the bird for Beth. The bird seemed alert and looked at me, but it held one wing strangely, I worried it might be broken. I didn't want to leave the poor bird out in the open on the deck where our cat Missy or a hawk might get it so still in my PJs and really at this point so cold I'm numb, I took a handful of snow with the bird sitting in it and carried it to the planter box by the gazebo. I brushed away the snow and set the bird among the dried plants safely camouflaged from any predator so it could rest and recover.

First order of business was to get out of my frozen PJs and into some warm clothes. I went back to the window to check on the sisken, and it was still sitting in the planter. It was moving its head around so that was good news. A half hour passed, and it was still sitting in the planter I was getting worried about it. I had a contingency plan running through my head, I would go out into the shed and get one of Jeanine's old bird cages and bring the bird into the house. I thought about where to put it away from Missy and what to feed it, and yes, I'll admit I was considering names for the little guy. But thankfully the little pine sisken flew away on its own!

Now I know you all might wonder when reading my stories if that really happened. Well, I swear it is all nonfiction.

Disclaimer: No birds were harmed in this story, although a crazy bird lady was nearly frozen senseless.

Birders Brigade

March 2015

I had an unexpected request recently. Mark asked if I would be willing to take him birding in search of the snowy owl. It seems he had read an article about the many sightings in our area and there had been news stories about the frenzy these Arctic visitors were causing. So Mark decided he wanted in on the action; he wanted to see a snowy owl too.

I was more than willing to take him out for a winter's day of birding. Of course, we went straight to my favorite birding spot, Plum Island. Problem was we have had so much snow that most of the refuge was closed off, the road wasn't plowed. This was going to be a challenge, but I was determined to find Mark that snowy owl!

The temperature was in the twenties, light winds, and overcast skies, pretty typical for early March. We parked at lot 1 and made our way across the snowy dunes to the ocean. I was flabbergasted, there weren't any birds! Usually there are dozens of shore birds and ducks in the shallows. All we saw were two loons and an unidentified grebe/ duck. There were four birders there, all trying to ID that one bird and none of us could. Winter plumage on birds is always confusing. I was getting worried I might not be able to deliver on my promise to find Mark the snowy owl.

I had done my research ahead of time, combed through the various reports of owl sightings and more than one report mentioned the owl being seen on Plum Island out on the salt pans between lot 1 and lot 2. So we continued along the road; I told Chris and Mark to scan the salt pans as I drove and to look for any "bump" that looked out of place. Sure enough, there he was the snowy owl! He was sitting on a piece of wood next to the open tidal canal, likely hoping to catch some dinner since that was the only open water. We have had such extreme cold and snow that all the usual open areas were frozen over solid.

We excitedly got out, and I set up the scope for Mark to get a really close up look at the owl. Ya know no matter how many times I see the snowy owl I'm still in awe at its grandeur. We stayed and watched the owl for a while then moved on to explore and see what else we might see.

Problem was the road was closed just passed lot 3, that was it we couldn't go any farther the snow was too deep. I was disappointed I wasn't going to be able to show Mark more of the island. We took the trail at lot 3 to see if we might spot another owl in the dunes. The snow was very deep and there was only a one-person wide trail stomped across the dunes and believe me you did not want to step off the trail and risk sinking into the deep snow. We made it to the ocean but yet again no birds in sight just empty shoreline and ocean. No snowy owl hanging out on the dunes.

On our way back, we came upon a man and two women, and like all good birders we shared our sighting of the snowy owl. They were very excited, they really wanted to see the owl and turned around to head back to see it. We headed back as well and set the scope up to share with others. It didn't take long for a crowd to gather. Two excited women even did the birders' happy dance when Mark offered to share the scope so they could to see the owl up close.

I think that was the most gratifying sight for me, to watch Mark enjoy the camaraderie of fellow birders all enjoying looking through the scope at the snowy owl. You'd think he was a seasoned birder, he was helping the others spot the owl and talking birding with those around him. We had a nice day.

I want to welcome our new recruit, Mark to the birders' brigade!

Secrets Uncovered

March 2015

The meteorological calendar may say it is spring but that's not what it looks like out my window. Those of you that don't live here in New England are probably tired of hearing about how hard the winter has been up here. Believe me we here in New England are just as tired of living through it! Cabin fever is raging, everyone is so anxious for the spring time weather to finally arrive.

Yesterday we had off-and-on snow showers all day. Today was forecast to be a nice sunny day with the temperature climbing to forty. I was itching to get out and do some birding, so I headed to Plum Island to see what I could see. The last time I was there with Mark and Chris to find the snowy owl most of the island was closed off due to the high snow, so I was hoping more would be open now that the snow was receding.

As we arrived onto the refuge, it was soon apparent that there was still a lot of melting that needed to happen. There was still a lot of snow and the tidal marshes were still frozen over. I wasn't too optimistic that I was going to see many birds today. A short way up the road we came upon three wild turkeys slowly walking along the side of the road. In the fall, I had seen a flock of more than a dozen turkeys, I wondered where the rest of the flock was. Were these skinny weak looking turkeys all that was left of the flock?

Luckily the road was open to the Hellcat Trails area, which is just about half way down the island. We decided to take the trail through the woods and across the dunes to the highest point on the island. This trail winds through the most wooded part of the island and usually is teeming with song birds. When you get to the top, it offers an expansive view of the island and ocean.

Unfortunately, the "trail" was in rough shape. It was little more than one foot in front of the other trail in the snow. But the sun was shining and the temperature was warming so we pressed on. The woods were quiet, no bird song, all I saw were a couple of chickadees and a hairy woodpecker. Along the trail, I came upon a few owl pellets that the melting snow revealed. I poked the pellets to see what the owl might have been eating, there were a number of small bones and some fur. Looked like Mr. Owl dined on rabbit most of the winter. Sad for the rabbit, but survival for the owl. That's nature's law.

We continued on to the high point on the trail. The observation platform offered a surreal view, a quiet snow-covered landscape stretched out before us, as far as we could see it was white. John even mentioned how strange it was that there weren't even any foot prints in the snow. There is a herd of deer on the island and these woods are where they can often be seen. The island did get hit hard by the numerous coastal storms that churned up the coast this winter. The area also saw some record-breaking cold temperatures. Spring was going to arrive late this year on Plum Island.

The trail loops back down through a wooded area to the parking lot. As we entered the wooded area, there on the side of the trail were the remains of two dead deer. The melting snow beginning to uncover the bodies to view. There they lay, next to each other, their bodies already been scavenged upon. The poor things, did the severe cold or the deep snow do them in? Perhaps the secrets to their death will become clearer as the melting snow uncovers the bodies.

Beware the secrets uncovered as the snow melts.

Benson's Park

April 2015

How many of you remember Benson's Wild Animal Farm in Hudson New Hampshire? My siblings that grew up in Pelham surely remember, as a trip to Benson's was a popular destination when we were young. My parents took my son there often. Unfortunately, the park closed down before my daughter was born so it wasn't a place she ever got to experience.

It has long since been closed down, the elephants, gorilla, and monkeys all gone. The land languished in litigation for years. Luckily the building boom busted and the developers were no longer interested in the property. So it finally was taken over by the town and transformed into a park for all to enjoy. This past Sunday was a beautiful sunny spring day, and I wanted to get out and enjoy it. Beth had invited me to a bird walk in the park, so I made the trip to Hudson to check it out.

I have heard a lot about the park and heard that it was very nice. They have a large steel beam from one of the towers destroyed in the attack on the Twin Towers on 9/11. I remember the news stories of when the beam made its way to New Hampshire and the dedication of the memorial. They did a great job of making a memorial to those that lost their lives in the attack. I have been wanting to visit it for a while now, and I'm glad I did it was very moving. I stood next to the burned and scared beam and touched it; I said a prayer for all those lives lost.

After paying my respects at the 9/11 Memorial, it was time to hit the trails. There are a lot of choices, trails that wind through the woods, along small ponds and across fields. Great opportunities for birding. The park was crowded there were families with children, young and old, walkers or bike riders, everyone enjoying the nice weather.

It was kinda eerie walking the trails, there was the old Gorilla cage, filled now with young children laughing and climbing the metal bars. Little do they know of the sorry existence of that poor creature that had to live in that small cinder block and metal caged enclosure. Over there wasn't that where the elephant circle was? I remember watching those huge beasts doing their tricks for our enjoyment chained to the floor. We passed the monkey house all boarded up and quiet now.

"The Old Lady Who Lived in a Shoe," her replica house still stands. And over there, was where the petting zoo was. Memories flooded me of the fun time I chaperoned my son's kindergarten class there. The original owners cared for the animals well, they just didn't understand it was wrong compared to today's standards. I'm glad they left some of the remains of the buildings, it is history. In its heyday, it was a jewel of a park.

We saw a total of fifteen bird species along our walk. We watched as iridescent blue tree swallows zoomed across the field like little fighter jets scooping up insects. We saw a small flock of yellow-rumped warblers hopping about the bushes along the water's edge. Our best sightings for the day were the pine warbler and the yellow warbler flitting about the tree branches overhead.

So it is official the warblers have returned! Spring has finally sprung in New Hampshire! I have recharged my batteries with a walk in the woods, feel more positive and ready for whatever the week brings. The power of fresh air is undeniable. If any of you get a chance, I highly recommend you visit Benson's Park, it's well worth the trip. Be sure to stop at the 911 Memorial to say a prayer.

You Snooze, You Lose

April 2015

The other day while watching the evening news, I noticed out the window my cat walking toward the house carrying something in her mouth. Now my little Missy cat is quite the hunter she does pretty well for an old kitty cat. She doesn't eat what she catches, she is way too fussy an eater for that. I had noticed that she had been sitting staring into a small hole in the ground under the old bird bath for a while. The cement bird bath doesn't hold water any longer, so I put mixed seed and old bread in it for the squirrels and larger birds like the turkeys. I guess she finally got whatever creature was in there.

As she got closer to the house, I could see it was a mole and that it was still alive, it was wiggling in her mouth. Oh great, she is probably going to bring it to me as a gift. She is known for presenting me with dead or half dead mice, moles or other disgusting half dead creatures from the woods. I consider going outside and making her drop the poor little thing but heck she has been cooped up all winter with the rest of us, I decide to let her have some fun.

She sits down and drops the mole then proceeds to chase it as it tries to escape. She throws it up in the air and is having a grand ole time with it. Soon she loses interest and begins to lick her paws to clean herself; she turns her back to the mole. Ah now is its chance, the mole begins to scamper away while Missy isn't looking.

Suddenly from the woods a Coopers hawk flies in, talons out stretched, and it lands on the mole with wings flapping, it grabs the mole and shoots off back into the woods! Missy, startled by the hawk, did a back flip into the air and with her tail puffed up in fright climbed the nearest tree in a flash. I couldn't believe what I was witnessing! Darn I was going to get the camera and video Missy playing with the mole but was lazy and didn't feel like going for the camera, now I wish I had. That was for sure a once-in-a-lifetime event to see.

So lesson learned by all: "You snooze, you lose." I was too lazy to go get my camera, so I missed out on a great video to share, Missy dropped her catch and turned her back on it, the mole wasn't moving fast enough to escape. But the Coopers hawk sure was the winner, hope he enjoyed his dinner, compliments of Missy cat. The circle of nature playing out yet again.

Blown Away

October 2015

This past Saturday, I had a chance to visit with Chris and Mark in Maine. There was a large storm just off the coast and the wind and waves were intense along the shore. Some times during extreme weather conditions along the shore a "fall out" can occur. This is when large numbers of birds are pushed ashore due to high winds; they are seeking refuge from the storm and are looking for a safe place to land. This particular time of year is migration for many of the inland birds who follow the coast line as they travel south, so the possibility was there that many birds could be seeking refuge along the shore. It was a good time to hit the beach!

I got to the camper before Chris did; she had a few things to tend to and planned to meet up with me in the afternoon. Mark was there but had gone to the library, so I had some time to myself to look for birds. That's okay by me! As soon as I got there, I headed out to the rocks to look for birds. Wow, was the ocean angry! I have been there during storms before, but this time was different, the wind was blowing harder than I had ever experienced, it was gray and damp. But there were birds! I had brought my spotting scope, so I could scan the rocks but the wind was so strong that it kept knocking over my scope.

I gave up on the scope and stuck with my binoculars. There were dozens of common eiders, herring gulls, ring-billed gulls, great black-backed gulls, and a small group of surf scooters all crowded into the cove riding the big swells. And there among them all was a male and female Canvasback. SCORE! A new bird sighting for me! (birders' happy dance) Mark had told me he had seen these shy ducks last year, so I was on the lookout for them this season.

As I was watching the birds from my perch on the rocks, a young man (maybe fifteen) came over and asked me what I was looking at. I told him about the birds gathered in the cove, he asked me what the little black birds were. I told him they were Surf Scooters and offered him my binoculars so he could get a closer look. He told me he had been on the rocks earlier and taken a picture of a cool-looking duck. He showed me the picture on his phone; it was the canvasback.

We talked birds for a bit, he seemed knowledgeable enough about the subject, and then he dropped the birders bomb on me. He says to me, "Oh, you should go over to Nubble Lighthouse, there are puffins gathered there on the rocks I saw them this morning." What?! Puffins! The Atlantic puffin has a very limited range along the northern Maine coastline, rarely seen on shore, frequents the small offshore rocky islands. I have wanted to see this rare sea bird but have not had the courage to go out to sea on a boat to find them.

Immediately, I say, "I'm outta here, I'm going to the lighthouse!" as I head for my truck. He walks along with me, telling me how to get there, I have been there before, but I was not quite sure of the directions. I consider waiting for Mark to get back so he can take me, but I can't take the chance of missing the puffins, so I head out on my own. I call my sister Chris on the phone, but she is still driving on the highway still a ways away. I'm too impatient I can't wait, I have her talk me through the directions turn by turn as I am driving. She is as excited as I am, she also would love to see the puffins and is going to meet me there.

As soon as I arrive at the lighthouse, I grab my binoculars and jump out of the truck.

I am immediately thrown back as the strong winds force the truck door shut. I wasn't expecting that, I push hard against the door and head for the rocks. The wind is fierce, the ocean is rolling and heaving huge breakers onto the rocks. The waves crash onto the shore and spray water high into the air, this is a scene I have not experienced ever before. The intensity and force of the wind was incredible. I made my way to the edge and tried to look over to the rock outcroppings by the lighthouse with my binoculars for puffins, but the wind was so strong that it pushed me side to side, and I had trouble focusing my binoculars on the rocks. Never mind focusing with my binoculars. I was having trouble even standing against the fierce winds, with each crashing wave I got misted with cold sea water. I could see birds there, all seeking refuge from the storm. Could there be puffins there among all those birds crowded on the rocks?

It was so frustrating; I could see many black birds on the rocks but many had their heads safely tucked under a wing to protect themselves from the cold wind. All I could see was a black blob sitting on a rock. Ahhh! Were they puffins or not? I decided to try getting back in the truck to get out of the wind to see if I could get a better view. But that didn't help much, the truck was rocking back and forth as each fierce gust of wind hit and the sea spray was covering the windshield, and I couldn't see out.

Finally, Chris and Mark arrived, now I had reinforcements. Mark was kind enough to be my stabilizer, and he let me lean back-to-back on him, so I could steady myself with the binoculars to scan the rocks. Unfortunately, most of the black birds ended up being just cormorants, bummer. My eyes were watering from the cold winds, so I gave the binoculars to Chris to see if she had any luck focusing on the black birds. All she saw were cormorants. But I just couldn't give up yet.

I decided to get closer to the edge of the rocks. Chris wasn't so sure I should, but I told her to watch the waves and warn me when a big one was coming in. I just had to see if there were puffins out there! I hear Chris yell, "Jane, Jane, get back up here!" as a wave crashes ashore and the cold sea water splashes my legs. Chris comes to where I am and tells me to take her hand, we are getting away from the edge.

There aren't any puffins out there. I was cold and damp, she was right there weren't any puffins out there. It was time to give up. It was a long shot anyways, I had to consider my source, did I really trust the word of a fifteen-year-old in his PJs hanging around the camp site telling me he had seen puffins at the lighthouse that morning? I describe to my sister the teenager that told me about the puffins. She tells me she is familiar with him; he is a nice kid but is known to play jokes on fellow campers.

Ummm, did I just get pranked?!

After all, I easily could have been blown away by those fierce winds while trying to focus on my search for the puffins.

Centered

December 2015

I just returned from a trip to one of my favorite birding spots, Plum Island. Here it is December 13, and we have no snow and the temperatures are topping fifty! Come on now when is that ever likely to happen again? I just had to get out on the trails in search of some birds, so I headed out by myself for a day of birding. A couple of weekends ago Beth and I were birding on the island, she had just purchased a new spotting scope and wanted to practice using it. And it does take practice to set it up and focus on your subject. Ah first step Beth is to point the scope at what you want to look at, not your chest.

So I was inspired by Beth to bring along my scope. I have not used it in ages, I usually only bring my binoculars. The only down side to carrying around a scope is that you become a magnet for other birders. They assume you must be a good birder and spotting something really good when they see you with your scope. I was a bit rusty but soon got the hang of it again and shared my scope with other birders so they could see some interesting birds up close. There were no sightings of the snowy owl, the rock stars on the island today were a flock of razorbills and a peregrine falcon.

I never would have spotted those razorbills if I had not used my scope. I was scanning the ocean off lot #7 with my binoculars and could just make out some blackish birds bobbing in the swells. But with my spotting scope I could zoom right in and see every detail and make a perfect ID! Of course, I still had to "confer and confirm" my sighting with another birder there on the viewing platform that also had a scope. There were many water fowls on the island—American widgeons, northern pintails, green-winged teal, blue-winged teal, and others. The scope brought them all up close and personal.

As I was driving off the island, it occurred to me that I had just spent a few hours enjoying nature and had not once thought of the black cloud that has been hanging over my head recently. I feel more centered now. I know that I am sadly not the only parent facing the same uncertainty and fears of a child in the military serving our country. May God bless all the brave Americans serving our country. It is a fear that can be very all consuming. But I am my father's daughter! I trust in God! I will weather this storm. I like to think of all of my family and friends as my rain gear to help protect me from the storm. I am not afraid of rain! I will take the steps needed to protect my family. Stay centered.

My mantra is, "Circle the wagons and raise the force shield, put on the rain gear."

Standing Up to Jonas

January 2016

It takes a powerful storm to earn a name and the current monster of a storm churning up the Mid-Atlantic coast earned the name, Jonas, aka Blizzard of 2016. Here in New Hampshire, we were spared; the storm stayed just to our south, we only had wind gusts and cold temperatures but no snow, bummer. So what else would a sane person do? Well, travel into the storm in search of birds of course.

Big storms can often cause a "fallout" of birds; literally, birds are blown ahead of the storm. The confused birds will look for a safe haven to ride out the storm, and Plum Island preserve, a small slip of land just off the coast can be that safe haven for storm weary birds. So the possibility was there that I could see some interesting birds or at least large numbers of birds gathered together.

Reports on the rare bird website listed some unusual sightings, like the short-eared owl, northern saw-whet owl, great horned owl, and snowy owl as all being on the island. Now it is well-known I have a weakness for owls! I just had to get on the island to search for these owls. I invited Chris, Becky and Beth to join me. Sisters Chris and Becky declined, due to the cold and wind. In retrospect, they made the right decision. Beth decided that the possibility of a "fallout" and possible chance to see an owl were worth braving the elements on the island.

And brave the elements we did! We arrived on the island, and it was void of all the usual birding crowd. We pretty much had the island to ourselves. It was nearly high tide, and it was expected to be a very high tide due to the full moon and the strong winds from the storm just off shore. The water was almost flooding the road, the salt marsh was doing its job of retaining the storm surge, but it looked like it wouldn't take much more to completely cover the road. I truly have never seen the water so high. I do hope the residents of the island can ride out the storm without much damage.

We checked out the North Overlook Pool for the owls to no avail, tried the pines trail and struck out there as well. We scanned the salt marsh at Hellcat Trails, no owls, though we were surprised to see a hermit thrush hopping around in the snowy underbrush. We walked the trail through the dunes at lot 5, but the strong winds drove us back. No owl sightings this trip. We saw birds, flocks of Canada geese, mallards, northern pintails, and robins. We saw a total of fifteen different species. But no owls.

We made our way over the dunes along an icy trail to the ocean. The force of the wind was incredible! Really, I mean it, the wind pushed us off balance, and it was hard to stand up against the gusts. Beth tried in vain to set up her scope, but the wind was too strong. There was a flock of small shore birds scurrying in the sea foam, I made my way across the sand to get closer to identify them, the wind-blown sand felt like shattered glass, but I did it I got close enough to tell they were sanderlings. There were also dunlin running in and out of the surf. I don't know how those little bitty birds kept from being blown away.

Washington closed down, New York banned all travel, the New Jersey shore flooded, and there is no question that Jonas is a powerful dangerous storm. I hope all those in its path make it through okay. As I drove off the island, the temperature gauge in the truck said it was nineteen degrees; there were light snow flurries, and my weather app said the wind gusts were 30 mph.

I have to give props to Beth, she braved the sandblasted winds, icy trails and frozen outhouse seats to help me try and find my owls. Together we stood up to Jonas!

I pray all those in the thick of it made it out safe and sound.

Lucky Pellet?

January 2016

After striking out in my attempt to see the short-eared owl during my last trip to Plum Island, I was considering another try. I had been watching the Plum Island Bird Report website and every day one to two short-eared owls were being reported as being seen, all in the same area of the North Pool Overlook and Fields. How was it Beth and I missed them? We were there, but the owls weren't.

After our shut out on the island, Beth came up with a possible answer, one I should have thought of. She suggested that maybe instead of trying to get onto the island early to see the birds, as is our usual routine that perhaps I should try to arrive later in the day. Most owls hunt only at night but the Arctic owls that winter on Plum Island hunt both day and night, so you can often see them in the day time. I did some research and yup, the short-eared owl hunts early morning just after dawn and late afternoon before sunset. That was all I needed to convince myself it was worth another trip to the island.

So Saturday, I made plans to get onto the island by 3:00 p.m., park in the North Pool pull off and wait for the owls. My plan was to pack a sandwich for dinner and just sit in the car till the owls arrived or the park ranger kicked me out. The last time we were there we saw other people parked, waiting, and now I knew why they were there. Some of the reported sightings were at 3:00 p.m. or 4:00 p.m.

I packed up the car with all my gear, spotting scope, binoculars, cold weather clothing, blanket, food and water. Just before driving away, I walked down the driveway to get the mail. As I was walking, I saw an owl pellet on the ground. I gave it a kick and walked past it, and then on my way back up the driveway, I stopped. I looked at the owl pellet, ummm, maybe it is a good luck sign, I decided to pick it up and bring it into the house. I didn't want to touch it barehanded; it was still fresh and damp, so I broke off a pine bough and scooped it up. I headed for the island with hopes of seeing the owls.

Saturday was the Super Bowl of birding events; this is a competition where birders compete to see who can see the most birds in twenty-four hours. It is a big deal, you win a trophy, and it is a fundraising event for Audubon. I considered competing but couldn't pull together a team. So I knew it would be crowded on the island, but I figured it would mean more eyes to point me in the right direction to find the owls. Sure enough, I arrived on the island to a crowd.

As soon as I got onto the island, I stopped at the visitor's center, cuz those that have been there know it is the last chance for a flush toilet. Off to the edge of the parking lot is a large crowd, with spotting scopes and huge cameras, and people pointing. Of course, I went over to see what was up. As I was walking toward the group, a birder came toward me, I asked him what's been spotted. He tells me a pair of American eagles are sitting together on an old piling sitting in the salt marsh. I wave my hand and say, "Ugh, just an eagle. I'm here to find the short-eared owl have you seen one?"

As soon as I say it and look at his face, I realize what a snob I sounded like. I try to recover, I say, "Oh, eagles are very majestic, I am fortunate that I get to see them often up north at my cabin."

"Umm, have you seen any owls?" He tells me no he has not and wishes me luck as he walks away. I don't even bother to look at the eagles, I am here for owls, and I must stay focused! I drive on.

Along the refuge road, I come upon another group of men, same scenario, spotting scopes and binoculars, people pointing. I stopped and ask, "What have you spotted?" One young man tells me in an excited voice, "Snowy owl! Would you like to take a look through my scope?"

I thank him but say no, "I've seen them before, I'm here looking for the short-eared owl, have you seen any?" One of the other men tells me, "Oh yeah, they're here, up at the North Pool Overlook. We just came from there. If you hurry, they may still be there." Wow, I exclaim, I thank them and turn to head back to my car when the younger man again asks if I would like to see the snowy owl.

He says, "Hey, even if you have seen it before when will you ever be able to say you saw two owl species in one day?" I laugh; again I have been a birding snob! I stop and look at the snowy through the scope, no matter how many times you see one they are beautiful. I rush along the refuge road to find my short-eared owls. Must stay focused!

I am almost there; North Pool Overlook is just around the next corner. I turn the corner and *bam*! There are cars at a complete stop, parked on both sides of the narrow refuge road and stopped in the middle of the road. People weaving in and out of the parked cars carrying spotting scopes and cameras. I am still almost a ¼ mile from the pull off for North Pool, this is crazy! The owls must be there! I gotta see them. Ahhh! I back the car up and do the best I can to park on the side of the road, I put the flashers on and jump out. I weave through the cars and push my way to the front of the crowd. Hey I am here to see the short-eared owl get out of my way! Warning obnoxious birder here!

And there they were! Not just one short-eared owl but two! A pair, they were gliding over the field in search of food, interacting with each other making circles in the sky. It was magical. I watched as one hovered over the grasses then dropped down. It came back up out of the salt marsh reeds with a vole in its talons. The crowd cheered, "He got one!" they clapped their hands, well a cold weather glove wearing birders' clap. I went back to the car and got my spotting scope, I set it up and offered other birders a chance to see the owls up close. I apologized to the couple I pushed out of the way in my rush to see the owls. I let them enjoy the spotting scope to watch the owls hunt.

I stayed there nearly an hour just watching the owls glide low over the field on their large wings. I watched as one caught a vole and then landed and enjoyed his dinner. I was so glad I went back for my spotting scope; it made the experience so much better. I was able to zoom in close and look the owl right in the eyes as it sat on the ground surveying the scene. Had to wonder just what they thought of all of us. But hunting was good for them, so I don't think they much cared about all us silly birders.

The park ranger came along on an ATV with a bull horn asking people to please move their cars. It was understandable; luckily, I was able to see the owls before he came along to break up the party. Just before leaving the refuge, I stopped to admire the sunset, I wanted to take a few pictures of the sky over the sand dunes as the sun began to set. I was standing there enjoying the view and thinking about what I had just witnessed, how lucky I felt to have seen those two owls hunting. I was thinking what could possibly top this day of birding.

As I was putting my camera back into my backpack, suddenly from behind me just over my head flies a snowy owl! Unbelievable! It was only feet overhead, it flew over my head and dropped down behind the very sand dunes I was just taking a picture of! Wow! I do indeed think that owl pellet I found brought me luck. When will I ever be able to say I saw two species of owls in one day again? When will I ever be able to say I experienced the behavior of two Arctic owls up close and personal again?

As I drove home, I thought the only thing that would have made today any better would have been if my birding buddies had been there to witness what I just had, maybe next time ladies, and maybe next time.

Island Christmas

I had a rather unconventional Christmas day I thought I would share. We actually celebrated the holiday on the Saturday before Christmas, Jeremy was able to come down from Vermont for lunch, and we exchanged gifts and visited. Thanks to technology we were able to Skype with Jeanine, and we opened each other's gifts. Both my kids gave me birding gear, Jeanine sent me a very comfortable to wear birding backpack and a folding walking stick. Jeremy got me a military grade Lock Down Optics Deployment System. Kinda a mouth full, but it is really cool. Sort of like having a covered case you wear on your chest, the binos attach to the straps instead of hanging around your neck. I just had to get out there and try this gear out!

So Christmas morning, I decided to head to Plum Island to do some birding. The Audubon Society holds a Christmas Bird Count each year, and they ask birders to count all the birds they see and report the totals. So while most of you were sitting around your tree and opening presents, I was bundling up and packing my gear for a day of winter birding. It was sunny on the island, temperature around thirty-five, but the wind was fierce. Blowing across the island with thirty-mile gusts, made it hard to stand on the observation platform. And I was sand blasted by the beach sand, it felt like needles poking me!

I wasn't on the island more than a few minutes when I spotted something rather unusual. There lurking in the tall salt marsh grasses was an American Bittern! What?! What was this bird doing here now? Sure, they live on Plum Island in the summer but not in December, sure hope he plans to head south real soon. There wasn't much snow and there was still some open saltwater in the marsh but that will be changing soon, and then all will be frozen including the Bittern if he doesn't fly to warmer climates.

There was a pair of northern harriers flying low over the tall grasses of the salt marsh. I watched as they hovered over the field and then dove down into the tall grass, I'm assuming for lunch. There was a beautiful red-tailed hawk just sitting on a bare branch along the side of the road. He sat there cocking his head side to side even when I got out of the car and took his picture. Maybe he was just too cold to bother moving. I left him alone and moved on.

There weren't a lot of different birds on the island but there were a lot of the birds that I did see. There were dozens of mallards and black ducks bobbing for food in open saltwater canals. On a hilltop, where the snow had been blown away, I counted ninety-two Canadian geese sitting in the dried grass! On the bare rocks along the ocean shore, there were huge flocks of gulls. Great black-backed gulls, ring-billed gulls, and herring gulls all gathered sunning on the rocks even as wind swept waves crashed over them. There were common eiders riding the crest of the waves like surfers.

So I guess you could say I had an Island Christmas. Maybe not the kind of island most of you would envision spending Christmas day on, but I enjoyed my day trying out my new birding gear. Thank you to Jeremy the Optics Deployment System worked great and was very comfortable. It was easy to use and nice to not have the strap pulling on my neck, and even in the steady wind the binoculars didn't bounce around. Thank you to Jeanine for the sturdy walking stick; it was very icy and the spike on the end of the walking stick made all the difference. I didn't fall! And the backpack was just the right size for my birding book, camera, water bottle and snacks. So maybe I was alone on a day most are with family, but I didn't feel alone. Being out enjoying nature always calms my soul and brings smiles.

Stink Eye!

January 2017

While my sister Becky's family was enjoying a tropical island get away her In-laws Carle and Al are house sitting for them. Carle invited me over for a Sunday brunch and to enjoy watching the flock of blue birds that call Becky's yard their home. And the birds did not disappoint! Becky has a large window feeder in the breakfast nook that she keeps full of the bird's favorite meal worms and suet nuggets. What can be better on a cold January morning than sitting by the window watching these brilliantly colored birds, the jewel tone blue of their backs and the rusty red on their bellies stood out against the white of the snow. At times, there would be three birds at once sitting on the feeder eating, just looking in at us. They weren't bothered by our presence at all. Though how they feel about Annie kitty sitting in the window is a different story. But Annie sure enjoys it.

A few weeks earlier, I was visiting with Becky, and she pointed out a strange behavior of the blue birds I certainly had never seen before. We were sitting at the table watching the birds eat, and she tells me, "Watch, the birds give me the stink eye every time they see me!" Umm, strange, I'm thinking gee little sister I'm not so sure the birds dislike you and give you the stink eye, you're the one that feeds them they should be grateful. But sure enough, one of the blue birds suddenly crouches down stiffens his wings and *stares* right at Becky. Yup, he is giving her the stink eye all right!

If it weren't for people like Becky, who put up roosting boxes for the birds and supply them with plenty of meal worms these blue birds wouldn't survive the winters of New Hampshire. Blue birds were once common in New Hampshire, but they have struggled in recent years due to the loss of their habitat and food supplies. Blue birds eat bugs, worms, grasshoppers, etc., and in the winters, they would eat fruits left on farmer's trees and shrubs. Farmers would set roosting boxes on each of their fence poles along their fields, the farmers knew the blue birds would help keep down the insect problems on their crops and the birds don't tend to eat seeds so they wouldn't bother the farmers new plantings. Blue birds are very territorial so they would chase away any other birds who might harm the farmer's crops. This was a perfect cooperation between man and nature for generations. But as is the sad truth of development, as the large open fields of farms were divided and sold off for buildings the blue birds began to leave New Hampshire.

As Carle, Al, and I sat at the table and enjoyed a few rousing games of Skip-Bo, I kept my eye on the blue birds landing on the feeder. Al was sitting in the chair Becky most often tends to sit in, and I was watching each bird watch Al. There was *no stink eye* for Al! Sorry Becky looks like the birds really don't like you. Becky's husband Christopher came up with an explanation I hadn't thought of that makes perfect sense. As far as the blue birds are concerned, Becky is a threat to their food supply. She is the creature that reaches out of the window and messes with their meal worms and suet nuggets. They don't see her as the provider, to them she is an enemy trying to invade their territory! So yeah, Becky, you are surely getting the stink eye from those birds. It's pretty amazing to think that they can recognize a face, really you should be proud that they give you the stink eye.

It was an enjoyable Sunday playing cards with Carle and Al and watching the birds in the yard. A large flock of turkeys came running into the yard and feasted on the seed on the ground below the feeders set up at the edge of the lawn… There were mourning doves, chickadees, tufted titmouse, and blue jays at the feeders as well. After the blue birds left the window feeder, a Carolina wren flew in as well as a purple finch, a gold finch, and even a red-bellied woodpecker stopped by to enjoy the meal worms.

Al was a first-time player of Skip-Bo, and he was the first winner; Carle won a game too. I was so distracted by all the bird activity I lost every game. I think we need to set a Skip-Bo rematch. But at least we all know that we won't get the stink eye from the blue birds, only Becky gets the stink eye, and she deserves it for messing with their food!

Everyday Birds!

This is a Barred Owl in my backyard.

May 2017

This past weekend we did not go the cabin, we stayed home, first time in quite a while. Our dog Shilo recently needed surgery; she had a disgusting growth removed that she has had to carry around for years now. She pulled through fine but was still in no shape to sit in the back seat of the truck for a four-hour drive to the cabin. And even when she got there, she wouldn't have been able to enjoy playing in the lake, which would have been pure torture for her. So I spent the weekend home watching the birds in my own yard as I went about with spring yard clean-up and the usual housework.

Here is the list of birds I saw, many as I was simply looking out the kitchen window:

Black-capped chickadee
Tufted titmouse
Northern cardinal
Bronze-headed cowbird
Gray catbird
Blue jay
White-breasted nuthatch
Downy woodpecker
Hairy woodpecker
Red-bellied woodpecker
Pileated woodpecker
Yellow-rumped warbler
Prairie warbler
American goldfinch
Chipping sparrow
Eastern towhee
Mourning dove
American crow
Red-tailed hawk
Barred owl

That's twenty different species of birds in my own backyard! No binoculars needed, no birding hat needed, no birding backpack with water, snack, and bird guide needed. Just casually looking out the window and in the trees as I moved about the yard doing those clean-up chores. I was bummed that I couldn't go to the cabin but home birding sure is a lot more productive than cabin birding. So what did I learn?

To appreciate the everyday birds around us!

Flat!

June 2017

I saw a recent news report on WMUR 9 and read a newspaper article about a very rare sighting of a brown booby at Corbbetts Pond in Windham, New Hampshire. Now this is exciting! I just had to try and see this brown booby for myself. Brown boobies are usually seen on warm tropical islands or at sea, not on a small inland pond in New Hampshire. So how did this brown booby end up in New Hampshire? Biologists speculate that its internal compass may have become screwed up and the poor thing got lost.

So I decided to travel to Corbbetts Pond to try to see this rare brown booby. I arrived at the location given, but I was surprised I didn't see any other birders there. I thought the place would be packed with birders all looking for this rare bird, but no one was there. I was worried that maybe I hadn't gotten the location right. I asked a couple of women sunbathing if they had seen the brown booby? They sat up quickly, holding on to their bikini tops, looked at me over their sunglasses and told me they had not seen a brown booby! Ummmm perhaps they misunderstood my question.

I decided to sit in the shade on a picnic table and scanned the water looking for the brown booby. A woman carrying an assortment of beach toys with a child in tow walked past me, she stopped and asked me, "What are you looking at?" I told her I was searching for a brown booby, an asked her if she had seen one. Yet again I think I was misunderstood, maybe I looked like a stalker or something. She gave me a strange sideways glance and quickly grabbed her child's hand and rushed away. I considered leaving, before I was asked to leave, didn't look like I was going to see any Booby today.

Just as I was gathering my gear to leave a small group of people came onto the beach, all with binoculars around their necks. Yay fellow birders! We all lined up along the water's edge all scanning the water for the rare brown booby. But no luck. Some had seen it the day before and had returned for another look, with cameras to try and get a good picture. I hung around an hour and a half to see this rare brown booby, but unfortunately, I came up *flat*. No booby for me, bummer.

But at least I tried. And heck, it sure was fun to say brown booby, it makes me chuckle to remember the look on those people's faces when I said I was looking for a brown booby—hahaha! Just what did they think I meant. I can understand that if you don't know birds well the names of some can seem strange and can be misunderstood. I still smile remembering our sisters' trip to Colorado and watching my sister Becky break into laughter every time I would call out, "Look, there's a bushtit!"

Birthday Bird Walk

July 2017

I spent my birthday doing one of my favorite activities, birding! My sisters and I went to Wild Cat Falls Conservation Area in Merrimack, New Hampshire, to enjoy the trails, sit by the falls and marvel at nature's beauty. We took the North Loop Trail, which winds through the tall majestic trees and along the Souhegan River until it meets up with the Falls Loop Trail. North Loop is a great trail to take if you are interested in spotting woodpeckers. On previous walks, we have seen the downy woodpecker, the hairy woodpecker, the pileated woodpecker, the red-bellied woodpecker and the white-breasted nuthatch. The area contains mature mixed hardwoods and pines, all the trees woodpeckers love.

Unfortunately, this day we didn't see any woodpeckers, though we did see multiple nest cavities that looked well used. But that's how birding goes, sometimes you just don't see many birds. Still, the walk through the trees along the ridge and past the river was peaceful. One interesting thing we did see was a turtle doing a belly slide down the hill toward the river! Not something you see every day. My identification of amphibious creatures is pretty rusty, so I wasn't sure what breed of turtle it was. My sister took a picture to get a better ID on the breed later. I do know it was not a snapping turtle or a box turtle. My guess was between a sun turtle and a blanding turtle. If it is a blanding turtle that would be great news as it is considered an endangered species and its presence would show conservation efforts by the Merrimack Conservation Committee are working.

As we walked along the Falls Loop Trail farther, we were serenaded by the raucous calls of blue jays and grackles and the constant calling of black-capped chickadees and tufted titmouse. Then add to the forest chorus the northern cardinal and American goldfinch to complete my birthday serenade by nature, the best birthday song ever! Soon the loud sounds of the swollen river rushing over the falls filled the air. The trail takes you to the top of the falls, where we sat on the rocks and took in the beauty of the surroundings. Even with the roar of the water rushing over the rocks, we could hear the sharp chip call of a pair of cedar waxwings searching the quiet eddies of the river for freshly hatched nymphs. Easy picking for the nimble waxwings.

I highly recommend this jewel of a park; visit it if you can as it was well worth the trip. Thanks to my sister Becky and all those town residents that volunteer their time to maintaining and protecting this park. It was an enjoyable day spent out in nature, one of the top birthday activities I would choose. And to top it all off I still got presents and cake!

Kite in the Wind

August 2017

Recently my friend Beth and I decided to meet up for a day of birding. The plan was to meet at a Park and Ride just off the highway so we could then continue in one car to Newmarket, New Hampshire. I had done some research into sightings in the area of a nesting pair of Mississippi kites. This would be a life list sighting for both of us, plus reports said there was one chick seen in the nest as well. It is rare for Mississippi kites to nest as far north as New Hampshire so it sure was worth the attempt to find the nest site.

The New Hampshire Rare Bird reports and Ebird both listed a street address where the nesting kites had been seen. There was not an exact location given just the street, so we weren't exactly certain where to go. Beth mapped out our route to get us to the area, and we headed out optimistic we could find the kites. Our hopes were soon dashed. We arrived at the street location to find it was a short loop in a residential neighborhood. We drove the loop more than once looking for any signs of a large nest in the trees. We looked for any possible places to pull over that didn't look like private property so we could get out and look around. We did see a small well-worn path that went into the woods between two houses. But there was no place to pull over or park, and it just didn't seem right to get out and walk through someone's yard so we left the area disappointed. No kites!

We decided to head over to Great Bay Discovery Center in Greenland, which was an area also listed as having sightings of the Mississippi kite seen flying over the marshes of the bay. The Discovery Center is just across the bay from Newmarket so it was plausible that the nesting pair would be hunting in that area. So off we went in search of the flying kites.

Before we got there, we made a quick stop at Chapmans Landing to scan the estuary. We saw some beautiful brilliant white great egrets. While watching them skulking through the tall marsh grasses for something good to eat we noticed in the sky a large bird flying toward us. It had dark wings and a light body could it be the flying kite!?

The flying bird was too far away to see well enough with our binoculars so Beth rushes to set up her spotting scope. Unfortunately, Beth was a bit rusty in her set up skills, she nearly dropped the scope while trying to connect it to the tripod. Then a knob fell off the tripod and some other small piece falls to the ground. But she did it and quickly zoomed in on the flying bird. But it was only an osprey, bummer no flying kite.

We headed on to Greenland still hoping to find those kites. We arrived and headed out on the trails of the Discovery Center into the Great Bay estuary scanning the sky for a flying kite. It was a beautiful day for birding along the bay, sunny with a brisk breeze to cool you off. We saw the usual residents of the area, gray cat bird, flycatchers, and assorted gulls. Then we spotted a large bird soaring above the bay, here we go again, dark wings and a light body, large wing span coming right toward us! We both zero in on the flying bird with our binoculars and soon agree, it's an osprey. No flying kite!

No, we never did see the Mississippi kite, but it was still an enjoyable day birding along the trails in the bay. Since our search for the kite ended sooner than we had expected we decided to head back to my house for an afternoon of local birding. I took Beth to a great blue heron rookery that was in my neighborhood. The rookery isn't as active as it once was before new residential building disturbed/damaged the area. But there were still two nests in the standing dead trees out in the marsh. But it wasn't the herons that got our attention. To the surprise and amazement of both of us, it was the tree swallows that left us both with our jaws dropped in awe of what was above our heads. A line of high-powered electric lines runs past the marsh and there sitting on the lines were hundreds of shimmering tree swallows. Yes, I mean hundreds! It was amazing, we counted 250 tree swallows sitting side by side on the lines their glossy blue/green backs shinning in the sun. And there were even more flying around the rookery, too many for us to count.

It was a perfect ending to a day of birding. No, we didn't get to see the flying kites but seeing hundreds of swallows flying above our heads made up for it. Both of us agreed that a day spent birding was better than a day at work no matter what we saw. And you never know, I might still have a chance to catch sight of a Mississippi kite flying in the wind over the bay. I'm still trying!

Thousands! Yes, Thousands!

A picture of the warning sign on the refuge
road on Plum Island Massachusetts.

August 2017

My sister from Florida was recently visiting New Hampshire family
and after reading many of my emails about my birding adventures on
Plum Island she asked if I would take her there. Of course, I would
be glad to! Parker River National Wildlife Refuge on Plum Island in
Massachusetts is one of my favorite birding destinations. Though

I would have to say visiting in late hot August was not the time I would usually choose to go. But it ended up being the perfect time!

The refuge on Plum Island is a migratory bird stop over spot. Which is exactly why there are so many interesting sightings there during migration season. It is a great place to see Arctic birds, like the snowy owl, as they fly south during the harsh Arctic winters, they consider Plum Island as their tropical getaway. Even as our local birds fly farther south to avoid our New England winters, they often stop on the island to gather into large flocks. It's all about timing, that perfect window when certain species of birds gather together to make the long journey to their wintering grounds.

As Sissy and I drove up to the gate of the refuge, there were signs warning drivers to "Beware of Swallows" and a second sign said, "Stop for Swallows Crossing the Road."

Ummmm not your usual road signs, we thought it was just a joke at first. But we soon found out it was no joke; it was a wonder of nature happening right before our eyes. There were large flocks of tree swallows everywhere! They were flying in groups back and forth across the dirt road in front of us, landing briefly in the low trees along the road then taking off again in a large swirling mass. What an amazing sight of beauty!

We stopped at hellcat trail to walk the boardwalk through the marsh and while crossing the dike flocks of swallows were flying back and forth from one side to the other right past us at knee level! As we stood still, they streamed past us chirping and chattering. I swear if we had put our hands out we could have touched one! Everywhere we went on the island we saw large flocks of swallows filling the sky. Even if they weren't flying, there were large groups of swallows in the low bushes weighing down the branches. The island has a lot of bayberry bushes, which is a favorite food for the swallows. Usually, the swallows eat mostly insects but to fuel up for their long migration to the Gulf Coast and Mexico they fatten up on the bayberries.

My sister tried to take a few pictures of the swallows as they flew around us, but they were moving so fast the pictures just came out blurry. There were plenty of fellow birders there some with nice fancy camera gear, I'm sure there will be plenty of good pictures of the tree swallows circulating out there. But we were enjoying the experience we didn't need a picture to remind us, it was an experience we will not soon forget.

Sissy and I tried to count the swallows, but it seemed impossible there were so many and all flying so fast. The day Beth and I saw the tree swallows sitting still on the electric lines it certainly was easier to count them. And I thought we saw a lot of swallows that day. But Sissy and I saw thousands yes thousands of tree swallows together! I know this because I checked the Plum Island birding page online, and on the day, we visited the refuge there were five thousand tree swallows counted! Then two days after our visit there were ten thousand tree swallows counted! Now that's what I call a major gathering for migration, surely a once-in-a-lifetime sighting.

Certainly, it was an "in the right place at the right time" kind of day of birding!

A Grebe for Me!

October 2017

This past weekend, I did something I haven't done in months, I went birding on Plum Island! It all started with a rare bird report of a sighting of the miniature northern saw-whet owl. This is one of the smallest species of owls, slightly smaller than a robin and very secretive and hard to find. Now it's no secret I have an obsession for owls. Gee my sweet niece Katie ends up in the hospital due to our efforts to find the great horned owl, I still feel so bad about that day's events. Then months later on a trip to Rocky Mountain National Forest in Colorado my sister Becky, and I were lucky enough to find a great horned owl nest with an adult and three owlets, right there off the side of the road!

I've traveled to Cape Coral Florida and have seen the cute comical burrowing owls nesting colonies. In Colorado, I stood on a high plateau in blazing heat watching burrowing owls pop in and out of their burrows. I've seen the majestic snowy owl on Plum Island as it migrated from the extreme harsh winters of the Arctic to the coast of New England. I've seen a pair of short-eared owls soar over a field hunting, watched as they dropped down into the tall grass and emerged with dinner in their talons. I've even held a barred owl in my arms! I rescued an injured barred owl and kept it in a box at home twenty-four hours while waiting for fish and game to pick it up to take it to a rehabilitation center. That was a once-in-a-lifetime experience, ya know what the owl said to me as I patted it and gave it some water? It softly hooted "who…who…who cooks for you…" But I have not seen the northern saw-whet owl so how could I *not* get onto Plum Island to try and see it!

Beth agreed to accompany me on my search. There also were reports of a great horned owl sighting and Beth wanted to see one.

Most often bird sighting reports for Plum Island list the date, time and location of each sighting. But this time for some reason the saw-whet owl listing said "location undisclosed"; in other words, shhh… it's a secret, stay away! I know that owl sightings can cause quite a circus on the island with paparazzi swarming around trying to get pictures and throngs of birders trying to set up their spotting scopes to get a good look. I've seen and been a part of the mayhem owl sightings can cause. So I wasn't surprised that it was going to be very hard to find the owls. Yet Beth and I were anxious to strap on our binoculars and search for birds!

It was great to get back into some serious birding. The refuge was busy with other birders, fishermen and people walking along the beach, everyone out enjoying the day. At one area we stopped at, numerous trucks pulled in together and guys in camouflage got out, pulling on knee-length rubber boots. Ah, what's going on?

My first thought was that they were a group of duck hunters. I couldn't resist I went up to one of the guys and asked him, "What's going on?" I didn't want to take a chance that they were all here to see an extra special bird, like an owl! Nope, they were all volunteers, seems the refuge was having a fall cleanup day out in the marsh. I thanked the guys for volunteering their time, and we headed out on the trail. No, we never did find any owls. But we still saw birds! The weather started out nice, sunny skies typical fall day but as the day went on the wind picked up and the clouds took over. The wind was getting so strong that it kept blowing our hats off! We would see a flash of yellow in the trees.

"Oh, what's that bird?"

Nope, not a bird just a yellow leave blowing in the wind. "Oh, what was that flash of red?"

Nope, not a bird, just a leaf. It did make inland birding difficult so we focused on the ocean side lookouts, but the shore was empty there were very few sea birds.

We continued along the dirt road and stopped at the bird blind, and we hit the jackpot! Because the marshy area opposite the ocean side was more protected, there were flocks of birds gathered in the open water, geese, cormorants, ducks, teals, and pintails There were other birders set up in the blind with spotting scopes, and they were nice enough to share their equipment so we could get good close up looks at all the birds. We were lucky to get a great view of a whimbrel walking along the top of the dike. We hung around in the blind for a while then headed on to the next birding spot.

Unfortunately, the weather was going downhill, getting windier and cloudier, the birds were all hunkering down for a storm, we just weren't seeing much. At our last stop, Beth was talking to some other birders who mentioned seeing some interesting birds at the Blind. Beth suggested that we go back to the Blind before heading off the island to see if anything new had shown up. Great idea, Beth! Turned out we did see something new among all the other water foal, a pair of immature red-necked grebes! It wasn't an easy identification it took us a lot of discussion and time searching through our bird guides to agree on what we saw. Birds in immature plumage are very difficult to identify.

This sighting was a life list bird for both of us! Yippee!

So our birding day ended on a high note. Enjoyed a day out in nature with my friend and experienced the camaraderie of fellow birders. No, we didn't find any owls, the woodland birds had migrated south and weren't around, and the ocean was void of birds. But as Becky often reminds me, "Birds fly, just because a report says a bird is somewhere on Monday doesn't mean it's still there Tuesday." Yup, birds fly! We watched the pair of red-necked grebes fly in and gracefully land in the marsh.

That's a grebe for me!

Columbus Day Search

October 2017

The school I work at had Columbus Day off, so I had the day off and had originally planned to do some fall birding on Plum Island. The warbler migration is in full swing and there have been reports of many interesting bird sightings. I was looking forward to getting out there to see what I could see.

Unfortunately, the weather didn't cooperate; our area was experiencing the effects of the remnants of Hurricane Nate. Although the storm was no longer a hurricane, we were still getting strong winds and heavy rains. Surely not a good day for birding on the island.

So in the spirit of the great explorer Christopher Columbus, I decided to explore the woods out behind the house for the nest site of the barred owls I have been hearing nightly. Our property abuts a large tract of wooded undeveloped land, just the kind of habitat the owls like. There was a break in the rain late afternoon, so I put on my rain slicker and headed into the woods. There aren't any established trails in the woods, but I followed a deer trail through the woods in search of the nest site. It was still very windy and wet and leaves were falling all around me, but I searched on. I passed a pileated woodpecker busy drilling for bugs on a dead tree. The pileated is one of my favorite woodpeckers I never tire of watching them. But no sight of the owl nest anywhere.

I walked a little farther to an area with tall old pine trees the kind of area the owls would like still hoping to find the nest but no luck. In the trees above me, I spotted a pair of hairy woodpeckers, and I saw a white-breasted nuthatch climbing the tree trunk. But still no owl nest, I walked on farther. I had been walking about an hour when the rain began to come down heavy again. Time to head back! I rushed back home soaking wet even with my rain slicker on, and never did find any evidence of the nesting owls. But time spent out in the woods exploring is still better than time spent inside sitting in front of a screen. The owls are out there somewhere, and I will still be searching.

Murder?

November 2017

What's in a name? Ever wonder why or how people came up with names for birds? I do. We all know a large group of birds is called a flock. But certain groups of birds were given different names to describe their gathering. For example, a gathering of geese is called a "gaggle of geese." A gathering of owls is called a "parliament of owls," and a gathering of crows is called a "murder of crows." Why did the crows get such a sinister name? Well, folklore says they were given this name because of the crows appetite for carrion. But the crow doesn't kill squirrels or rabbits; they just clean up the leftovers of road kill or from four legged predators. Unfortunately, it seems crows got a bad reputation for their culinary choices.

The American crow is actually a very intelligent bird. I know this from my personal experiences with a family of crows (I can't bring myself to call them a murder) that live in my yard. For the past few years, they have built a large nest in the tall pine trees in the back wood lot. And I swear they recognize me! I have an old leaky bird bath that I use as a feeder for the birds since it doesn't hold water any more. I usually put out stale bread or cereal, etc., for the birds rather than throw it away, and I also add seed and cracked corn in the winter.

The crows will sit in the tree above the bird bath and call out, *Caw! Caw! Caw!* if there is no food out. Even when I walk out to put something in the bird bath for them, they will sit on the branches above me and cock their heads as if inspecting my offerings. They seem to know my schedule too, when I get home from work and check the mail at the end of the driveway there is often one sitting in the pine tree watching me as I get the mail. As I drive up our long driveway, I've even looked in my rearview mirror and saw the crow flying up the driveway behind me. It's like it knows I am the one who leaves them food in the bird bath. When I get out of the car, the crow will *Caw! Caw! Caw!* at me while flying overhead. It's like it is asking, "What's for dinner?"

They are undoubtedly a very noisy and social bird species. But I have really enjoyed having a family of eight crows living in my yard. Watching them raise a family and teach their young the ways of the world. Even when four or five gather at the feeder, they never fight; they take turns snatching a piece of bread and flying off to sit on a branch and eat. I've watched an adult grab a piece of bread and walk over to a young bird and offer it to them.

So what's in a name? A murder of crows? *Not* my family of crows!

Snowy!

December 2017

My sister from Florida was visiting New England family for the holiday and one of the things on her to do list was to get to see the snowy owl. The Arctic snowy owl migrates to Plum Island, Massachusetts, each winter and is always the star attraction for birders on Plum Island Parker River Wildlife Refuge. So I had my mission set: to get my sister Sissy a snowy owl sighting!

The pressure was on; I had been following the reports of sightings online, I knew the owls were on the island, now to get my sister there to see them. So I loaded up the truck with the spotting scope, binoculars, walking stick, and backpack with supplies. I threw in an extra hat, scarf, mittens, and coat and wind pants to ward off the biting cold winds to be sure to keep my sister warm. What were the chances she packed or even had enough winter weather clothes for her trip from warm and sunny Florida? Of course, there is no guarantee in birding that just because a bird has been seen one day doesn't mean they will be there the next day. But the chances were pretty good, the owls were about as predictable as possible to be there. Fingers crossed.

Winter birding is not easy. I have been on Plum Island numerous times the past years during the winter with family and friends searching for the snowy owl. It is a cold activity, often with strong biting winds coming of the ocean. The trails across the dunes are snow packed and slippery. But we have been rewarded with great sightings of the snowy owl making the discomfort worth it. But I was worried, how would my sister from warm and sunny south Florida adjust to the harsh conditions of winter birding on the New England coast?

Turns out it didn't matter what the weather conditions were like, she didn't have to trek across the snow to find the owl! We passed through the entrance gate of the refuge and drove barely a couple hundred feet and there on the ocean side of the road was a small group of people. It was obvious what they were all there for, as they had spotting scopes set up, large lens cameras, binoculars around their necks and everyone was pointing into the dunes. Yup! There sitting on the snow-covered sand dune was a snowy owl!

Wow that was a record fast sighting! And we didn't even have to get out of the warm truck to see the owl. Though, of course we did, the fellow birders were very nice and shared their scope that was already focused on the owl so my sister got an up-close look. Honestly, I was a little disappointed it was such an easy sighting. I kinda wanted my sister to get the full experience of New England winter birding and to experience the satisfaction of spotting the snowy owl after spending hours in the cold searching the dunes. But she sure was happy she got to see an amazing new bird and really that's all that mattered, she saw her first snowy owl!

City Birding!

June 2018

I met up with my friend Beth in Nashua, New Hampshire, this past Wednesday to do some birding. This was about to be a new experience for me, birding in a city. She has been seeing chimney swifts flying over the old mill buildings across from where she works. Also, some have been seen at her church circling the bell tower. I was anxious to see some for myself. Because of the loss of habitat, the swifts are becoming rare, they need tall stone or brick chimneys to nest in. And as the old brick mill buildings are torn down for new development the chimney swift population has declined.

First, we drove to the church to see what we could find. A majestic historic stone church on the top of the hill on Main Street. Beautiful architect, granite arches, inspiring stained-glass windows and a tall granite bell tower. Even if I didn't see the swifts, it didn't matter. I was in awe of the beauty of this church and the positive calming vibes I could feel just from being there.

The sky was overcast and gray which hopefully would make the silhouette of the swifts stand out good. Beth explained to me how different the swift was compared to the shape of the swallow, and she told me to listen for the high-pitched chattering of the swifts as they flew high above. It is said that the chimney swift looks like a flying cigar, its body is long and rounded at both ends and dark against the sky. The swift doesn't flap its wings like most other birds but glides barely moving its wings at all, it actually vibrates its wings in quick short movements. We walked around the church yard for a while and sure enough Beth heard the swifts chattering, and she pointed up in the sky and yells, "There they are!" Their shape indeed was very distinctive. They were flying so fast and so high I couldn't get a good look at them with my binoculars, but I did see them! What a magical moment watching the swirling flock of chimney swifts circling the tall church bell tower.

Next, Beth took me to where she works to try and get me a better sighting of the chimney swifts. Her office building is along the old canal, across the street from the old mill buildings that had been turned into offices. We sat on a table in the courtyard under some trees and enjoyed our picnic lunch while watching the sky for flying cigars. Didn't take long before they showed up! First there were three, and then two more, then another group flew in all circling in unison above the trees along the canal chattering loudly. I ended up seeing dozens of chimney swifts—yippee, a new life list bird for me!

All thanks to Beth for inviting me to do some city birding.

Adventures in the Great North Woods

This Loon plaque my husband made to represent
our cabin The Skimmersplace.

This chapter is about my birding adventures at my cabin on Lake Francis in Pittsburg, New Hampshire. The northern most town in the state along the Canadian border. It is a special area secluded from the hustle and bustle of larger towns. The serenity and beauty of being surrounded by nature can't be beat!

Another Season Begins

April 2013

Well, the cabin made it through another winter season in one piece. There were the usual trees down, the spruce forest is dying, and it has been for years since it became infected with the spruce beetle. You can hear them eating away at the trees at night, nothing can be done but wait for nature to run its course. John was able to take some extra time off, and I was on school vacation so we were able to spend six days at the cabin. We arrived on a Friday to cold wind; overnight it rained like crazy, and we lost power. We awoke to flash flooding Saturday, no power, and temps hovering below thirty, cold and windy. We didn't get power back till late in the afternoon near supper time. Because of the flooding, John wasn't able to do any fishing.

The only bright spot in the day was a surprise visit from Jeremy and Crystal, they drove over from Vermont to visit. It was nice to see them, Jeremy helped his dad cut down a couple of trees in the front of the cabin, and they did a great job and felled the trees without hitting any others. They brought their dogs, Bella and Dexter, along for the visit, and Dexter was one happy lab playing in the icy water, fetching the sticks Jeremy tossed.

I did get to see the first loon of the season to return to the lake. Because the river was running so high, our cove was the only spot on the lake where the ice was beginning to break apart. A couple of days later, there were five loons in our cove, two pairs and one bachelor. By the following Saturday, the temperatures had warmed, the winds died down and the flooding abated, and it was officially ice out for Lake Francis. The loons were yodeling and calling all night, it was comforting to hear them back.

On Sunday, we awoke to fresh snow on the ground and flurries in the air. It was cold and windy with temps in the high twenties.

Not the best birding or fishing day. But I was determined to get out and do some birding. I wore my ninja birding outfit, covered up head to toe with only my eyes visible, I had to ward off the bitter wind somehow. I was walking along the shore and was in Gray Cove when I noticed a deer walking across the ice. The wind had pushed a large flow of ice up against the shore near the lighthouse and the deer walked onto the ice from there. I watched as it trotted across the ice toward the shoreline near Seal Beach. But as it got to the opposite shore it stopped when it noticed there was a gap between the shore-line and the ice that was open water. The deer walked back and forth trying to jump onto land without having to swim through the icy water. I was getting worried it might fall through the thin ice.

The deer trotted back in the direction it had come but the wind had now pushed the ice flow away from the shore on both sides of the lake. Now the deer was adrift on the ice flow. I couldn't watch any more, I was so worried it was going to fall into the icy water and die. I walked away hoping the poor deer would survive. I couldn't do it. I went back to see how the deer was and luckily it was off the ice flow. It must have been able to jump the gap or swam to shore. I checked out the ice with my binoculars and didn't see any open holes that the deer might have fallen through. So in my mind, he made it back to shore. I'll know by the next time I go up, I'll walk the shoreline and see if a deer's body washed ashore.

Back at the cabin, I saw a strange little fellow. It appears to be an albino red squirrel. He was running around and frolicking with the other red squirrels, but it was pale blond, not red. There aren't any gray squirrels at the cabin; he was definitely the same shape and sounded like a red squirrel. He was pretty freaky looking. I don't know if he will be able to survive without any camouflage from pred-ators. I'll keep my eyes open for him. Hope he survives.

Come on ladies it's all about the shoes! John knew I had been looking for a good pair of rain boots for Pittsburg's fifth season, mud season, and he saw a pair of Boggs at the trading post and bought them for me. Thank you, Johnny. Thanks to the boggs I was able to track down the elusive winter wren in the mucky bog and get a really good up-close look at him. Those of you with birding apps you need to look this bird up and listen to his beautiful song. He is a small five-and-a-half-inch brown bird but his song resonates through the forest. I got a quick look at one last year, but this time I was able to really enjoy the sighting, watching him sitting atop a stump singing his heart out for all to hear.

By the last day, the weather had improved greatly, it was sunny, temps near sixty. The spring migrants were beginning to return. I was able to spot a blue-headed vireo and a Philadelphia vireo high in the treetops. These are two of the most beautiful treetop singers ever. Once the leaves all bloom it is almost impossible to spot them as they live high in the canopy. I saw the first warbler of the season, a yellow-rumped warbler as I was walking along the river. All in all, it was a great vacation. John caught some good fish, and I saw some nice birds. The weather was cold and windy to start but finished sunny and warm. And so another season began.

Shhh...

May 27, 2013

While up at the cabin I was doing some birding in my favorite spot when I came upon two men set up with scopes looking out over the water. I approached them and asked if they had spotted anything of interest. They told me they were trying to establish if a certain bird was nesting in the area. I thought one of the men looked familiar but couldn't figure out why. He introduces himself as the state birdman and asks if I remember him. Ah, now I remembered; we worked together over ten years ago on the Osprey Project. He looked a little different but then we all do as time passes.

I felt proud as he explained to his associate all about the volunteer work I did for the state to document the return of the osprey to Lake Francis. That I had documented the first known nest on the lake, and it is recorded as Neskey Nest #1. A little back history for you here, you see the osprey were in decline and on the endangered list because pesticides had gotten into the water ways and contaminated the fish they live on. The toxins didn't kill the adult birds, but it caused a defect in the egg shells and caused the eggs to crumble and crack soon after being laid, so there were fewer and fewer baby birds surviving and the osprey numbers declined sharply. After years of study, documentation, and debate, legislation was passed banning the toxic chemicals. It took years for the damage to be repaired but finally the osprey numbers were rebounding. So the discovery of an active nest was big news.

We talked about my current volunteer work on the loon project. The loons face a similar problem now, they are being poisoned by the lead sinkers fishermen use. There is currently legislation (SenateBill89) up for passage to ban the use of such lead fishing tackle to protect the loons. It has passed in the House and is next up for

186

debate and vote in the Senate then onto the governor to be signed. I have been in contact with my local representatives and signed petitions showing my support for the bill and urged my representatives to support the bill. Let's hope the lessons learned from the Osprey Project will help save the loons of New Hampshire.

Mr. State Birdman then asks me if I would be interested in helping him with the State's newest project, Air Force One Project. The state is trying to document the return of the bald eagle to the Lake Francis area and search for any active nests. The bald eagle like the osprey had been in decline in our state but has also made a successful return to our rivers and lakes. But there had not been any nests located in the Lake Francis area. Of course, I would love to help out on the project! I tell Mr. State Birdman that I have been keeping a birding journal for years and have documented every time I have sighted an eagle. He is very interested in this information and asks me to email him all sightings and activity for the past three years.

When I got home a few days later, I emailed Mr. State Birdman all the info I had collected over the years. I was surprised that after I emailed my sightings to Mr. State Birdman, he replied, asking for my discretion in this area. He hoped I would understand the need to keep all information on this project on the down low. He emailed me the name and phone number of a fellow "agent" on the project that I was to contact for further instructions.

A couple of days later, Mr. State Birdman sent me another email telling me that he had found Air Force One's home base. With the help of a small plane, he was able to fly low over the large area and using heat seeking technology he found home base and verified that there were occupants present. Don't worry New Hampshire taxpayers this project was funded by a UNH grad student grant, no tax payer's funds were used. This was very exciting news indeed! I received an email with the coordinates of Air Force One's home base and asked to continue to document any sightings *and* asked to be very discrete in doing so. He asked me to *not* set up a scope and to *not* draw any attention to myself so as not to draw a crowd of other birders or photographers. Air Force One's home base was deserving of the highest security protection.

So I am bound by avian ethics to keep the location of Air Force One's home base a secret. I will guard Air Force One's home base to my last gray hair. Yeah sure, I've told you the story, but I haven't really told you the complete facts. Even if some of you break my code, I won't reveal the location of Air Force One's home base even if you try to tickle me with a lobster claw.

Shhh...Agent 008 out.

WWCD

I was able to spend ten days at the cabin over the July 4 holiday, which gave me a chance to explore some new trails I had been wanting to try. There was one along Moose Ally that went down to the river and to a waterfall that sounded interesting, so I headed out early one morning. After my adventure on Mt. Agamenticus (WWCD), I was sure to leave a note at the cabin telling John where I went, I packed my bird bag with water, molasses cookies, a cheese sandwich and the trail map. It had rained hard the night before, but it was nice and sunny as I headed out.

The trail head is marked by a small sign along Rt. 3 where you pull over and head into the woods. My car was the only one there as I headed onto the trail. It was very muddy which was no surprise considering how much it had rained the night before, so I tread carefully along the slippery muddy trail. I continued to follow the blaze yellow markings on the trees till I came to a grassy meadow. Then the trail was marked by boards laid down across the tall wet grasses winding through the swampy area. I was hoping to see a Lincoln's sparrow or swamp sparrow, they both like wet meadows and woodland bogs but no luck. Though it was hard to be looking for birds when I was balancing on moving boards laid across the soggy swampy meadow.

At the end of the meadow was a small foot bridge crossing over a stream, which was moving fast due to the recent rains. As I was crossing the bouncing bridge, I could hear some chickadees calling, and I'm always on the lookout for the boreal chickadee who lives in the north and sounds almost the same as our common black-capped chickadee. But I didn't dare stop to look, the bridge was swaying and bouncing and the small rain swollen stream was moving fast. So I listened to the little voice in my head (WWCD) saying, "Keep moving," and crossed the bridge fast.

The trail led back into the dense spruce trees and along the river. I could hear the raging river but could hardly see it because the trees were so dense. There were a couple little foot paths down to the river's edge to access the water. John had told me he had fished along the trail before, so I cut down one of the paths to get a better look at the river. Wow, was it ever running fast! The river was swollen by the rains and running brown from the runoff. I could hear the rocks being tumbled by the rapids. It was awe-inspiring to see the power of nature, to hear it and feel it up close. I walked along the river's edge and carefully climbed over a couple of big rocks to get closer to the river. I took a few pictures and headed back up to the main trail.

Well…I thought I had cut back onto the main trail; it sort of looked like a trail, or was it? I admit I was a little spooked, all I could hear was the roaring river, I couldn't see any yellow blaze marks on any trees. I didn't own a cell phone at this time and wouldn't have mattered anyways, there was no cell service in the area. There weren't any human or animal prints in the mud below my feet, but it sort of looked like a trail. I stuck a couple of sticks into the mud and decided to go forward a little ways, and if I didn't find any yellow blaze marks, and then I would turn around and follow the sticks back, and then try another way to find the trail.

Phew…there ahead was a yellow blaze on the tree. I could hear my younger sister Chris's voice in my head (WWCD) making me promise not to do anything stupid after my adventure hiking Mt. Agamenticus. Right then and there I turned around to head back to my car. No more looking for birds, I didn't even make it to the water fall, I had taken enough chances this morning, that was it I was done.

I retraced my steps and came back to the wet meadow and as I was crossing the planks through the grass, ahead of me I see something moving in the tall grass. I see a black head. OMG, a bear! I freeze, it doesn't see me. Quickly I think what do I do, I'm standing in the middle of a wet meadow of tall grass balancing on a two-by-ten of wood. The nearest tree is yards away there is no way I can out run a bear. Okay, think…I decide I'm gonna reach down and grab the two-by-ten I'm standing on, and if I have to, I'll use it as a weapon. I'm gonna scream and yell and swing that board at the black head in the grass if it comes at me.

I hear a loud whistle. I think, umm, that's a new bird, I quickly snap back to reality and that black head in the grass. Then I hear a man's voice yell, "Bear!" My heart is ready to explode, the black head is moving. I stand in the mud holding the board over my head ready to strike out at the creature in the grass. God help me! The black head lifts out of the tall grass, and I see a red collar, suddenly a man comes into the clearing of the meadow. He whistles and calls, "Here, bear, come, boy." He sees me and waves, he waits for me to cross the planks to his side, the planks are a one-person crossing. When I reach him, I tell him his dog scared the heck out of me, that I thought he was a bear and I was ready to smack him in the head. The guy laughs and tells me, "Yeah, he looks like a bear that's why he called him Bear." I tell him I didn't think it was so funny. I'm sure he enjoyed scaring the daylight out of me and had fun telling the story of the crazy old bird lady standing in the mud swinging a two-by-ten over her head to his buddies over a few beers. I don't know dog breeds, but I swear this dog looked like a bear. Big, black and I see him alone in the woods rooting around in tall grass.

I was never so glad to get back into the safety of my car. I just sat there trying to calm myself. I never did see a single bird, I didn't make it to the waterfall I wanted to see, my feet were covered in mud and who knows how many ticks were in that tall grass. I sat in my car and ate all four molasses cookies I had packed. I think I deserved them.

My new mantra is, *What would Chris do?*

Please Be Careful on the Lake

July 2013

There are only a couple of times a year when Lake Francis could be called busy, and the Fourth of July weekend is the most popular. This year was no different, the campground was full to capacity. There were people everywhere, they had blankets and lawn chairs on every available inch of grass at the boat launch/picnic area. People were enjoying the lake, the smell of grilling food wafted through the air, teenagers tossed footballs back and forth to impress the young girls sunning on beach towels.

The boat traffic was incredible; there were boats of all sizes and sorts on the lake. An unusual occurrence on the lake indeed. Most of those on the water were by human power, others open fishing boats slowly trolling along. But there was always one or two boats that just don't fit in. One such boat was a souped-up, twenty-one-foot speed-boat circling the cove. This was one nice-looking boat, and you could tell there was a lot of money invested in it. The guy had the ski pylon all decked out with an assortment of gear; he had a wake/knee board, double skis, single ski, and a two-person tube. It was a hot and sunny day, and they were on the lake to enjoy the water. That boat roared as he opened it up over the water.

You could tell the three guys in the boat knew what they were doing. I was watching them on and off all day. The skier was cross-ing the wake behind the boat and doing twists and jumps. Each of the guys took a turn showing off their skills. They were putting on quite a show. Unfortunately, their activity wasn't appropriate for the campground cove. The boat was making an awful wake, canoes were being tossed around, and kayaks were being swamped. The repeated waves were chewing up the shoreline. John said the guy needed to adjust his trim tabs to cause less wake, the boat was way too big to be circling in the cove. Where is the marine patrol when you need them?

The most inappropriate activity pushed me to the brink. The cove loons have hatched a young, and the family was doing its best to stay out of the way. A baby loon can't dive to get away from trouble and the adults won't leave it on its own. The baby was riding on its parents' back when one of the guys riding behind the boat on a tube swung far to the side putting the loon between him and the boat. I thought he was going to decapitate the poor loon with the tow rope. I gasped and covered my eyes in fear. As the boat roared away, I searched the surface for the loon, I could see it bobbing in the wake. It survived. Something had to be done about these guys. But what can I do? I understand they are here enjoying their holiday. I don't want to ruin anyone's fun. I consider my choices when finally they set anchor and take a break. I think good, maybe they're done for the day and will leave the cove and our poor loons alone.

No such luck. After a short break, they're at it again. This time one of the guys is on the wake board doing tricks as the boat speeds toward the campground. The boat turns sharply and is coming toward me close along the shore. I'm watching in my binoculars as the loon and the baby are also swimming toward me just ahead of the boat. I yell up to John sitting on the porch of the cabin that the boat is headed straight for the loons. The baby loon is falling behind its parent as they are trying to swim out of the way. Oh, God, no don't let the boat hit them! I'm yelling and waving at the boat, but it's futile they aren't looking my way at all.

The boat skims by the loons with inches to spare, the wake boarder leans far to the side and causes a rooster tail of water to splash up, and it hits the loons. I watched as the water swamped the loons and saw the parent loon stretch up out of the water and let out a loud yodel. The wake boarder laughs and calls out to the others in the boat, "Hey, did you see that? I got the duck good." I can't see the baby. By now, I'm screaming, trying to get their attention! John yells down to me to try and get the bow numbers off the boat. Perfect timing, just as they get just off shore from me the wake boarder falls into the water and the boat stops. I yell out to the wake boarder that he nearly killed the loons, that they are a protected bird, and it is a federal offense to harass them (16 USC 703-712). He laughs and says, "Whatever."

The boat has circled back now, and they yell out to the fallen skier, "Don't worry about the old lady, she can't see the bow numbers, get in." Oh, they messed with the wrong old lady, I put my binoculars to my eyes and yell up to John the bow numbers. The boaters are "waving" the universal symbol of disrespect to me and yell, "Forget you, you don't have my bow numbers."

I yell back, "Oh yeah—MAXXXXX!"

Again, I yell to them, "MAXXXXX!" The boaters are scrambling to help the skier into the boat and pull in the line. I'm screaming to John, "DID YOU WRITE THAT DOWN? MAXXXXX…"

The boaters speed away into the open lake faster than I thought was possible for a boat to travel. I'm scanning the water trying to find the baby loon. Praying it survived. I can't find it. I run up to the cabin and grab my keys, I rush down to the campground office to report what has happened. The park ranger agrees they had been causing problems, and he had been wondering how to handle it. The marine patrol was very busy farther south handling water rescues due to the swollen rivers. Three people had died in the waters of New Hampshire over the holiday weekend and there were many water rescues as people misjudged the rapid rain swollen waters. The park ranger was hoping to catch the boaters when they pulled the boat out of the water at the launch. I told him the launch area only had cars and trucks with roof racks for canoes or kayaks, there were no vehicles with boat trailers. That meant the boaters must have put in at the other larger launch along Rt. 3.

The park ranger calls 911 the dispatcher says our situation is a non-emergency, marine patrol is busy so she connects us to NH Fish and Game. They are also busy and the park ranger leaves a message. He asks me to write out a report of the events so when F&G gets back to him, he can relay the information on my complaint. Before I even finish the report, F&G calls back and talks to me. F&G agrees this is a serious offense, he asks me if I have seen the baby loon since. Sadly, I tell him no. The F&G officer tells me he is in Colebrook trying to take care of a bear issue but will head up to Pittsburg as soon as he can. He said he would stop by the Rt. 3 boat launch and see if he can find the boat, if not he will run the bow numbers, and he will be in contact with the owner one way or another. He takes my number and thanks me for watching out for the loons.

I head back to the cabin with a heavy heart, I can hear the mournful call of a loon, but it goes unanswered. I go to the water's edge to search for the loons. I'm upset over what has happened. I'm not that kind of person who screams and yells at people. I don't like confrontation but the loons can't speak, so I guess it was up to me. I've watched these loons for months and now the baby we were all so excited to see is gone. Then I hear a loon return the others call, there is much yodeling and calling from the loons. I rush to the water's edge, and yes, it's true, the baby is there! The family is together calmly swimming across the lake in front of the cabin. Well, safe for now till the next time.

The next morning, I get a phone call from the F&G officer. He tells me that he caught up to the boaters along Rt. 3 in Stewartstown after they had pulled the boat out of the water. The bow numbers matched and the owner admitted he was on the lake. He was from out of state and said it was his first time in Pittsburg on Lake Francis and that he didn't know there were protected loons there. The F&G officer asks him why he was repeatedly going around the campground cove when there was more than two thousand acres of water he could have used instead. The boat owner said the main part of the lake was too rough so he stayed in the calm cove because it was safer for the skiers. He said the loon popped up after he went by and that the wake boarder couldn't avoid it. He apologized and denied any disrespect to me. The F&G officer said none of them were intoxicated and the owner had all the proper paperwork and equipment.

The F&G officer gave them a copy of 16 USC 703-712, which is the US Migratory Bird Treaty Act. Harassment, trade, death of a protected bird can carry a five thousand dollar fine and 6 months in jail. The F&G officer told me he believed my account of what happened over the excuse the boat owner gave him, he said he was sure the boaters wouldn't repeat their mistake again. He told them that if the baby loon turned up dead he would be talking to them again. I was glad to be able to tell him that the baby loon was safe and the family was together again. He thanked me for taking action and told me not to hesitate to call him again if any other incidence happen. I just hope I never have to call him again! Boaters, please be careful on the lakes!

Back on That Horse

August 2013

About a week before family reunion, I was at the cabin alone to get things ready. The weather was pleasant, so I decided to take a hike on the trail along the river to look for birds, it's about a four-mile loop. The lake has been very high for this time of year and the high water left a lot of debris along the trail as it receded. The trail was muddy, with all sorts of rocks and branches and even fallen trees littering the path.

As I was walking along, suddenly my toe got caught on a branch across the trail. In what seemed like slow motion, I fell hard onto a pile of logs and branches. I tried to break my fall by putting my hands out but my hand pushed right through the soft wet wood and I hit the side of a log face first. The log pushed into my cheek and I could taste blood. At the time, I wasn't sure if I had bitten my tongue or the inside of my cheek, but it sure hurt either way.

My bird bag that I had across my shoulder came around and hit me hard in the back of the head. My binoculars swung forward and hit me in the side of my jaw. I laid there in a tangle for a few seconds trying to assess the possible damage. My knees and legs were cut and bleeding, my right wrist hurt really badly, the back of my head hurt, but the worst was my cheek. I still wasn't sure where the blood I was tasting was coming from.

Of course, then I'd do the typical "Look around; did anyone see me do that stupid thing?" move. But I was alone on the trail, it was a quiet week day. So I slowly stand up and brush myself off and get my bearings. Okay, now what, I'm about two miles from the cabin, I've got to walk back I have no other choice. I sit on a rock for a bit till I stop shaking, I have a sip of water to rinse out my mouth. Then there is no other choice I stand up and start the hike back to the cabin.

That was the longest walk back to the cabin ever! As soon as I got back, I checked out my mouth, it seems I bit the inside of my cheek pretty bad but the bleeding had stopped by then. I washed myself off, put ointment on all the scratches and wrapped my wrist. I sat in the rocking chair on the porch with a cold ginger ale and read a magazine. I figured I deserved it.

I was concerned that my face would be bruised for family reunion and I would have to explain my appearance to everyone. But luckily the discoloration on my face didn't last long. I had some bruising and cuts on my legs, but it was so cold over reunion week-end I kept pants on most of the time and no one noticed. I did share my experience with family around the campfire, all agreed that I had to stop taking chances, to be more careful. All made me promise *not* to go off on my own in the woods any more. After all, I was sixty years old now; no spring chicken any longer, just an old hen.

Well, I tried to follow their advice. I was at the cabin alone for four last days of summer before going back to work; the weather was great. I sat on the porch, I sat by the lake, I took leisurely walks along the dirt road. But *darn it*! I have wasted too many years battling anx-iety and panic attacks, always in fear of doing anything! Afraid to go anywhere! Always waiting for something bad to happen and sure it would if I didn't dot my Is and cross my Ts perfectly and never ever stepping on a crack in the sidewalk! Afraid always afraid. DARN IT! I just turned sixty, and I'm glad to still be alive. I have to except that I'm more than halfway done my time here on earth, that I'm closer to death than I am to birth.

So I put on my hiking shoes; strung my binoculars around my neck; slung my bird bag stuffed with my bird book, plastic baggie with tissues, water bottle, and molasses cookies across my shoul-der; and headed back to the trail along the river. What's that saying? "When you fall off the horse, you gotta get right back on." Well, I got right back on that horse! I hiked along that muddy debris littered trail on a quiet week day all alone. I clambered over the wet rocks at the river's edge and sat enjoying the sound of the rushing waters. I slipped and slide along the muddy trail into the cool dense woods. I had a great day alone in the woods!

Of the nine possible woodpeckers I could see in our area, I saw six along that one walk. From the smallest downy woodpecker to the largest pileated woodpecker. I saw the yellow-bellied sapsucker, hairy woodpecker and the northern flicker. The best sighting was of a black-backed woodpecker, with his glossy black patent leather looking back and head topped by a blaze of yellow. He was so busy searching the dead log for bugs he paid no attention to me as I stood and watched him for a good five minutes. I saw this bird because I did it, I ventured into the dark dense dead parts of the forest where he lives. I did it, I got back on that horse! Giddy up…giddy up… giddy up…

Loon sightings on Lake Francis 2013

An adult Common Loon & young.

I take part in the annual loon survey put on by the Loon Preservation Committee here is an example of the reports I submit to help protect the common loon of New Hampshire. I have a cabin on the lake near the state park campground. I usually go for a kayak paddle for an hour each morning, afternoon and early evening. I mainly observe the loons that are in the cove where the Connecticut River comes into the lake. I often see an additional loon or two when I paddled farther into the main part of the lake.

April
19: 1 adult
20: 1 adult
21: 1 adult
22: 1 adult
23: 1 adult
26: 2 adults
27: 2 adults
28: 2 adults

Sometimes saw two adults together, other times in separate parts of the cove.

Approx. total time spent observing: 10 hours

May
3: 2 adults
4: 2 adults
5: 2 adults
17: 2 adults
18: 2 adults
19: 2 adults
24: 2 adults
25: 2 adults
26: 2 adults
27: 2 adults

Often saw one adult at a time in the cove, was much calling at night.

Approx. time spent observing: 30 hours

June
7: 2 adults
8: 4 adults
9: 3 adults
14: 2 adults
15: 2 adults

16: 3 adults
27: pair w/ 1 young
28: pair w/1 young
29: pair w/1 young
30: pair w/1 young
Approx. time spent observing: 30 hours

July

1: pair w/1 young
1 adult in separate area
2: pair w/1 young
3: pair w/1 young
1 adult in separate area
4: pair w/1 young
5: pair w/1 young
6: pair w/1 young
1 adult in separate area
7: pair w/1 young
12: pair w/1 young
2 adults in separate area
13: pair w/1 young
14: pair w/1 young
18: pair w/1 young
1 adult in separate area
19: pair w/1 young
20: pair w/1 young

Watched 5 adults swimming and feeding together in the area where Amy Brook enters the lake; it was a frenzy of feeding.

21: pair w/1 young
29: pair w/1 young
30: pair w/1 young
2 adults in separate area
31: pair w/ 1 young
Approx. time spent observing: 51 hours

August
>5: pair w/1 young
>6: pair w/1 young
>1 adult in separate area
>7: pair w/1 young
>1 adult in separate area
>8: pair w/1 young
>10: pair w/1 young
>2 adults in separate area
>11: pair w/1 young
>Approx. time spent observing: 18 hours

Hope for the Future

June 2014

I had an encouraging sighting recently at the cabin in Pittsburg, a ring-necked pheasant. What makes this a hopeful sighting is that NH Fish and Game has been trying to reintroduce pheasant to the Great North Woods for years now. Though its main reason is to provide game for hunters they also had hopes that some of the birds would survive hunting season and the harsh winters to establish themselves in the area. I will admit that in my late teens I did partake of pheasant under glass (tastes like chicken) but that was before I knew better, chalk it up to youthful ignorance.

I have been searching for this pheasant since late April. I was at the campground watching the flocks of ducks that had gathered in what little open water there was near the mouth of the river, as the rest of the lake was still covered in ice, when a man approached me. He saw me with my binoculars and asked if I knew a lot about birds. I told him I knew a fair amount but was always learning more, he asked if I could help him identify a bird he just saw.

He describes the bird as chicken like, brown streaked body, long tail, greenish neck, and a bright red patch on its face. He said he had just seen it walk across the road by the campground sign. He tells me he has never seen such a beautiful bird in the area before. I knew right away what it had to be, I told him it sure sounded like a ring-necked pheasant. I told him why this could be such a hopeful sighting, and he told me he wasn't a bird hunter as he held up his fancy camera. He said he would be on the lookout for the bird again and hoped to take some pictures.

So of course, I headed right to the area he had seen the bird. There was still snow on the ground in the woods, so I was hoping I could track the bird, or at least find tracks to confirm it was a pheasant. As I was tromping through the snowy woods, looking for tracks, I heard a strange unfamiliar sound, I've never heard a pheasant, so I wasn't sure if that was what I heard or not, but I knew it was different than any other bird I've heard. Unfortunately, the noise I was making crunching through the snow and snapping branches was surely scaring the bird away. The snow in the woods was getting deeper and was over my boots, my feet were getting wet and cold. I was getting farther into the woods, that little voice in my head told me it was time to turn around and follow my own tracks back to the cabin.

When I got back to the cabin, I listened to the call of the ring-necked pheasant on my bird app, and yup, what I heard was the pheasant. Since that day in April, every time I have been to the cabin, I have been on the lookout for that pheasant but to no avail. I heard his call a few times but couldn't spot him. Then this last visit to the cabin I scored! I heard his call, closer than ever this time, I rushed out and there in the pine grove he was in all his colorful glory. The ring-necked pheasant! Ah, there was hope for the future this bird survived the winter.

Over the next few days, I saw the male pheasant a number of times. He was always calling, it felt sad, he was searching for more of his kind, were than any others out there? You would think such a colorful bird might have trouble hiding from its enemies. But one day I spotted the bird in the tall wild flowers of the field, one of their favorite habitats. The wind was gently swaying the colorful yellow, red and white wild flowers. There in the field was the pheasant. All that was visible was his face and neck, his green neck blended with the greenery and his red face patch looked just like a flower, now his coloring made sense. I saw him again later in the woods out of the sun, now I could see that his neck and face patch were more subdued, again he blended in easily, his brown body and long tail looked like the branches around him and his face patch looked like a fall leaf.

After the excitement of seeing this beautiful bird wore off, I began to wonder if there really was any hope for the future of this bird. Was it just a fluke that this farm raised bird released in the fall had survived the harsh winter in the Great North Woods? Were there any others out there? More important were there any females out there in the woods? For there to really be any hope for the future we all know Mother Nature's rules, it takes a male and a female to ensure a species future.

One morning, as I walked past the field, I flushed the male pheasant, he startled me and I jumped. Then suddenly a female pheasant ran out of the tall grass and followed the male across the road! Could I really believe my eyes? Wow! Then before my heart rate could even go down, I flushed a second female from the tall grass, and she also ran across the road toward the others. This was incredible, three pheasants made it through the winter. There was in deed hope for the future now!

I won't be reporting my sightings to NH Rare Bird Hotline or recording my sightings on E-Bird, this species is too delicate to draw attention to their location. Now I'm not knocking you hunters out there; Daddy was a hunter. I live with hunters. I understand that it is the very money that Hunters spend on the extra pheasant stamp that funds the Fish and Game efforts to bring these birds back to our woods. I understand that Hunters bring much-needed money into the struggling economy in the Great North Woods. It is a mental tightrope walk to balance my feelings on these issues. But for there to be hope for the future we have to learn to compromise.

So remember, when daily life seems stressful and hard, when the evening news is full of doom and gloom, when the future seems bleak and uncertain, we have to hold on and believe there is hope for the future.

Ferns to Your Nose, Dolly Goes Everywhere and Jersey Doesn't Slide

July 2014

Beth was able to join me at the cabin for a four-day marathon of birding. She hoped to see the gray jay, a life list bird for her. I have seen them in Pittsburg before, they only live in the higher elevations in the north. I did as much preplanning as I could to try and ensure she got to see the birds she hoped too. I checked out Ebird, I checked out NH Rare Bird Alerts, I traveled to the spots I had seen them before and left bait (peanuts and raisins) hoping to draw them into view. There had been sightings of gray jays in the area so we were optimistic we could find them.

On Saturday, we set off on the winding maze of dirt logging roads in Pittsburg with high hopes of finding the gray jays. There are no road signs in the wilderness, I had a piece of paper with the directions and Beth was copilot. We traveled to Scotts Bog, East Inlet, made stops along Magaloway Rd and bounced along the narrow dirt road to the Magaloway Mountain fire tower trail. But still no gray jays. We spent the whole day searching we left offerings of peanuts and raisins, we tried to call them in with bird calls all to no avail. The bird that is known to except food from an out reached hand remained elusive today.

On Sunday, we decided to try one more place that Ebird listed gray jays as being seen, Fourth Connecticut Lake. I had never been there before; the lake is only accessible by a trail along the US/Canadian border. Before leaving home for the cabin, I tried to print a map of the trail, but it didn't come out right, half of the map was missing. I could read most of the directions, it said the trail was two miles, rocky and steep and warned to be careful to *not* cross into Canada as the trail followed the boarder. The website said to be sure to sign in at the border patrol station and that maps were available at the kiosk at the trail head, so at the time I wasn't worried that we didn't have a good map.

I have not been to the boarder in a while. I had heard that they replaced the old building and that new security measures were in place. But what I found was not what I expected. The old crossing had a building about the size of the cabin, and we used to go inside, talk to the border patrol and use the bathroom. Years back when I was a GS leader I had taken the Girl Scouts there a number of times. Wow! This was not the border crossing I remembered this was a fortress! I understand we live in a very different world now but still I was blown away by the new building, it has to be about four times bigger with high chain link fences topped with barbed wire. Huge metal gates block the boarder and cameras are everywhere. Signs told us to stay on a thin trail along the fence and to *not* try and enter the building or speak to the guards. We followed the fence, crossed the road and went to the trail head. But there were no maps, no sign in.

But we were two determined birders on the hunt for the elusive gray jay. At the trail head, there were some walking sticks other hikers had left, I picked one up, and we headed up the trail. Well, we headed up all right but to say we were on a trail would be stretching it, we were in a jungle. As Beth said, "Ferns to your nose," the trail started off steep and only got worse. It was so overgrown that it was hard to even see just how steep it was. At times, it was like climbing up a ladder; I could feel gravity pulling me backward. I didn't take any pictures on the steepest part because I didn't dare turn around and look; I was focusing on where to next place my foot and looking for something to hold on to.

In the partial directions that I had, it said that when you came to the USA/Canada marker in the ground to turn left and follow the trail down to the lake. Well, when we got to the marker there was no trail off to the left. There was a barely-there trail to the right. But that crossed the border into Canada, and also, we could see that it was still climbing even higher. I decided to wait on the USA side of the boarder and Beth climbed ahead into Canada to see if she could see any trail markers or the lake. Beth disappeared into the thick brush and I continued to look for the trail on the left. I came back to the marker, it was very quiet, very eerie, and where was Beth? I couldn't see her, I called her name, but she didn't answer. I called louder still no answer. Okay, now I was getting worried, my heart rate was increasing, I was getting scared, where did Beth go? She had disappeared into the "ferns to your nose" of Canada!

I yelled even louder and finally Beth answered me! I couldn't see her but at least now I could hear her. She came back across the border and said that she had climbed over two more rises and still didn't see a lake or a trail off to the left. We had been climbing for over an hour by now; the map I had said the turn left was supposed to be in 0.4 miles. Surely, we should have come to it by now. We had brought our passports because we planned to cross the border and have a picnic lunch after our hike, but we didn't have them on us now, we had left them in the truck. I had a bad feeling about this, my knee was aching, it was time to listen to that little voice in the back of my head, it was time to go back. So Beth the illegal international boarder crosser agreed with me, and we gave up our quest for the gray jay and started the arduous trek down.

As we began the trek down, suddenly two dogs come bounding out of the brush. I immediately step in front of Beth and raised my walking stick while yelling at the dogs, "Hey, hey, get outta here!" Now I need to explain that Beth is afraid of dogs, nothing wrong with that I certainly can relate I have enough of my own fears. We can't see any people but a voice below calls, "They're friendly!" Shortly a young couple with a little girl come up over the edge. The first thing I notice is that they seemed prepared, they are all wearing good hiking shoes, unlike the couple we passed on the Magaloway Mountain trail, that women was only wearing flip flops, she wasn't going to get very far up that steep trail that's for sure. The man had a backpack with a Gatorade bottle on the side, I also noticed that he has a doll with black hair tucked under his arm. Not what you would expect to see a man carrying on a hike.

He asks us about the trail, we explain that it is very steep and very overgrown. We tell them we didn't find the lake and turned around because we couldn't find the trail. I give him the map that I have and explain that it isn't complete, but it's better than nothing. He also said he was expecting there to be a map at the trail kiosk. While I am talking to him Beth is talking to the little girl. She asks her, "How nice, Dolly gets to come on the hike."

And Dad answers, "Oh, Dolly goes everywhere." The man asks if there is any water along the trail for the dogs, and we tell him not that we saw, Beth gives him her water bottle for the dogs. That's Beth for ya, she doesn't like dogs, but she is still willing to give up her water for them. We wish them luck and warn them to be careful then we continue climbing down.

As we come upon a particularly steep section of rock, we decide that the best and safest way down is to slide down on our butts. Beth goes first, she is wearing hiking pants made of a smooth fabric, and she slides down the rock like it was ice. Next, it's my turn; I'm wearing baggy jersey shorts. I sit at the top of the rock face and try to slide. But the fabric sticks to the rock, it won't slide. Slowly I can feel gravity pulling me downward and my shorts are rolling up to my waist. Now I am sliding down the rock on my underpants. Beth is laughing, but hey, I don't care; "jersey doesn't slide," underpants do.

We made it back to the truck in one piece and since we were already at the boarder we decided to cross into Quebec. The boarder guard asks us where we had been, we tell him we had hiked the Fourth Conn. Lake trail. He chuckles and in his French accent says, "Oh…very steep."

We replied, "It sure is!" We stop at a picnic area on Magnetic Hill and enjoy the view. We discussed our morning adventures; we never did get to see the gray jay or find the lake but Beth did get an up close and personal view of a winter wren. I was able to call one in close, they are very territorial birds, and he wasn't happy we were in his yard so he flitted back and forth chattering at us on the trail until we left his yard.

Beth enjoyed the magical feeling of hiking in a jungle of "ferns to your nose." We smiled when we thought of that obliging dad who carried his daughters Dolly as they climbed the trail. Like he said, "Dolly goes everywhere." It was nice to see a young family out enjoying nature; though, I'm not sure how well Dad would make it up that rock without using both hands. Maybe Dolly wasn't going to get to go everywhere after all. And of course, Beth was still laughing at the sight of me sliding down the rock face on my underpants...but hey, "jersey doesn't slide." You know you can't put two gray-haired birders in the woods for four days and there not be stories to tell.

Feathers a'Flyin

The Merlin family at dusk.

July 2014

Since April, I have been watching a pair of merlins in the pine grove by the cabin. Merlins are a jay-sized falcon, which feeds on small birds. I watched as the pair made circles together while screeching loudly, and then they would dive toward earth and pull up suddenly. It was quite a sight to watch, they are amazing fliers and very fast as they would zoom through the trees. Each weekend I was at the cabin I would watch them trying to find out where they had a nest. It took a while, but I finally located the tree they had a nest in.

As the adult was incubating the eggs, I could just make out the top of the bird's head. At pretty regular intervals, throughout the day, the birds would switch nest duties. I knew when they were changing sitting on the nest because one bird would fly circles over the area screeching. Then the other bird would leave the nest and the two of them would circle screeching and screeching. One would fly away and the other would settle back into the nest. I watched each time I was at the cabin anxiously waiting to see if the eggs hatched.

After a few weeks, I was excited to see little heads peeking out of the nest. I watched as the adult birds would make trip after trip to the nest with chickadees in their talons. Chickadees seemed to be their favorite food. I watched as the merlin held the little bird in its talons and plucked the feathers, there were feathers a'flyin everywhere in the wind. Then offered the little bird to the young. It was sad to know the chickadee lost his life but that's the circle of nature. Soon I saw the merlins on the edge of the nest or on the branches beside it. It wouldn't be long before the young left the nest now.

Birding is all about being in the right place at the right time. When Beth was at the cabin with me was the perfect time. We watched as the adult birds would fly in with a little bird and drop it in the nest. The fledglings would screech and fight each other for the kill. There were feathers a'flyin! The whole nest area was covered in feathers stuck to the edges and in the branches around the nest. We watched as one of the birds tore the feathers from the chickadee and watched as the feathers floated to the ground.

At one time, as Beth and I were watching the adult brought in a bird and two of the merlins began to fight over it. One fledgling jumped on top of the other, and they were screeching and wings were flapping. Not sure which one finally got the bird, but it was a pretty intense sibling rivalry going on in the nest. Later Beth and I were sitting on the porch of the cabin when we heard the loud screeching start. We knew this meant the parent bird was coming back with dinner for the young ones. We headed over to the nest site to watch.

As we were watching the fledglings sitting on the edge of the nest screeching for food, suddenly the parent bird flew from over our head. The parent was coming in fast; it flew into the nest at full speed and right into the fledglings sending them tumbling out of the nest. I watched as one of the young fell head first down the tree. I was stunned! I was so worried it was going to hit the ground head first. Suddenly the young bird caught a branch with its talons and swung around to an upright position on the branch. Phew...I thought it was going to die. That adult merlin literally kicked them out of the nest!

Beth was watching the other young one which fell onto a branch just below the nest. There was much commotion going on with all the birds screeching. We decided to leave the nest area to let them calm down and not add to the drama happening. I worried all night if that young one I saw tumble would be able to make it back up the tree into the nest or if the parent would still feed it where it sat.

We checked the nest tree before leaving the next morning and I was encouraged to not see the fledgling still sitting near the base of the tree. I nervously walked around the base of the tree in fear of finding the dead body of the merlin but all was clear. We were not sure at that time where the birds went to, but I was hopeful they were alright.

I returned to the cabin two days later and was encouraged to hear the screeching of the merlins as soon as I arrived. There were thunder storms with torrential rains so I wasn't able to get out and look for the birds till later, near 7:00 p.m. I found them, the family all sitting together in one tree. They were dripping wet from the heavy rain, I could see the water dripping off their feathers, but they made it through the storm. Now the young are following the parents calling for dinner. They are doing what merlin young are supposed to do, watching their parents, learning to fly and catch food for themselves.

It was amazing getting to witness the young fledge, and I'm glad a fellow birder, Beth was able to enjoy the sight. I may not have been able to find Beth the gray jay, but I hope the up close and personal birding made up for it. We were both in the right place at the right time to see feathers a'flyin.

Try 'n' Try Again

September 2014

As I described in a previous story, I have been trying to find the gray jays of the far north in Pittsburg. Beth and I searched for two days to no avail. I took her to all the places that Ebird listed sightings for and the places I have seen them before. I have not seen a gray jay in over two years. Gray jays are similar to blue jays, but as its name implies, they are various shades of gray. They only live in the high elevations of the north. The legend is that they are the spirits of lost hikers roaming the mountains. They are friendly birds and will seek out humans. Many have taken pictures of these friendly birds sitting in their out stretched hand to enjoy offerings of peanuts or dried fruit. I know they are there somewhere! I just gotta try 'n' try again to find them.

This past weekend, we were in Pittsburg to do some fall maintenance. The cabin has slipped off some of its supports and John needed to jack up the edges and reposition the posts. He needed to crawl under neath and restack the cinder blocks that had fallen. After working at it for a while, John decided to take a break and offered to take me to the places he had seen the gray jay last hunting season. He and the guys even had them eating out of their hands, so he was confident he could locate them again for me. Of course, he also wanted to scout out good hunting spots for when the guy's head up in October.

So we headed out to Scotts Bog in search of the gray jay. We saw nothing, no jays, just silence. It was strangely quiet. I wondered if the fact that the State had to replace the worn dam holding back the bog had disturbed the bird life. The area is different now. I believe it has made a difference. I guess I'll have to try 'n' try again till the birds return to the area. But for now, we struck out, no gray jays.

We headed to East Inlet to continue our search. There was bird life there, there were flocks of golden-crowned kinglets flitting about. There were regal great blue herons walking along the shoreline in search of frogs for dinner. There was a Mink that came down to the water's edge for a drink, we saw a red fox along the road side. There were northern flickers around every corner but no gray jays.

John wasn't ready to give up yet, there was another place he wanted to try 'n' try again. We bounced along Macalloway Road at what John called "road-hunting speed" to the spots he said they had fed the gray jays last fall. We stopped and I searched the trees, I shook the bag of goodies I had for the birds, I threw some bits of food on the ground hoping to draw their attention. These were all techniques that have worked before but not this time, no gray jays flew in for dinner.

I know they are out there people have seen them, but it wasn't in the cards for us that day. When we got back to the cabin, a cold drizzle had begun. I sat in the cabin in the rocking chair in front of the window going over my bird guides. I thought to myself, *Why am I bothering searching for the gray jay?* I've seen them before; I've counted them in my birding life list. What does it matter if I see them again or not? I'm being silly wasting time searching for a bird that doesn't want to be seen; there are other more pressing things I should be doing with my time. So the gray jay wins, and I lose this round.

As I'm gazing out the window doubting my choices, there on the ground is a Bicknell's thrush! I have been trying to spot this thrush all summer. This is also a bird that only lives in the higher elevations and is known to be very secretive and hard to spot. I've heard his song but I'd been unable to spot the bird in the trees. When Beth visited the cabin, we heard one singing and I was trying then to spot him but didn't. It was as if the bird was teasing me all summer; I would hear him singing but as soon as I got close it would stop. Then I would hear him off in another direction, and as soon as I would get there again, he would stop singing. I had given up hope of ever seeing one! And now here he was on the ground right in front of the window. Add another new bird to my life list. It's funny how things can work out that way, you think you've failed then nature will surprise you when you least expect it.

I plan a couple more trips to the cabin before winter sets in, and I'm gonna try 'n' try again to see those elusive gray jays! I'm not ready to give up on finding those gray jays yet. Another life lesson learned: Don't give up; try 'n' try again!

Still Trying

September 2014

Recently John and I were able to spend a beautiful fall weekend at the cabin. The foliage was spectacular! John was very confident that he could find the gray jays for me so we set out on the hunt along the northern back roads of Pittsburg. Now I use the term "roads" loosely, these are narrow, bumpy dirt trails through the woods. He took me to the places he and the other guys have seen the gray jays while hunting, in fact one of the guys even had the birds land on his hand to take some food.

We set out along Magalloway Mountain Rd first, there were multiple reports of gray jays being seen in this area recently so we were encouraged I would finally get to see them. But no luck, we bounced along the side roads with our windows open listening for the jays. We scanned every treetop and overhanging branch but to no avail. We gave up on this area and moved on.

We drove along the dirt roads to Scotts Bog and East Inlet still searching for the gray jays. We came to an intersection and stopped, thinking about which way to turn. When suddenly, a loud ruckus erupted from the woods along the road. I jumped out of the car, and yup, they were gray jays squawking and chattering in the trees! *But* they were staying under cover; we could hear them but couldn't see them. I walked to the right following the loudest bird which seemed closest to the edge of the road and John walked straight toward more of the squawking birds.

Don't ya know I chose the wrong way. John calls out, "Here they are! Come quick!" I ran back to the intersection and turned toward him but only caught a fleeting glance of two gray silhouettes as they flew across the path deeper into the woods. Darn! Missed them. I walked back and forth along the road holding out my hand with goodies for the jays, but they didn't come back. We thought maybe if we left and came back, they would too, so we drove along farther.

We stopped at Scotts Bog, saw nothing and decided to try driving the back road around to the other side of the bog. I was nervous this "road" was barely two tracks in the woods. The trees were brushing against the car on both sides and some branches were hanging low over the trail, and we just made it underneath them. I suggested that maybe it was time to turn around, which wasn't an easy thing to do it was much more than a three-point turn. John was worried we may have to back up a mile or so to the intersection, but luckily, we were able to turn around.

As we were heading back toward Scotts Bog, suddenly I see a blur of a jay-sized gray bird streak across the trail overhead. We stop and I jump out. I can hear the bird squawking in the tree but can't find it. I decide to walk off the road into the brush to find the bird. I step into the thick brush up to my waist only a few feet when I hear something growl! I can't see the creature, but it sounded big! It growled and ran through the brush with a whoosh! I in turn scream and run back to the car! I ask John, "OMG, did you hear that animal!"

He says, "No, I heard you scream, but I thought it was because you saw the gray jay."

Needless to say, I had had enough for the day. It was time to get out of the woods. Technically I did hear the gray jays, and I kinda sort of saw them. But it wasn't a good enough view for me. I'll be back north at the end of the month and I'll be still trying to see those gray jays! I'm not ready to give up yet.

Still trying!

Happy New Year, Chickadee

January 2015

John and I spent most of New Year's week at the cabin. There wasn't much snow and the snowmobiles had packed down the road to the cabin so we were able to drive right up. With just a little bit of shoveling, we were able to get into the driveway, which is a first for the winter time up there. Even though there wasn't much snow, it was extremely cold and windy, high temp was about twenty and the low -5. The cabin was in good shape, a couple of trees fell, but nothing hit the cabin. We were snug and warm.

I took a walk one morning and a small flock of chickadees seemed very interested in my movements. They actually followed me, hopping about in the trees alongside the trail as I walked. A couple of them even buzzed my head, I was sure they were going to land on me. They don't have a fear of humans, they just don't see enough to have developed a fear of us. They are a curious bird. I stood still and put out my hand and sure enough one landed in my hand.

The little bird sat in my hand, cocked his head, and chirped at me as if to say, "Okay, here I am, where's my treat?" I felt bad I didn't have any seeds to offer it. When I got back to the cabin, I asked John to stop at Young's store and pick up some bird seed when he went out to try fishing the river by the dam. When he returned, I put some seed in my hand and stood outside with my hand raised. It didn't take but two minutes before the first chickadee flew in and landed in the tree beside me. I stood still hand stretched out, camera ready in my other hand then the first bird flew in and landed on my hand.

Before I knew it, there was a flock of eight chickadees buzzing around me! At one time, there was even two birds on my hand at once. They didn't seem to mind the camera at all; though, it was so cold my camera shutter was moving very slowly so I could only get a few shots. I tried taking off my gloves to feed them, but they didn't like landing on my bare hand. Their little feet felt so gentle as they sat on my fingers. Then a bird landed on my head! I think it actually was a red-breasted nuthatch by the sound of it and out of the corner of my eye I saw the blur of blue streak by.

I know that it can be dangerous to the birds of the wild to become dependent on humans to feed them. Especially since I won't be there often during the winter to refill a feeder. I had brought up with me a large ten-by-twelve suet/seed block that we hung for them. That should last till we get back in a couple of weeks. Each day, I was there I spread a few seeds on the ground for them too. Not too much that they get dependent on an easy meal, but just enough to sustain them. I watched as the chickadees and nuthatch would grab a sunflower seed and fly off to a pine tree and shove the seed into the bark. You see the birds have learned to store food like squirrels do in the winter, and they remember where they are when times get lean.

So the first bird I saw of 2015 was everyone's favorite little bird the black-capped chickadee, sitting in my hand looking back at me. What a great way to start a new year. Happy New Year, little chickadee!

All-Night Diner

July 2015

When I am at the cabin by myself, I often leave a light on overnight. I know at my age I shouldn't be afraid of the dark but at the cabin there are all sorts of things that go "bump in the night" and with a light on at least I have a chance to see whatever it is making the "bump." This last trip up it was hot and humid at night so I left one of the windows facing the lake open, which happened to be next to the light I left on overnight. Yeah, you know what happened, I woke up to the screen full of bugs and moths attracted to the light left on. Yuck!

While eating breakfast I made the mental note *not* to do that again! When suddenly, a chickadee flies onto the screen and holds on with its tiny feet then plucks a moth off the screen. It flies off then a second chickadee does the same thing. I watched out the window to see where they were flying to and saw that they were going into the bird box near the water's edge. They must have babies in there! Cool! Those bird boxes have been there for years and never been used before, now it looked like I am hosting a chickadee family.

After breakfast, I went down to the water's edge carefully, and as I approached the bird box, I could hear the young squawking. I thought about getting the camera and taking some pictures but decided not to disturb the birds. I went to get the kayak out from under the cabin for my morning paddle when I noticed a pile of translucent wings laying on the ground. I heard a chickadee in the tree above me and watched as it took a moth and plucked the wings off then flew into the bird box. Being the crazy bird lady that I am I say to the chickadee, "Hey that's not good manners, you don't just throw on the ground the food you don't want. I'm the one that left the light on and provided you with all those yummy moths and bugs." But hey, I suppose moth wings would be a bit dry and hard to swallow without something to wash it down.

So that night, I decided to leave the window open and the light on again. I thought about it, maybe the light will draw in the delicate green luna moth or the boldly marked Ceracopea moth. I haven't seen either of those huge beautiful moths in a long time. And since both of those moths are larger than a chickadee I wasn't worried the bird would eat them. I went to bed thinking the chickadees would have a buffet of moths and bugs available for them in the morning to feed their young and I could watch the show at breakfast time.

I awoke during the night when I heard a strange fluttering coming from the window left open. I thought, *Oh, cool maybe it is the Luna or Ceracopea.* I walked over to the window carefully to see what was there when I noticed it was a *bat*! Ahhh! I should have known! Day time birds aren't the only creatures that dine on moths and bugs. Here it is 2:00 a.m., and I'm yelling at this bat clinging to the screen, "You get away from there those bugs aren't for you! Those are dinner for the chickadee family."

Poor bats are stereotyped, they are considered evil or wicked just because they are covered in black and creep around at night. But hey they are just another of God's creatures trying to survive. They do some good, they eat a lot of bugs that would otherwise be dinning on us around the campfire. I thought of that just as I was about to swing the broom at the screen to scare away the bat. Well, actually what stopped me was the thought that it was just as likely that if I hit the screen to scare the bat that the screen would fall out of the window and the bat could fly into the cabin! I didn't sleep well that night.

You know you are never too old to learn a life lesson. I learned that if you plan to run an all-night diner with an electric light proclaiming "OPEN" then you can't complain about the clientele you draw in.

Still sleeping with a light on and window open.

911 Loon

August 2015

Well, I had an interesting couple of days at the cabin recently. I am the loon volunteer for Lake Francis, I am considered a citizen scientist, and I collect data and file reports for the Loon Preservation Committee and New Hampshire Audubon Society on the loon population on the lake as well as the osprey and bald eagles. It is my eyes on the ground that help protect these birds and hopefully show that when the time comes to dole out the funds for programs and protection that the Connecticut Lakes region wants in on some of that grant money.

This past Saturday while watching the lake I saw a loon just off shore from the cabin that just didn't look right. I focused my binoculars on him and I could see something was stuck on his hind leg where it joined his body. It was a green color and looked like fringe or hanging grass or something. Oh no! As I watched, he leaned to one side and began to poke at the object stuck on him. He needed help! I had my camera in my bird bag so I took a few pictures to document his injuries.

I ran up to the cabin and called the loon biologist that I had been working with all summer, but it was his office phone and only went to voicemail. I left a message but time was limited that loon needed help! I jumped in the car and drove to the ranger station to see if they could contact the fish and game officer for help. I figured this would be faster than trying to get a call through to their office on a Saturday and the rangers helped last time I had to get help when the water skiers were harassing the baby loons. When I got there, the ranger said I would be better off going down to the school in the center of town, it was Old Home Day and the Fish and Game had a booth set up, the local conservation officer would be there.

So I quickly drove to the school; yikes, there were a lot of people at the Old Home Day activities! I had trouble finding some place to park, I had to park about half mile away and rush over to the school yard. I located the Fish and Game booth and there was only one young man standing there wearing a "volunteer" T-shirt and a Fish and Game hat. I asked him if the conservation officer was around, he tells me that he and Smokey the Bear just went to the town green for the governor's speech. I ask him if he can call the officer, that there is an injured loon, and that I need his help now. The volunteer tells me that he doesn't have a radio to call him with, that I should walk up to the town green and look for him.

So I rush to the town green, which isn't very far thankfully 'cause it was hot out that day, and there were people everywhere; never seen so many people in Pittsburg at once before. As I approach the town green, I can see the Governor standing on the stage (well, on the back of a flatbed truck with speakers on either side), and there on stage with her is the conservation officer and Smokey the Bear. Great, now how am I supposed to get the officer's attention?

I carefully weave my way through the crowd, making my way to the back of the flat bed. I'm not listening to the governor, people are clapping she is just blah blah blah to my ears right now. I was focused on getting closer to the officer, I had a loon that needed help! When suddenly, a man stood in front of me and says, "Excuse me, madam, may I help you?"

Oops, I think I found security. I tell him I am trying to speak to the F&G Conservation officer, that there is an injured loon on Lake Francis and I need his help. He says, "An injured what where?"

I repeat myself. He asks me if I have any ID on me. I explain that I left it in the car, I had just grabbed my bird bag when I left the car. I mean I wasn't going to go anywhere without my binoculars, water bottle and a snack. He asks me, "What is in the backpack?"

I empty my bag trying to juggle its contents without spilling it all over the ground, but I was nervous when my jackknife tumbled onto the ground. I was a GS leader for years. "Be prepared" was the rules of the woods. I take out my binos and hang them around my neck, put my hat on my head and take out my jelly sandwich. I had wrapped my sandwich in tin foil cuz I didn't have any baggies at the cabin. The man says, "Excuse me, what is in that? Please unwrap that carefully."

Jeepers, it's only a jelly sandwich. I can understand why I may have seemed strange; the security guard was only doing his job. Meanwhile, a local volunteer fireman comes over and asks if he can be of any assistance. I tell him my name and that there is an injured loon on Lake Francis and that I need to talk to the conservation officer. He immediately talks into his radio and calls dispatch requesting the rescue squad. He asks me the name of the injured person. NO! It is a bird that is hurt not a person! He calls dispatch back and says, "Cancel rescue squad."

Yes, yes, I have officially become the "crazy bird lady of Lake Francis." The firefighter takes me to the side, he is very nice he listens to my full story, and then he uses his radio and calls the conservation officer, who by now has left the stage and is mingling with the crowd, and everyone wants a picture with Smokey the Bear. Soon the officer makes his way over to the fireman and me. I explain the whole story to him. He is very concerned, he tries to call the head honcho at Audubon in Concord, and he also gets voice mail. He calls dispatch to ask for a cell number or private phone for him but is told they do not have any listings other than the office number.

The officer tells me that he cannot leave right now, that he is needed to direct traffic. This I can understand there are a lot of people milling about and ATVs zipping up and down the road and the governor is still present. He tells me that he gives me special permission to try and catch the loon if I think I can. You see the loon is a federally protected species, and it is a federal offense to even touch one unless you are Fish and Game or Police. He tells me that after the governor leaves, he will meet me at the cabin to see what he can do.

So…back to the cabin I go. I barely get there when the phone is ringing, it is the office of the biologist calling back. I explain yet again the plight of the loon off shore. I am told that they have limited resources to help me right now, that they do not have anyone who can travel to the area so far north, they do not have a boat, the budget is bare this late in the season. I explain that I contacted the Fish and Game conservation officer and that he will be coming here soon. Concord is happy about that and asks me to send any pictures and a report of what happens.

Next, I did something very stupid. Yeah, I launched the kayak and tried to catch the loon. I got up real close, the loon just floated beside my kayak looking at me, I swear it was asking for help. I had my knife, could I just reach out and cut that thing off his leg? Could I do this? Could I reach over and grab the loon? Ah, *no*! As I'm trying to lean over, my kayak flips over into the water, my foot gets stuck under the seat. The injured loon hurries away from me. I splash around and make my way back to shore dragging the overturned kayak. I just sprained my ankle, and bruised my pride.

The officer arrived a couple hours later. I told him of my unsuccessful attempt at rescuing the loon. He stood on shore with me for a while, we watched the loon who by now had moved to the opposite shore, I am sure that was my fault. He agreed with me that the loon looked like it was in trouble. It would be dark soon so the officer said he would launch his boat Sunday morning and see what he could do for the loon.

He returned on Sunday, I watched from shore as he circled the loon in his boat. He reached out with a long net but missed. He floated in the water for a while just watching the loon. He drove the boat over to me on shore and explained what he saw. He confirmed that it was a fishing lure stuck to the side of the loon's body where its leg was. He said that he did see the loon dive into the water and resurface with a crayfish in its mouth. This was all good news. Because the biggest concern was that the fishing lure stuck on his body might prevent him from diving and feeding. The officer said he got close enough to see that the wound area where the fishing lure was embedded looked clean. It did not look red or infected. The decision was made to watch and wait. The officer said he would keep an eye out for the loon whenever he was on the lake. Unless the loon became listless or appeared weak we would just hope the fishing lure hook would rot, and he could get the lure off himself.

I went to the visitor center at the State Park campground and filled in the ranger on what was happening with the injured loon. He put up a notice for the campers and boaters to keep an eye out for the injured loon and to report to the office any sightings. The next day, I was out on the lake in my kayak paddling along the shoreline of the cove watching for the injured loon. Ahead of me I noticed a man in a canoe close to shore pointing and could hear him yelling something to a boy on shore. As I got closer, I paddled closer to him and asked if he needed any help. He tells me his son is trying to get some tangled fishing line with a lure attached to it that they saw in the bushes at the water's edge as they were paddling by. I call over to the boy to thank him for retrieving the tangled fishing line. The man tells me they are staying at the campground and about the notice he read about an injured loon on the lake. The young boy excitedly yells, "I GOT IT!" while holding up the tangled mess. We talk about loons for a while and I tell them about my volunteer work for the Loon Preservation Committee. It was encouraging to know my eyes weren't the only ones watching the injured loon and working to protect them all. I thanked them both, and we all paddled on across the lake.

I watched the injured loon for days and each day I saw him I could tell the lure was slowly coming apart and watched as the loon would pick at it and drop pieces into the water. The loon was swimming fine, still diving and eating. He did finally get the last pieces out of his body and all seemed well with him. With the help of caring responsible people on the lake there is hope no other loon or duck ever has to deal with that kind of danger to their life again. So fisherman out there, please remember, if you get your fishing line stuck in a branch or bush along the shore, *be sure to remove it*!

Red Snow

We recently returned from a stay at the cabin. For late March standards it was mild, there was very little snow on the ground, and we were able to drive right up to the cabin. The first morning we were there I saw a coyote running across the ice on the lake from the far shore toward the cabin. I often see them and hear them in the summer, but this was the first time I had seen one out on the ice. I made a mental note to be very careful when we let our dog Shilo out to do her business.

We had about four inches of fresh snow fall overnight and I awoke to a winter wonderland of snow-covered trees. The sky was bright blue and the sun shining on the snow made it look electric. It was a prefect winter day for a bird walk. I hadn't even gotten out of the yard when I spotted the first fresh footprints in the snow of deer, looked like at least three had crossed through the yard. A little farther on, I came upon a set of pheasant tracks that crossed the trail that was a good sign, it meant that the pheasants the state fish and game were trying to stock had made it through the winter.

There were flocks of noisy pine siskens flitting about the pine trees and I was enjoying watching them. But then the sound of angry crows filled the air. I know that crows often group together to annoy larger raptors or owls just for the fun of being annoying. They don't actually strike the larger birds they just cause a loud ruckus and dive at the larger birds just to torment them. So of course, I had to investigate to see what all the ruckus was about.

As I was making my way through the woods toward the loud crows, I came upon another set of fresh tracks in the snow. This time it was of a rabbit that was heading down toward the lake, the same direction I was going. I stood still for a few minutes and followed the tracks with my binoculars to see if I could spot the rabbit, but I couldn't. I was getting close to the crows, they were really loud but then I spotted more fresh tracks. This time it was the coyote, its tracks were parallel to the rabbit tracks, oh no doesn't look good for the Mr. Bunny. I stood still, looked around but saw nothing, only heard the loud cawing of the crows. I continued making my way through the woods to the lake.

When I broke out of the cover of the trees onto the open shore, I immediately saw something very troubling. RED SNOW! Yikes! The snow was all turned up, I couldn't identify any footprints they were all mushed together, but it was obvious that some kind of mortal battle had taken place. I assumed poor Mr. Bunny had met his demise. The loud angry sounds of the crows drew my attention farther down the shoreline. I continued on, just as I came around a curve in the shoreline, I saw the crows flying and jumping along the shore between large boulders.

And more *red snow*! There below my feet was a trail of blood in the snow. I looked up and saw lying between a couple large boulders the body of a deer! Before I could even register what I was seeing, suddenly a coyote lifted his head up from the back side of the deer. It was his kill! I immediately drew my pistol from my pocket. I stood still and pointed my gun at the coyote. I didn't want to shoot the coyote, but I was ready to if I needed to. The coyote stood up and looked right at me.

For what seemed like minutes but was only seconds, we stared at each other. I found myself talking to the coyote. I said, "It's your deer you can have it. I don't want it. I don't want to shoot you please don't make me." I didn't dare try to run or back away, the shoreline was icy and rocky I feared I would only fall down. The stalemate was ended by the coyote. He ran off across the ice toward the opposite shore. Phew! Any questions now as to why I carry a pistol with me when I am walking in the woods?

I watched (from a safe distance) the carcass of the deer over the weekend. Although it is a shame the poor deer was killed its body provided food for many. I saw a Mink pulling bits of meat off the body and the crows finally had their turn to dine as well. Also I watched as an immature bald eagle torn bits of flesh from the body and flew off into the treetops to eat. And yes, the coyote returned, he deserved it, it was his kill. Though I may think twice now about following the sounds of angry crows. And we have all heard the warning about "Don't eat yellow snow." But I think it is much more important to heed the warnings of "RED SNOW!"

Gray Jay Day

June 2016

Earlier this month, when we were at the cabin, I went target shooting in a sandpit off East Inlet Road, which is a back country dirt road in Pittsburg. John has often told me of the times during hunting season when the guys would see the gray jays when they were shooting, that the birds seemed to seek them out and would take food right from their hands. I have been searching for these birds for a while so I thought I would try John's suggestion and see if I could draw the birds to me. It is known that these birds are drawn to the noise of humans and since in the back woods of Pittsburg that often means gunshot noise; I thought it was worth a try. Besides, I wanted to practice shooting my pistol anyways.

It worked! After shooting about a dozen rounds, we noticed in the trees besides us three gray jays sitting looking at us. I put some trail mix in my hand and held it up and the bird flew down and sat in my hand. I swear it would have landed on my pistol if I had put food on it. It carefully picked through the assorted nuts and candy and took just the piece it wanted. I had to admit John was right. He found the gray jays for me!

So this past weekend, I wanted to see if I could do it again; could I draw in the gray jays at the sandpit? It was a cold dreary damp day, but I decided to give it a try. We set up the target and I shot about two dozen rounds but no gray jays this time. Maybe it was too cold. I shook the bag of trail mix and tossed some around on the ground by the edge of the trees but to no avail. Oh well, at least I was getting in some practice, my aim is getting better, and I am getting more at ease handling my pistol.

As I was driving back to the main road, we came upon three cars pulled off the dirt road and a crowd of ladies were all standing around looking up. As we got closer, I could see that they all had binoculars strung around their necks, and they were bundled up head to toe as if it were the Arctic. They looked as if they all just stepped off the pages of a LL Bean catalog in their coordinating outfits. It could only mean one thing, they're birders, most likely looking for the fabled gray jays of the Great North Woods just like I was.

I stopped and put the window of the truck down so I could talk to them. I said, "Hello, what are you looking for? Seen anything good?" The ladies all looked at each other and at me then at each other than one brave one spoke to me. Gee, did I look that threatening? I had my Ruger shooting hat on and my old beat-up sweatshirt; was it that strange for an old lady to be driving a truck on the back roads and stop to talk to strangers?

She answers, "Oh, we were just taking a lunch break." I noticed that two of the vehicles had Massachusetts plates I couldn't see the third. Come on was I supposed to believe that? There are ten ladies ranging from age forty-plus, all in matching outfits with binoculars hanging around their necks but they're just taking a lunch break on the side of the dirt road? I didn't see any lunch bags.

So I say, "Well, keep your eyes open. You may see the gray jays. I saw a group in the sandpit just up the road last week." I tell them I was just at the sandpit target shooting hoping to draw the birds in, but they didn't come this time. Again, the ladies all nervously look at each other than at me then one says to me, "We heard the gunshots! That was *you* shooting a gun?!" The written word cannot describe the tone she spoke in or the look on her face. One of the ladies says to another, "Get him, where is he, what should we do?" then I see that a man exits the last car and comes over to us. The ladies crowd around him and tell him I was shooting a gun and saw gray jays. At this point, I realize he is their guide, the ladies likely hired him to take them birding in the Great North Woods with the hopes of finding the gray jays.

The man comes over to the truck and speaks with John and I, we tell him where we saw the gray jays. The ladies all crowd around him and one says, "We have come a long way to see gray jays can we go where she saw them?"

John tells him to toss trail mix or peanuts on the hood of their cars and wait to see if the birds will fly in. As John is telling him this, I throw a handful of trail mix out the window and onto the roof of the truck. I reach out the window and offer them the trail mix to do the same, but they decline. One of the ladies gasps and grabs the arm of another lady and says, "Oh my, did you see what she did!" Really ladies am I that weird? We wish them good luck in finding the gray jays and drive away.

As John and I are driving away, we are both laughing. John says, "You scared the hell out of those old ladies!"

"You just shocked them out of their stereotype of what a New Hampshire redneck looks like."

Really? Am I scary? We drive a mile or so along the road and suddenly at a trail intersection we see an immature gray jay sitting on the sign post! Then two more fly in. Bingo! Gray jays! John yells, "Stop the truck let me out I'll keep the jays here with food you go back and tell the old ladies!"

John jumps out of the truck and I do a quick three-point turn on the narrow dirt road and speed off in search of the ladies. Later John told me I took off a little too fast and kicked up a cloud of dirt and rocks and that he had to duck to keep from getting hit by flying rocks, oops! I speed off back in the direction of where we last saw the group of ladies, but they were no longer on the side of the road. Darn! Where did they go? I drive a little farther along the road figuring they went to the sandpit we told them to try.

I get to the path (I mean a path; it is not even a dirt road but a small path through the trees that leads to the pit) to the sandpit and can just see the back end of the last car driving in. I blare the horn and flash my lights; the last car stops. I jump out of the truck and run up to the car yelling, "We found some gray jays! Follow me!" The women actually screams—out of fright or excitement, I'm not sure. I run up to the second car and repeat, "We found some gray jays back at the trail intersection, my husband is holding them there with food.

Follow me!" The passenger in that car gets out and runs up to the first car, by now the man is getting out, she tells him I have found gray jays what should they do?

The man waves to me, yelling, "Follow her!" The three cars fall in behind me, I take off fast, and we are losing time here. Within seconds I have lost them, darn ladies come on speed it up! I stop and wait for them to catch up, uhhh, they will not go over 15 mph, I am hoping John can keep the jays there long enough for us to get there he didn't have much left in the bag of trail mix. We finally arrive back at the trail intersection but John is not there. Yikes where did he go?

I stop and the caravan of cars pulls in behind me. All the ladies spill out of the cars and gather together, nervously chattering, "What do we do?" "Where is Scott?" "You go." "No, you go." I approach them, saying, "I promise I am not crazy, my hobby is birding too. Believe me it is okay, the birds are just up here." Gee, I guess in every horror movie the bad guy tells you he is okay, maybe I am scary. The man (who I gather is Scott) calms the ladies down, tells them to quiet down and follow him, he will go first.

John steps out of the woods and motions for the ladies to come forward. He tells them the gray jays flew away from the road and are just off the trail back in the spruce. All the ladies are behind Scott but then one brave lady breaks away and runs up to John. He hands her some trail mix and directs her into the bushes. I can hear the other ladies gasp. She stands with her hand out and a gray jay flies down and sits in her hand! She turns back to the group and says excitedly, "Did you see that!"

Now all the ladies want to experience the same thing. Scott hands out peanuts to all, the ladies break apart, and each stands in the bushes, hands raised to the jays. One lady has an iPad raised high and is taking pictures. They all get to see and feed the gray jays, they all giggle and smile with excitement. If you think the sight of me doing a happy birders' dance is a laugh, you should see ten ladies standing in the bushes dancing with excitement! Scott came up to me and thanked me for coming back to find them and lead them to the gray jays. The ladies all thanked John and I, everyone was so excited to score a life list bird. Guess I'm not so scary after all.

On the long ride back home from Pittsburg, John and I laughed about the whole thing. John said it was the most fun he ever had birding. Gotta wonder what the story all those ladies will be telling their friends about the crazy Great North Woods bird lady that found them the gray jays. John said that the guide thanked him for our help because it meant his clients were happy and that meant he got a good tip. In retrospect, yeah, I might have come off a bit loony. But the next best thrill to seeing a life list bird is helping someone else find a life list bird. A great gray jay day was had by all!

Hunting Crew

A Gray Jay in the cabin yard.

I recently returned from a very relaxing couple of days at the cabin. The weather was fantastic! Temperatures were in the low seventies, and it was sunny, very unusual for so late in October in the Great North Woods, but I'll take it. The trees are all bare now, the leaves have all fallen so birding was good it was easy to see into the woods. But it is hunting season now and the sound of gun shots rang through the air, so it wasn't a good time to be wandering around in the woods looking for birds. But I didn't need to go anywhere to find some great birds.

I did something I haven't done in a long time: I did nothing. That's right nothing! I just sat in the yard and watched the birds around me. Thanks to the all the work the Hunting Crew did I didn't have to stack any wood, they did it. I didn't have to haul any brush, they did it. I didn't have to burn any large piles of brush, they did it. Thanks to the work the guys did we didn't have to fix the broken pipes in the bathroom, they did it. They dragged out the ladder and put up all the plastic on the screened porch to winterize it for the season. They did most all of the work we usually need to do to button up the cabin for the winter. That meant we had nothing to do but relax!

And that is just what we did. I put my Adirondack chair in the middle of the yard in the sun and watched the loons on the lake. I turned to the left and watched the pileated woodpecker busily drilling for bugs in the standing dead tree trunk. I turned to the right and watched a small flock of red-breasted nuthatches searching for bugs among the spruce trees. A noisy group of three blue jays came flying in and landed on the feeding stump and readily gobbled up the offerings I had put out. But still no black-capped chickadees or boreal chickadees visited the yard, their absence is still a mystery.

As part of the end-of-season cleanup I need to empty the cupboards of unused food, I can't leave anything in the cabin over the winter because of the extreme cold. So I emptied out the half-eaten box of cereal and the stale crackers, etc., on a tree stump for the birds. I tossed out a bit of seed as well. It didn't take long for the blue jays to find the food, and they were busy gathering as much as they could in their beaks before flying off into the woods. They soon returned for more.

But much to my surprise the blue jays were scared off by a pair of gray jays! Yes, gray jays were in the cabin yard! I usually have to travel deeper into the woods and farther north to see gray jays, though I have seen them a few times near the cabin it is unusual to see them in the yard when blue jays are also around. Gray jays are my favorite northern bird, folklore says they are the spirits of lost hikers that raid campsites for food. They seem to seek out humans and are very curious birds. They will eat right out of your hand if you offer them food, they especially like trail mix. I grew up calling them Canadian jays and old-timers call them Whiskey Jack or Camp Raiders. It was a thrill to sit and watch them repeatedly fly onto the stump and gather food. They would use their beak and shift through the food to find just that perfect piece of food. They seemed to like the golden raisins in the trail mix the most.

So thank you, John, Jeremy, Stanley, George, Andrew, Ralph, and Jacob for all the work you guys did around the cabin during your hunting trip. Thanks to you, guys, I was able to sit and relax and watch the birds. I enjoyed a gray jay day thanks to all of you!

ZERO

We just returned from spending the holiday at the cabin, as we have for many years now. We usually make the trip to the cabin at least once a month in the winter to check on the place and shovel the snow off the roof. Although we have had mild winters the past few years this year is starting out to be a more typical north country season. River Rd. from the camp ground to the cabin is not plowed in the winter, but it is a groomed snowmobile trail and often we are able to drive up. We park where the groomer turns and makes a good-sized cleared area to park. Still the walk into the cabin can seem twice as long when you're trudging through the deep snow. The path we usually take through the pine grove is now an open field since the devastating storm that knocked down dozens of trees and the snow was up to our knees! Didn't realize how much the trees would hold the snow and prevent it from getting as deep.

We haul in all our water, food, and other supplies by sled. But poor Shilo couldn't walk in the deep snow at all. She took two steps and was up to her neck in snow! John had to shovel a path for her. A walk that would usually take mere minutes took nearly an hour. The weather was nice when we first arrived but soon clouded up and began to snow. The temps were in the teens and the wind was howling. Right about now most of you are saying, "What are you crazy? No, thank you, not the way I want to spend a holiday weekend." But the new fishing season opens the first day of the New Year and John just had to be on the open river below Murphy Dam to catch his first fish of 2017!

Although he put in hours of fishing, trudging through the snow just to get to the river and standing in the freezing cold water (even in insulated waders don't tell me it isn't cold in that water!) he got skunked. No fish! He blamed the poor weather conditions, said it was too windy, he had trouble casting his fly. Though he did get a couple of bites he never hooked a fish. Zero.

I spent my time birding as usual. But I didn't have any better luck than John did. I followed the snowmobile trail through the woods searching for birds, but the wind kept blowing the snow off the trees and causing near white out conditions. I just couldn't see anything; I was so bundled up only my eyeglasses were exposed and the blowing snow kept getting them wet. I tried sitting in my make shift bird blind bundled up in an old sleeping bag to watch for birds in the yard but still nothing. Zero.

I checked my birding records from previous years and usually over New Year's weekend I would see flocks of pine siskins and dark-eyed juncos. I hang a large seed block and usually would have red-breasted nuthatch and downy woodpeckers visit. And usually, I can stand in the yard with seed in my hands and have the chickadees land on my hand to eat. But this year nothing, nada, zero! Not a single bird anywhere, no chirping in the trees. No wildlife at all. I checked my records, usually I would see the otter playing on the ice, zero. There usually is a small herd of deer that pass through the yard; this year, zero deer, other than the dead one by the boat launch (poor thing). There were no tracks in the snow of rabbit, fox, coyote, or squirrels, nothing but untouched snow. Zero.

I find the lack of birds and wildlife very concerning. You have to wonder why; do they know something we don't? Have they all traveled farther south because they know this winter is going to be harsher than usual? Is it because the habitat has changed in the yard since the tornado? Skimmers Place is no longer a cabin in the woods it's now a cabin in a field. All the pine trees are gone, which means all those pine cones and pine seeds are no longer there for the birds and squirrels. The cover the low branches of the pines offered for the deer are now gone. Or is this a more ominous sign of a silent spring? (a book by pioneering conservationist Rachel Carson about the negative effects of man on nature). What I do know is that I have never spent three days at the cabin and seen nothing! Zero birds or wildlife! ZERO!

Scolded by a Wren

July 2017

I recently returned from an extended stay at the cabin, it can be such a different world it truly awakens my senses and renews my soul to spend time in the woods. It's hard to believe but on the nineteenth of this month it will have been one year since that freak storm ravished the cabin trees. And I'm still hauling brush and burning it! I'm looking forward to everyone visiting for family reunion all are going to see such a difference in the cabin yard. I know everyone will rave about how wonderful it looks but truth be told if I could turn back time I would, to the day before the storm and put all those trees back in place.

Now as unpleasant and dirty a job hauling year-old brush is I actually enjoyed the experience because of what took place around me as I was pulling brush out of tangled piles in the woods. When the linemen cut the fallen trees that were around the electric lines, they stacked it all into a big pile, which was nice of them but sure made for an ugly mess of dead stuff. So this past stay there, my goal was to attack those piles and clean it up. I know some are saying, "Why clean it up, just leave it to rot"; problem is, it can take years for those piles to rot and in the mean time they kill all the smaller ground cover plants and look darn awful and can be a fire hazard.

So I suited up and gathered my hedge clippers and doused myself in bug spray and started to haul brush. When suddenly a small bird flies from inside the pile and nearly hits me in the face! Yikes! The little bird settles on a branch above my head and begins to squawk and chatter at me, it was a winter wren. He did not want me there I was in *his* territory. I have heard this secretive little woodland wren in the yard for weeks but had been unable to spot him. They like to live in tangled brush and make their nest low to the ground in the dense tickets of fallen brush. Okay, now what am I supposed to do? I don't want to disturb the little bird's home, but I want to get the mess cleaned up. Umm, birdy won, I moved on to another pile for now.

I successfully removed a messy brush pile across the driveway from the wrens home but the whole time I was working he sat in the tree and scolded me. It made for nice back ground music to hear his song, but he was still unhappy about me being near his home. I'm sure there was most likely a nest in there that he was protecting. But as unhappy as the wren was to have me hauling brush a family of blue jays were excited about my activity in the woods. I had the brush pile cleared and was barely out of the woods when a family of blue jays nosily flew in and landed in the freshly cleared area. They began to hop about and scratch at the ground and peck at the bugs and worms they were finding. I mean you don't think about what lives in or under such a mess but there seems there was life under there for some to enjoy. But it only made me go "EWEE!" How many bugs and spiders were in there, and I might have touched one!? A hot shower was needed ASAP!

After my shower, I was walking along the driveway admiring the day's work to clean up the brush piles and I was happy to see the wren was sitting atop his brush pile quietly preening. He saw me and let out a song with his head thrown back then he hopped into the dense pile, all was well with him now. I kept my distance from his home and gave him the space he wanted. Then I noticed that in the area of the brush I had just cleared there were two ravens, they were flipping the leaves over and poking at the ground with their large beaks. One raven grabbed a grub and fed it to the other raven, which must have been a young one. It flapped its wings and begged for the grub with its mouth open.

So you know what, I wasn't the only one who benefited from cleaning up the dead mess of branches; the birds enjoyed the bounty of easy pickings of those creepy crawlies that were hiding under the brush. I know some are wondering, how can you call that a vacation? Spending days dirty and sweaty, hauling brush from the woods. But ya know what, yes, it is hard and dirty work; but when you slow down and look and listen to what's going on around you, even the nastiest job can be enjoyable.

And there was still time to do some birding; there always isn't there. I met a nice couple from Massachusetts at the camp ground who were enjoying birding in the area. Lucky guy he spotted a boreal chickadee along the river, I took the trail later but never got the chance to see the boreal chickadee, darn. They were telling me about a bald eagles nest in their town and all about the efforts to protect the site. It's encouraging to hear of people's efforts to help protect the birds and wildlife that we share this world with.

You know what, I don't need a gym membership I have branches to haul and logs to lift. I don't need a life coach to help motivate me to "Give me ten pushups! Let's tone those abs!" I don't need an iPod with earbuds to zone out the outside world. I've got the sounds of nature surrounding me. I've got a wren scolding me to keep moving, get that job done, and get out of here!

Rotting Banquet

I have lamented for ages now about the change in the cabin habitat due to the 2016 storm damage, it broke my heart. That freak tornado caused such devastating damage to the environment; though thankfully, there were no serious injuries. I wasn't sure the land would ever recover. But yet again, Mother Nature has amazed me at the rate of recovery the area has made and how fast the new growth has rebounded. I do know that if we had not spent the time and money to clean up the storm damage it surely would have taken many more years for the area to recover with new growth.

As part of the cleanup process, we purposely left some dead standing trees, the ones that lost their top third to the winds and were nothing more than a branch less trunk. We also left some of the fallen trees laying on the ground; we just limbed them and hauled away the brush. Leaving the piles of dead brush would have smothered the earth and made it even harder for new growth to begin. I knew this would help replenish the area and that leaving the dead tree trunks would offer food and shelter for the woodland critters. And it worked!

In one day in the cabin yard, I counted seven different species of woodpeckers! Though they weren't all actually technically woodpeckers, they were all tree climbing bug eating birds. Starting with the smallest, I saw red-breasted nuthatches, white-breasted nuthatches, downy woodpeckers, hairy woodpeckers, yellow-bellied sapsuckers, a black-backed woodpecker, and the pileated woodpecker.

I watched all of the birds as they were enjoying the rotting banquet of bugs, worms, and ants that were in the year-old dead trees. Some of the different species of birds I even saw together on the same standing dead tree sharing the rotting banquet. So it is important to remember that even dead trees have life to offer. It's good to try and leave a couple of standing dead trees for the birds when you can.

Saturday Survey

July 2017

Saturday July 15 was the annual Loon Protection Committees Loon survey on New Hampshire lakes. Again, this year I am the volunteer for Lake Francis in Pittsburg. Basically, I watch the loons all season as much as possible and record what they are doing and how many I see. If an emergency arises and there is an injured loon or if there are issues with a loon being harassed by boaters I act as a contact to the committee and state biologist to help the loons. I don't have any legal power myself, I'm just a set of eyes and ears on the lake to alert the proper authorities if needed.

The loon survey is done once every year; there are dozens of volunteers across the states many lakes who submit their sightings. The information gathered helps in the efforts to protect the common loons and as information on the health of the loons. I was glad this year to have seen five adult loons on Lake Francis. Unfortunately, the pair that calls the State Park Campground Cove their home did not nest this year. Unsure why they didn't, perhaps it was because of same issue that has destroyed their nest in previous years, their nest gets flooded out by rising waters. The pair usually nests by the mouth of the Connecticut River where it enters the lake along a narrow strip of land which often floods due to the sudden increase of water entering the lake from the river. The Loon Protection Committee has more than once installed a floating nest site for the loons, but they have just not accepted the location for their nest. I have seen adult loons sitting on the nest platform but none ever establish an active nest site.

As part of the survey, I drove to the Rt. 3 boat launch area by Murphy Dam to set up my spotting scope and scan the area for loon sightings. This area is at the opposite end of the lake as my cabin, not an area I can paddle my kayak to, just too far for me. When I got there, I met Darrell and Lynn who are the Lake Francis Lake Hosts. They set themselves up there on a picnic table near the boat launch to greet boaters. Darrell told me all about his volunteer work to help educate boaters on the dangers and how to prevent the spread of aquatic invasive species that threaten our lakes. Very interesting information, they are doing a great job; it's comforting to know that there are good people like Darrell and Lynn in this world who care about our environment and volunteer their time.

Of course, our talk soon turned to birds. I explained about the loon survey and asked if either of them had seen any loons that morning. Darrell tells me yes, that he saw an adult and baby loon earlier that morning. Wonderful! I was so excited to hear such good news. To know that there was a second breeding pair of loons on the lake made me feel better about the campground pair not having any young this year. There was hope for the future of the loons on Lake Francis!

Darrell agreed to fill out a loon survey form for me to submit. I carry extra forms with me to hand out to anyone who wants to help with the survey. The more eyes on the lake the better outcome for the loons. I scanned the lake for a while with my spotting scope for the mother loon and her young, but no luck. I saw a couple single adult loons but no sighting of a baby loon. Oh well, I will stop by the boat launch again and try to spot the mom and baby. I'll check in with Darrell and Lynn again, I hope they get to spot the baby loon again as they are there along the lake more often than I can be.

In fact, from this day forward I will name that baby loon, Darrell.

Chasing Darrell

July 2017

On a recent visit to the cabin, I had planned on focusing on searching for the baby loon that was seen on Lake Francis near the Rt. 3 boat launch. It's not that I doubted the reported sighting, I was just jealous, I wanted to see the baby loon with my own eyes and hoped to be able to get a picture as proof to share with the Loon Protection Committee.

So I decided to devote the whole day to searching for the baby loon (a.k.a. Darrell). Early morning, I dragged my kayak to the water's edge in front of the cabin and headed out onto the lake paddling along the north shore. I knew this wasn't the area that Darrell had been seen but the lake was calm and I thought I'd give it a try and see how far toward Murphy Dam I could get. I told myself I would paddle for an hour then turn back. I made it to the point where the campground cove opens up to the main part of the lake, I could see the dam in the distance, but it was still a long way off. Now that I was out of the cove and into the open main part of the lake, the wind was stronger and choppy waves were starting. Reality told me it was time to turn around and paddle back to the cabin. I did see one pair of adult loons swimming together in the middle of the lake and a single adult loon on the opposite shoreline. But no sight of Darrell!

I paddled back to the cabin, dragged the kayak out of the water, and back up the hill to the cabin. I loaded up the truck with my spotting scope, binoculars, a picnic lunch and all my other birding gear and headed to the Rt. 3 boat launch to search for Darrell. I pulled in to the far end of the launch area where there are a few picnic tables close to the water so I could set up my spotting scope and scan the water for Darrell. There was a young couple there with their dog, sitting in lawn chairs by the water's edge enjoying the sun, while the dog was playing in the

248

water. I asked them if they had seen any loons in the area and if they had noticed any baby loons. Surprise! They tell me they hadn't seen a baby loon today but had seen one last Saturday in this same spot. That was the same day Darrell (the human) and Lynn had seen the baby loon. Great news now that's four people who saw the baby loon on the same day in the same area I just have to find Darrell for myself!

I hung around the area for a while scanning the water. I did see an adult loon but no baby loon, I'm still searching for Darrell. I did talk with Darrell and Lynn who were there at the boat launch helping boaters. I told him about the other couple who had also seen the baby loon the same day they did. And I told him I had named the baby loon Darrell after him, he was fine with that. Having no success at the boat launch I decided to move on. Thought I would give it a try at Murphy Dam, knowing that from the top of the dam I could get a good view of the south cove area. Still searching for Darrell.

I park at the dam and start to pack up my gear to take the path up to the top of the dam. It's an easy trail to the top, nice and wide and smooth, but it currently was very hot out so I decided not to carry my spotting scope with me. I debated should I or shouldn't I bring it? Figured I had a fifty-fifty chance I was making the right decision. I got to the top of the dam and scanned the water with my binoculars and soon spotted a loon on the far side close to shore. That was a good sign, if the loon was close to shore it was possible it was there because it had a young with it and was staying protected from any overhead Raptors by staying closer to shore.

I focus on the loon, wait do I see what I think I see? It almost does look like there is a smaller grayish blob next to the adult. Oh, could it be Darrell?! I just couldn't see well enough with my binoculars. Yup. I had to rush back down the trail to the truck to get my spotting scope then rush back to the top of the dam! Of course, once I finally get back, set up my spotting scope the loon was gone! Was it only an adult loon which had dived under water and was gone? Or did the loon turn into the small cove to the right which was out of my viewing area? Was it an adult with a baby? Guess I'll never know for sure. Hope to find Darrell soon. So I'm still chasing Darrell!

May I Have This Dance?

August 2017

I have been watching the common loons on Lake Francis for more than twenty years now. I record how many I see, what they are doing, if there are any nesting pairs or any young present. Then I submit my observations to the NH Loon Preservation Committee, the biologists then compile all the submissions they receive from across the state to get an idea of the status and health of New Hampshire's loon population.

You would think that by now I would have seen every possible behavior of the loons on Lake Francis. I have seen them diving for dinner, preen in the morning sun, swimming gracefully across the lake, not so gracefully attempting to take flight and comically come in for a landing. I have watched them pair up, build a nest and rear their young. I listen to their loud yodeling calls each night and hear them call back and forth to each other with soft hoots during the day.

But yet again nature has amazed me. I recently witnessed the loons performing a "circle dance" on the lake! There was a group of ten loons gathered on the lake, a group of loons is called a raft. The raft of loons were swimming in unison along the shoreline and all the while they were hooting to each other. At times, they would all stick their head in the water and turn in a circle. Every now and then, one or two of the loons would rise up out of the water flapping its wings and yodel loudly. The whole raft glided along the shore, turned and glided up the opposite shore making a complete circle in the cove.

I knew this was something special but didn't know why, so I asked the loon committee biologist for an explanation. I was told I was lucky enough to witness the phenomenon known as the circle dance of the loons. It happens every year as migration begins, but it is not always seen as it occurs in different locations and times every year. Lucky for me this year, the loons held their dance right in front of my cabin as I watched!

The biologist explained that loons are a social species and each year as they prepare for migration, they will gather on one lake. She explained that the two loons I saw rise up from the water and flap their wings while calling were likely the hosts of the dance, they wanted to be sure all the other loons understood that this was "their" lake. The other loons may have flown miles from other lakes to gather on Lake Francis to dance.

The biologist also explained the behavior of the loons dipping their heads in the water and making a circle, that it was a defensive action. The loon was checking to be sure no other loon was underneath them trying to attack from below or behind, which is how one loon would attack another. The constant hooting back and forth was as simple the loons just "talking" to each other. Just sizing each other up, deciding who is single and who is not. It was all so *fascinating*!

The loons danced this way for a couple of days in the early morning and again in the early evening. All this took place just before our annual family reunion which is held at the cabin. I was so excited to show all my family this wonderful spectacle of nature. Unfortunately, the loons stopped dancing the day before the family arrived! I was so disappointed they weren't going to witness the circle dance of the loons. But I was so grateful I got to watch such an amazing display of nature. Even now, I can close my eyes and see the loons circling, I can hear the music of nature and imagine myself joining in. May I have this dance?

Food for Thought

I have something that I've been wondering about for a while now, the question is, where have all the chickadees gone? I have not seen a black-capped chickadee at the cabin since April 26. Which is very unusual, I usually have a small flock of five to eight chickadees that frequent the yard of the cabin at the lake. They usually move through the yard in a mixed flock with red-breasted nuthatch and brown creepers. I have seen the nuthatches but not any creepers either, since March 16.

I know all this because I keep a nature journal when I am at the cabin. I record all the birds and animals I see each day and make notes of any unusual or interesting behaviors I witness. Other than my binoculars and bird guide I consider a notebook one of the most important items to have in my backpack. Sure it's old school; in today's tech world, I'm sure there is an app for that. *But* there is no internet, cable, tv or cell service in the Great North Woods as far north as my cabin so I have to rely on good old pen and paper. I have been keeping a journal since early the 1990s and I can look back and read that consistently there have been black-capped chickadees in the cabin yard.

So where are they now?!

My first thought was that it was because of the change in the area habitat since we lost so many trees to the freak storm last summer. During the winter months, I would offer seeds to the birds when I was there to help them through the harsh conditions, the little chickadees would even eat from my hand. I know there is the constant debate about if it is good or bad for the wild birds to feed them, if you're not able to do it regularly. Since we don't spend as much time at the cabin in the winter, to try and find a middle ground on the issue I wouldn't hang a feeder but would toss mixed seed out on the ground here and there whenever we were there. I continued tossing seed out on the ground over the summer but still no chickadees! Where have they all gone?!

In early August, I thought I had a possible explanation. While sitting on the cabin porch enjoying my morning coffee, I heard the call of a bird that suddenly gave me an answer. Merlins! The merlin belongs to the falcon family, this small powerful flier catches its prey in midair then flies back to its perch to consume his dinner.

The main diet of the merlin is small birds, aka chickadees! There has been a pair of merlins nesting in the area for a couple of years. This year the merlins have a nest high in the pine trees just across the dirt road from the cabin.

A couple of years ago, I even saw a merlin catch a chickadee in midair, and then with my binoculars, I followed the merlin to its nest site and watched as the merlin tore apart the poor little chickadee and dropped it into the nest for its young. Sad for the chickadee but life for the merlins, circle of nature. So is that why there are no chickadees in the yard? Because of the merlins? Did they eat them all? Oh, wait! Or did I contribute to the demise of the local black-capped chickadee population by feeding them and drawing them into the yard in groups? Thus, supplying the merlins with an easy-to-catch food supply? Would that be why the merlins have nested in the area repeatedly? Oh no, tell me it isn't so! I love birds I certainly hope my actions haven't caused such a sad scenario. But where are the chickadees?!

Feeling very guilty and sad I flipped through the pages of my nature journal back a couple years to the last time the merlins nested in the area. With a sigh of relief, I read the daily counts of birds and the chickadee population remained stable at five or eight sightings a day! Even with the presence of the nesting merlins. So maybe it wasn't mine after all? So if it wasn't my fault, and it wasn't the merlins' fault, then why are the chickadees gone?

Yes, the habitat around the cabin has changed but Mother Nature has renewed the woods, and we cleaned up most of the dead trees and new growth has sprung up. The pine trees that are left standing are healthy and bearing many pine cones. The low bushes have numerous berries for the birds and animals to feed off. There does not seem to be any lack of nature's food for the birds and wildlife. So the question is still out there: where have all the chickadees gone!?

Pheasant Under Glass

I recently returned from a fall trip to the cabin. The Great North Woods are in full fall splendor! The colors are amazing, the red and orange leaves of the hardwoods and the yellow leaves of the birch trees all complemented by the green pine trees. It's like Mother Nature's patchwork quilt covering the landscape. Add to that the reflection of the fall foliage across the blue water of the lake. A breathtaking view I never grow tired of.

Typical for this time of year the temperatures were cool during the day and near freezing at night. Saturday morning, I decided to take a kayak paddle across the lake to a small marshy area to do some birding. The morning started out sunny but clouds soon moved in and the wind picked up by the time I made it to the opposite side of the lake. I did make it to the area I wanted to and there were numerous birds flitting about the low marsh bushes. Unfortunately, the water was so rough due to the wind that the kayak was bobbing up and down and back and forth violently. It was pretty hard to focus on any one bird with my binoculars I was rocking so badly.

I did manage to spot a small flock of about five birds I was able to focus on. But I couldn't stay still long enough to get a good look at them. I could tell they were warblers by their small size and dull olive above and a pale yellow below. They were calling, *seet…seet… seet…*back and forth to each other. Looking through my bird guide the closest ID I could come up with was that they were blackpoll warblers in fall plumage. Still, I didn't count them as a sighting since I really couldn't get a good look at any of them as I was bobbing around in the kayak so much, I was even getting splashed by the water.

Indeed, it was time to head back across the lake before the weather got any worse!

Later in the day just before dusk I decided to take a walk to a Wildlife Management Area about a half mile from the cabin where the NH Fish and Game stock ring-necked pheasants. I flushed a Ruffed Grouse from the tall grasses as I was approaching the area. As I was walking along the trail, I suddenly heard a strange sound and heard rustling in the underbrush. It was a sound I couldn't identify. It wasn't the bugle of a Moose, or the snort of a deer, or the growl of a Bear. Whatever it was wasn't large as it was staying hidden in the underbrush. I have seen coyotes in the area before, but it didn't sound like them, and even when I did see them their tails would give them away as it stuck up above the low bushes. It wasn't a fox. I have foxes that have a den near my home and I am quite familiar with their sounds. What was it?

I couldn't identify the sound, but I knew I needed to exit the area ASAP! I tapped my walking stick on the ground and hit some of the low tree branches to make noise as I slowly backed away from the area. As silly as it may sound, I was talking to the "whatever" was in the bushes, telling *it* I meant no harm to *it* and was leaving. Please leave me alone. *But* it was still moving toward me and making that strange sound! I hurried back to the cabin as fast as my arthritic knees would carry me!

When I got back to the cabin, I explained to John what had happened and tried to recreate the sound I heard. He mentioned an animal I hadn't thought of, *it* could have been a bobcat. John reminded me that the Fish and Game had just stocked the area with pheasant two days earlier, and that bobcat would prey on pheasants. And that opening day for pheasant hunting was the next day. Ummmm, maybe *it* was a bobcat?

Very early the next morning I was awakened by the sounds of gunshot. BANG! BANG! BANG! And again! And again! Yup, the hunters were out there. Well, is sure sounds like someone is going to be enjoying pheasant under glass for dinner. I sure hope the bobcat gets a chance to enjoy some. Nature's circle of life.

Sharing with the
Next Generation

This is a picture of the banner the students made for
me to thank me for teaching them about birds.

This chapter is a few stories of my chances to share my knowledge
and experiences birding with youngsters. Family members and
strangers. Encouraging our future members of society to get out
there and explore the world around them. To appreciate and protect
Mother Nature and all of God's creatures. Their reactions to me were
uplifting and inspiring.

She Is Okay!

I was excited to travel out to Western Massachusetts to visit Katie, she had invited me to come and explore some of the natural areas around her in my search for the great horned owl. She said she knew where the locations were that Ebird had listed as spots to find the owl. We tried a couple of the listed locations but to no avail, we saw some nice birds but no owls. Katie suggested we try out the last place listed, the Station Rd rail trail, she entered the location in her GPS, and we headed out.

We arrived, and it was a very nice spot, an old railroad bed turned into a narrow biking/walking trail. There was a large expanse of swamp on one side perfect habitat for ducks and birds. We saw a couple of Hooded Mergansers with the male proudly displaying his crest in hopes of impressing the females nearby. The usual mallards and kingfisher were present, but no sign of any great horned owls or active nests. The weather was overcast, windy and cold, but we were having a nice day. I was really enjoying spending time alone with my niece just exploring.

We walked along the trail for a mile or so and decided to give up the search and head back. Katie mentioned that she saw a woman ahead of us that had stepped off the trail and was sitting on a stone bench looking out over the swamp, maybe she was a fellow birder and had some info on the owl's location. Good idea, I get most of my best sightings from fellow birders. We catch up to her (we named her the cat lady; she had a cat on a leash with her) and she is a local and tells us where she has heard and seen the great horned owl. Cat Lady tells us to go back about half mile and just after the end of the swamp to look for a narrow side trail with some wooden planks across the marshy ground. She tells us in the pine woods is where she has seen and heard owls though she wasn't aware of any nests.

I look at Katie, I tell her I don't care either way, I'm fine if she doesn't want to look any more and head back to the car, or I'm willing to push on if she is. Katie says it's only a little after one o'clock, we're here let's just give it a quick look. So we head back up the trail in search of the great horned owl. We follow the edge of the swamp and find the wooden planks and cross onto the muddy side trail. A bit down the side trail, I notice a set of footprints in leftover snow leading into a group of trees. I suggest we follow them; they lead up to a large pine tree, and I look up and there about ten feet up is a large nest. Could it be true have we found the great horned owl nest we have been searching for all day?

I strain to see the top of the nest but can't see anything as we are standing directly under the nest. We search around the tree on the ground for any signs of bird activity. I see some bird droppings, and a few fine feathers, I don't see any owl pellets. Katie notices a low branch with scratches across the top, where you might envision a large taloned bird sitting. All the signs were pointing to this being an active nest of a large bird. But we couldn't see anything in the nest.

We are both walking around the large pine talking, searching for a clue, Katie is at the back side of the tree, I can't really see her. She says, "How about I climb the tree and see what's in the nest?"

I call back, "Oh, Katie, I can't ask you to do that, you don't want to disturb the owls if they are in there."

She calls back to me, "You're not asking me, I want to see this owl."

In turn, I call out, "No…Katie, I don't think that's a good—" SNAP! I suddenly hear the sound of a branch as it breaks!

I rush over to the back side of the tree, I'm calling, "Katie, are you all right!"

She answers, "Aunt Jane, I think I hurt my foot bad." She is kinda leaning against the tree, I ask her what can I do for her, she says she just wants to sit down for a minute and catch her breath. I grab her and lower her to the ground. Katie has such a poker face I really didn't think she was hurt that bad, she said she just wanted to sit for a minute. She wasn't crying or grimacing in pain, she wasn't bleeding. I offered her a drink of water and a molasses cookie that I had in my pocket.

Right away, I go into planning mode. Okay, how am I gonna get her out of these woods and back to the car about a mile away. I start to look around for a large branch I can fashion into a cane to help her support herself. I continue to talk to her, ask if she is okay. All I can find are dead rotten branches that keep breaking when I put weight on them; as I'm searching, I ask her if she thinks she can hobble back using my shoulder for support. She answers, "Aunt Jane, don't bother with that, call 911, I'm gonna pass out." I rush to her side and help her lay down, her face is pale, I keep talking to her as I'm reaching into my pocket for my phone.

I ask her what town we are in; she says she's not sure just tell 911 we are on the rail trail. I know that is a very broad location, there are miles of rail trails. I look at Katie, she is conscious, her color looks better, I tell her I'm gonna run back about couple hundred yards to the main trail where there is a trail marker for our location. As I'm running through the bulk brush, I hear the jingle jangle of a dog's collar. I call out for help as I see a man and his dog through the bushes up on the main rail trail running past. I explain my niece has hurt her foot, I am from out of town and have no idea where to tell 911 dispatchers we are. He takes the phone and explains to the dispatcher exactly where we are, town, street, mile marker in, he was a great help. Such a nice man, he offers to run back to the parking lot and wait for the ambulance.

I stay with Katie, and I tell her the EMTs are on the way is there anything I can do for her. I offer her some water and a molasses cookie from my pocket. She tells me she is getting cold. I take off my jacket and wrap her in it; of course, she tries to shrug off the jacket telling me, "Oh no, Aunt Jane, you need this you're gonna be cold." I tell her not to worry; the EMTs will be here soon. I'll be fine. But minutes seemed like hours as we waited for help.

I look at Katie she looks okay, I tell her I'm going to go back again to the intersection of the side trail and the main trail and see if I can see the EMTs. It's not very far but the bushes and trees are dense. I continue to call out to Katie even when I am out of sight, to keep in touch. I get onto the main trail and I can just make out the flashing red lights way in the distance, I realize we were a lot farther from the parking lot than I first thought. I call back to Katie, "The Calvary has arrived." I run back to check on her, offer her some water and a molasses cookie from my pocket.

But minutes seemed like hours as we waited for help. I run back to the main trail again, and it doesn't look like the ambulance is any closer, I'm puzzled. I look through my binoculars, and I can see the ambulance coming up the trail backward and that two EMTs in fluorescent yellow coats are standing behind it. I was worried that they had stopped at the wrong side trail, we had passed a couple. I take off my sweater and begin to swing it over my head and I start to yell, "Hey, *help* over here!"

But they don't seem to see me. I run back to Katie to check on her, I tell her I can see the EMTs they'll be here soon. She says okay.

But minutes seemed like hours as we waited for help. I run back to the intersection of the side and main trail and the ambulance doesn't look any closer. I again swing my sweater over my head and yell. This time one of the EMTs waves back! Now I can hear the backup bells of the ambulance. I run back to tell Katie they will be here soon. I offer her some water and a molasses cookie from my pocket.

I run back to the trail intersection when we can see the flashing red lights through the trees to guide them in to where Katie is. An EMT is opening the back doors of the ambulance, and he walks toward me with a blanket open motioning to wrap me in it, he says, "Lady, are you okay?"

I tell him no, it's not me; it's my niece back in the woods, and I motion for them to follow me. The EMTs quickly surround Katie and start to tend to her. One of the first things they want to do is remove her boot to check out her hurt foot, Katie has been so brave, but I can tell she is getting scared it is going to hurt. I do the only thing I can think of to comfort her, I drop to the ground behind her and hug her tight from behind and tell her to hang on, it will be over soon.

One of the EMTs takes my jacket off Katie and hands it to me, he tells me I'm welcome to go back and get in the front seat of the ambulance to warm up. I know Katie is in good hands now so I go to warm up. Soon they are carrying Katie out of the woods and into the back of the ambulance. The driver jumps in, and we begin the slow trip back to the parking lot. He again asks if I'm okay, I tell him I'm fine. He asks what we were doing out here and I tell him we were looking for the great horned owl. We talk about birds as we slowly head back to the parking lot.

It was only after a very nice police officer helped me get Katie's car to the hospital, and I had checked on Katie that I went into the restroom and saw myself in a mirror that I understood why the EMT might have thought I was the patient. I was a mess! In the process of running back and forth through the bushes, I did remember something poking me but paid no attention to it at the time. But it seems a branch must have caught the side of my pants, and they were ripped open from my waist to my thigh and my granny panties were exposed for all to see. My hands were all scratched and my knuckles were bleeding. I was splattered with mud from my toes to my knees. I must have been quite a sight to the EMTs jumping up and down waving my sweater over my head.

I wouldn't share this story without Katie's permission; she even asked me to document our adventure with pictures. They are hers to share if she sees fit. I explained to Katie, my actions may have seemed frantic, but they weren't. I knew time was against us, we could only stay out there in the cold, wet woods for so long before hypothermia was a real concern, I was beginning to shiver that's why I kept running back and forth to stay warm. No way would I even think about taking my coat from my dear niece. I was really concerned that it was taking the ambulance so long to get to us that's why I felt I needed to make some noise and get their attention. I kept asking Katie if she wanted any water and a molasses cookie from my pocket to test her. She remained clear headed, she answered me, and she laughed at me, so very proud of how well she handled it all!

Bottom line is Katie is okay. The hospital took x-rays and checked her over good, nothing is broken. She has some torn ligaments and must remain off the foot as much as possible and use crutches. I had a great day spending time with my niece, we had some fun adventures. Obviously if I could I would go back in time and erase the moment Katie attempted to climb that darn tree. Hindsight is always twenty-twenty. But I wouldn't change anything else. Thank you, Katie, for a very special day!

Hooked Another One!

December 2013

Perhaps you hadn't noticed, but it is in the news, the snowy owls are back! In fact, there have been as many as fifteen seen on Plum Island Wildlife Refuge. That's more than any previous year, so I knew the chances were good that we could find one. Jeanine was home for the holidays and wanted to see a snowy owl to add to her life list. My niece Emily had expressed an interest in also seeing one. Any excuse I can find to venture out on the island in search of birds sounds like a perfect outing to me, so we arranged to meet up with Chris and Emily for a day of birding.

It made me feel all warm inside to see how genuinely excited Emily was to embark on her first birding adventure. It made me smile when she told me about telling her friends she was going birding in search of the snowy owl and her friends questioned rather "birding" was even a word, that they laughed at her and thought she was making it up. No, birding is a real word and a very real activity. I often talk about the excitement and camaraderie among birders in my stories, all of which the girls were about to experience firsthand.

We arrived on the island and before even getting out of the car at the first stop the girls were saying their toes were cold. When we stopped at the refuge entrance, I asked the park ranger if there were any snowy owl sightings. He told us that there were multiple sightings on the island, that lot 1 reported three. He suggested that we skip lot 1 and head to lot 2 as the large crowd at lot 1 ended up scaring the owls, and that they were flying toward lot 2. Excited we headed to lot 2 in hopes of scoring a good sighting. Chris took over driving duty so the girls and I could scan the salt marsh for the owls, with binoculars raised we were on the hunt.

We park and head out across the meandering board walk into the sand dunes. It was indeed chilly, as usual, the wind is always strong coming off the ocean and the trail was icy. We pass a few birders carrying scopes and ask about owl sightings, none. We pass a young boy who tells us that he had just seen one out in the salt marsh sitting on a post. There is a group of birders lined up along the narrow boardwalk with large camera set ups and scopes all searching the dunes, we walk up and ask about owls but still none seen. We decide to head to the area the young boy suggested and rush back to the car, I think the girls were wondering if we birders are all delusional or if maybe the cold has frozen our senses. I knew the girls were cold but at the same time I think they were beginning to catch the enthusiasm of the hunt. They looked so cute all bundled up with their binoculars hanging around their necks chatting about birds as we walked along the icy trail.

Sure enough, as we drive toward the marsh there is a large group of cars all parked in the road and along the side. There are people lined up with scopes and cameras, and there is the young boy and his dad setting up a scope. We walk right up to them, and they offer the girls the use of the scope to get a really good up-close look. There out in the salt marsh sitting on a post is the magnificent snowy owl! The girls first sighting, yeah! We hang out and talk to fellow birders, enjoying the circus as people jump out of their cars and rush to see the owl. As we head back to the car, Emily mentions how she is surprised to see so many different people out birding, young and old, women and men, families. All enjoying the birds, everyone excited about the star of the island the snowy owl.

I was hoping to get a better closer look of the owl for the girls so they could get a few pictures so we drive on to try a few more likely spots. We stop at the wardens shed when we see a group of birders all scanning the scrub brush, that's always a good sign of an interesting sighting. The girls were out of the car and excitedly walking toward the group before I was. They were defiantly getting into this. Turns out what the birders were looking at was an immature (third year) bald eagle sitting on the ground protecting a fresh kill while off to its left was a merlin sitting on a stump waiting to pick up any scraps. Emily was enjoying the show, asking questions about the birds and the girls were talking to the other birders. I was enjoying watching the girls watching the birds.

I was determined to get the girls a closer view of the owl, because of the snow the island road was closed at the half way point, Hellcat Trails, but there was one more trail across the dunes I wanted to try. Chris and the girls were cold so it was decided that I would head out on the trail, and if I saw anything good, I would come back to the car and get them. Off I went along the narrow snow-covered board walk scanning the dunes for the owl. About a quarter mile along the trail, I come upon a group of birders, yup, there sitting atop a windblown sand dune is a snowy owl! I ran (well, more like trotted) back across the icy path to get the others waiting in the car. We all rush back to the dunes and the girls both get a chance to take pictures of the regal snowy owl just sitting on the ground atop the sand dune looking at us.

We head back to the car; the girls share their sighting with fellow birders they pass along the trail with sincere excitement. We stop in old town Newburyport for a warm lunch and talk about our day of birding on Plum Island. Emily sends a text to her friend with the news of her exciting sighting of the Arctic snowy owl. I felt joy to know she honestly had fun with her Aunt Jane birding in the cold when she felt the need to share it with friends via text. :) Jeanine got to add two new birds to her life list, the snowy owl and the merlin. And I think I can safely say that I hooked another one, Emily seems to have caught the birding bug. I hope she will join Chris and I some day on the island in the spring to enjoy another day of birding.

Beach Boyz

July 2014

Thanks to Chris and Mark for offering me the use of their camper in Maine during the weekdays. I was able to meet up with my niece Jessica and her son Ryan on one Monday and that same week on Wednesday I enjoyed the company of Carle, her daughter Kym and her grandsons Liam and Declan. Unfortunately, the day Jesse and Ryan visited didn't start off to good, we had rain in the morning. Which wasn't really a problem for Jesse and I as we had plenty to talk about to fill the time waiting for the sun to return.

Ryan did what any self-respecting eight-year-old boy would do stuck in a camper in the rain with his old Aunt and mom yacking away. He built himself a fort in the bottom bunk in the camper using all the lawn chair cushions. He was happy as pie in there, he had a light and a few of his action figures to play with. It was a "no girls allowed" zone. He was very proud of his handy work as he well should be it was a nice comfy hiding spot. It brought back fond memories of all the forts Jeremy used to build, boy's imagination can be so resourceful. They can build a "fort" out of most anything anywhere.

Just about noon the rain stopped and the sun began to come out so we hit the beach to search for sand dollars. Ryan likes to collect shells so he was excited to search among the rocks for shells and odd shaped rocks. I enjoyed spending one on one time with him wading in the surf in search of treasures from the sea. It made me feel old and young at the same time.

The weather was much better on the Wednesday that Carle and family visited Cape Neddick. As soon as the car door was opened, the two boys made a bee line for the beach. They were excited to search along the rocks for shells and interesting shaped rocks. Somehow most of them seemed to be shaped like a butt or toilet? I thought it looked like a heart but then I'm not a young boy. The boys were having a great time riding the surf on their boogie boards and drifting along on the current that runs across the beach.

After lunch, I set up my spotting scope on the rocks and let the boys use my binoculars to check out the birds bobbing in the swells. Liam was calling out the description and colors on the bird he was viewing. Then we would look it up in the bird guide together to decide which bird it was. They were Terns sitting on the buoys. Declan focused in on a large black bird he saw on the water, he described the orange neck he saw. We looked it up in the bird guide, and he decided he had seen a cormorant. It was nice to get to share my love of birding with them.

I had a great time with my Beach Boyz! I enjoyed sharing my knowledge with them and getting to know them each a little better. It was nostalgic, I miss those days with my kids. Jesse, Kym, I know you two moms can get tired of the constant energy and questions of your boys. The never-ending "Mommy, Mommy, Mommy!" Been there, done that. But take it from a mom that's an empty nester now, the constant chatter and questions was music to my ears. My time spent at the beach with your son's was the best Beach Boyz concert ever!

Birding with Ella

June 2016

I was quite surprised but also thrilled when my niece Liz contacted me and asked if I would be willing to take her daughter Ella birding. She said Ella asked her if Aunt Jane would take her birding and show her some birds! As I have said before finding a life list bird is thrilling but next to that is helping someone else find a new bird. Here Ella was a clean slate, she was just starting out on her adventure in birding. That was a lot to live up to. Could I help her find some birds and pique her interest in the hobby of birding? Could I keep a six-year-old interested enough in searching for birds to actually find some high in the treetops? Ahh the pressure was on! But I was determined to satisfy her curiosity in nature and make it exciting as well.

Monday was the first day of my school vacation and what could be a better way to spend it than taking my brothers first granddaughter out in the woods to find birds. I arrived at their farm to find Ella packed and ready to hit the trails. She had her backpack stuffed with all the essentials, bug box, net, hand sanitizer, water bottle, snack and the bird book I had given her for her birthday. I brought along a small pair of binoculars for her to use. After a little practice using the binoculars by focusing on her chickens in the yard, she was ready to go. Liz had detailed directions to a rail trail in town she thought would be a good spot to try. We both put on our birding hats and got a spray down from Liz of bug spray and were on our way.

Unfortunately, it was a very hot day, temps in the mid-eighties, I knew that meant the birds would not be moving around a lot, I sure hoped we would find some. We soon arrived at the rail trail; I admit I was a bit nervous. I was about to head out on an unfamiliar trail with my young grandniece, could I meet her expectations of what birding with Aunt Jane was all about? We weren't far down the trail when she spotted a prize. A huge frog! It wasn't a bird, but it was a creature she was excited to see, and she quickly got out her critter net and bug box to catch it. Unfortunately, there was a hole in the net and the frog escaped. But as we were standing there in the tree above our heads three cedar Waxwings were hopping about the branches. I showed her a picture of them, and we talked about how they got their name. That the tip of their tail and wings are smooth waxy looking and bright yellow and red and look like they were dipped in wax. By explaining the details of the bird to her, I hope it will help her remember the bird next time she sees one. It's all about teaching the next generation, pass it down.

We stopped for a snack along the river about a mile down the trail. While sitting there I could hear a gray catbird and a common yellow throat calling from the bushes along the far shore. I directed her attention to the bird song and showed her how to mimic their calls. She did great! Both birds were soon answering her calls, but they still wouldn't come into view. Ella skipped rocks across the water and watched the water bugs skating across the surface. Of course, she asked if maybe she could catch them, but I reminded her the net had a hole in it (thankfully) so that idea was nixed quickly.

We continued along the trail. She spotted a tufted titmouse first and directed my eyes to it. Great job, Ella! We saw a song sparrow and chickadees. We had been on the trail for an hour, it was time to turn around. Before we headed out, I explained to Ella that we should keep track of the time and be aware of how far we had walked so that we didn't end up farther away from the start than we were prepared for. She would have gone farther, but when I had her look back, and she realized she could not even see the beginning gate of the trail she understood what I meant. I wasn't trying to scare her or make her think we were lost, I just wanted her to be aware of the distance/time we had traveled.

We came upon a trail intersection, and she was interested in going up the new trail, but I explained we had already walked a ways and about staying on the main trail, that some other day with her family she could explore the new trail. We took a trail map from the kiosk, and I showed her how to follow the red markers on the trees of the trail. I know it was a lot of information for her to absorb, but I wanted her to understand that she should not just go running off to explore a new trail off the main trail, to stay on the main trail. She was excited to find a caterpillar crawling up the wooden sign and soon had it in her bug box. Attention diverted.

As we were heading back, she suddenly spotted movement in the bushes. It was the gray cat bird! She got a good look at it, and she called, "Meow…meow…meow," and it answered! She later said that was the highlight of our trip. She only saw seven birds in a two-hour span but each one meant a lot to Ella and that's all that counts. On the ride back to the house, she sat in the backseat of the truck talking to her caterpillar, boy did that bring back memories of my daughter Jeanine. I dropped her off at home sweaty and dirty. I told Ella that meant we had a good day! And I did have a good day birding with Ella!

Best Sighting Ever!

I have shared many stories of my birding adventures and exciting bird sightings for a while now. But today I had the best sighting ever! I got to see a miracle, a newborn human, I got to visit with Katie and Shawn and meet Alice. I was so honored when my niece had told me that their newborns middle name was Jane, after me. The special bond that formed between Katie and I might not have happened or been so strong if it weren't for our birding adventures in search of that great horned owl and more.

The day started off rough that's for sure. It was a long and arduous three-hour drive across the Berkshires in a spring snow storm. It wasn't a heavy snow fall but worse, the wet slick couple of inches that grease up the roads and make driving a challenge. As I passed vehicle after vehicle that had slid off the road, I began to question my sanity to continue, maybe I should call and cancel and turn around while I could. But *no*, I was on my way and determined to make it out to see baby Alice in person.

I arrived safe and sound and after being approved for entry by pup Hazel I was warmly greeted. And there on the couch by Mom, nestled in her little nest of soft blankets, wearing pink PJs decorated with little blue birds was tiny Alice. Gosh you forget how small an infant is, there she was sweetly sleeping, this tiny human.

While Alice was sleeping Katie gave me a tour of their new place, what a nice house, the area is beautiful. Katie took me into the nursery which she painted a happy color of green. There are silhouettes of tree branches on the walls and Katie hung colorful little bird houses on the ends of the branches. There were silhouettes of birds all around the room. What a delightful inspiring nursery, I want to sleep there!

Now I have to admit that I'm not a "baby" person. I mean I don't go all goo-goo gaga over a baby and have to cuddle and squeeze them. But I have to be honest and tell you that when I held Alice in my arms I was completely smitten, mesmerized by her little face as she looked at me. I felt an instant connection, as if we had known each other for ever. It was quite an experience.

For truly the birth of a child is the most wondrous event nature can provide.

I look forward to watching her grow as her loving parents lift her up to soar. And watching as time goes by and Alice learns to stretch her wings and fly to become the person her loving environment has allowed her to be. I look forward to the day I can take Alice out in the woods for her first day of birding with Aunt Jane! (I wear that title proudly.) Congratulations, Katie and Shawn, on becoming parents, you have brought a beautiful little girl into this world. May God bless you all.

Brrrrrr...ding!

This is a picture of an American Robin nestled in a wild
berry bush on Plum Island during a wintery day.

My daughter Jeanine was home from Colorado over college break
for the holiday, and we had planned on a winter birding trip to Plum
Island in hopes of seeing the snowy owl. She hadn't been on the refuge since she was a child and that was only during the summertime,
to play on the beach or other times to ocean fish off shore with her
dad and brother. So this would be her first winter time visit to the
island. She is an avid skier and hiker she is used to the cold Rocky
Mountains and was well prepared for winter conditions. But we had
not planned on the weather conditions being so extremely cold. Sure,
we had planned on cold weather but when we woke to a temperature
of -5 and the temperature for the day topped off at four. Looked like
it was going to be a "car birding day."

I was on the island a few days earlier with my sister, and we had an easy sighting of the snowy owl. I had been checking out the sighting reports and the owl was still being seen in the same area just near the road. So we were hopeful to get a good sighting. We bundled up, loaded the truck with all the necessary equipment, and headed to Parker River National Wildlife Refuge on Plum Island Massachusetts. Unfortunately, the weather only got worse, when we arrived the wind had picked up, and it was snowing lightly. *Burrrrr... burrrrr...burrrr.*

I had received a really nice new camera set-up from my husband, and I was anxious to try it out to get some close-up pictures of the birds. I threw the truck into four-wheel drive, and we slowly drove along the snowy refuge road in search of birds. We saw large flocks of American robins feasting on the winter berries that grow on the island. Also saw some cedar waxwings and starlings, got a few pictures of the birds as they enjoyed the bountiful berries. There were plenty of dark-eyed juncos flitting about.

Jeanine did want to walk out to the ocean to watch the waves crashing along the rocky shore. She said she did miss seeing the ocean now that she lived out in Colorado. So we headed across the snowy boardwalk toward the ocean, and the strong wind coming off the ocean blasted us as we got to the open shoreline. *Burrrr...Burrrr... Burrrr...*

Well, we never did see the snowy owl; we talked with other birders we came across, and no one had spotted the owl. I'm sure the extreme cold and high winds had something to do with that. I'm sure the owl was hunkered down somewhere safe to ride out the storm. Oh well, that's just how it goes in birding. But it really didn't matter, we had a nice day spending time out in nature, birding together. That's what it's all about spending time together doing some winter brrrrr...ding!

Who...Who...Who...
Cooks for You...

January 2018

The elementary school I work at as a lunch lady has a very nice open courtyard and many of the classrooms circle it and have large windows with a great view. Some of the teachers have set up bird feeders among the small trees in the green area. The gym teacher even holds classes outside there now and then. She holds a spring cleanup class where the students rake the leaves and prepare the area to plant flowers, all so everyone can enjoy the calming area. There always is an assortment of birds flying about. It is no secret that the lunch lady is a birder. At times, teachers have seen birds they weren't sure what species they were, and they would ask me if I knew what kind they were.

I was recently asked to speak to a kindergarten class about my hobby of birding. The students are learning about backyard birds and their teacher thought they would enjoy hearing about some of my birding adventures. So I came in early before I started my shift in the kitchen to prepare school lunch to visit the class. I brought along my scrapbook with stories and pictures of the places I traveled the birds I saw when I was participating in my Big Year bird count. I kept it simple and just flipped through the pages to show the students a snapshot of my adventure, they were all very interested and asked questions about some of the bird pictures.

I played a little game with them. I played some bird songs on my Nook without showing them the pictures to see who could identify what bird was singing. I played the songs of very common backyard birds, and we talked about how the songs sometimes sound like talking, and how it can help identify a bird even if you can't see it. I played the song of the black-capped chickadee and pointed out how it is calling, *chick...a...dee...dee...dee, chick...a...dee...deee...deee*, telling you its name. They all excitingly repeated the song! An hour flew by fast, and it was time for me to get into the kitchen to start making the pizza for lunch. I played the sound of the barred owl and pointed out it sounds like it is saying, "Who...who...who cooks for you?!" Then I told them how much I enjoyed spending time talking with them all, but it was time for me to get into the kitchen to cook lunch. As I stood up to leave, I sang, "Who...who...who cooks for you..." They all clapped and repeated my song as I waved goodbye. Sure brought smiles to my day!

For days after my classroom visit when the students would come through the lunch line every now and then one of them would call to me, who...who...who cooks for you...then smile and point at me and say, "YOU DO!" And sometimes a student would tell me about a bird they saw in their own yard and how proud their parent was that they knew what kind of bird it was. Their teacher had thanked me very much for my visit, and she said that she was planning on taking the students for a short nature walk along the woodland perimeter of the school yard. She said that since the class was currently so interested in birds that she put together a chart of about a dozen common birds the students were likely to see to count. What a great idea, practice counting out in nature, these are young kindergarteners, sounds like more fun than sitting in the classroom. I told her that to add to the fun if she wanted to give me the list totals that I would submit the sightings to Ebird for the class. She liked that idea and even signed herself up on Ebird, and she submitted the sightings and shared the map with the students. They were all so proud to see their school listed on the Ebird map with the sightings they all took part in.

I so enjoyed sharing with the next generation my hobby of birding. The students were all very polite and showed great interest in what I was telling them. They all are obviously good students and learn from their teacher about the birds around them.

Sure, I became known as the bird lunch lady who cooks for you. But it was heartwarming to know that there is a whole new generation out there ready and willing to explore the world of birding!

A Cheer for Me!

April 2018

I had the opportunity to speak to another kindergarten class about my hobby of birding. I pretty much stayed with the same format that I used for the first class I spoke to. I explained to the students that I spend my summers volunteering for different organizations, like the Loon Preservation Committee, counting and observing birds to help save and protect them for our future. I shared some pictures of the common loons on Lake Francis and some of the survey information I had gathered. I could tell by the looks on their faces, they were listening, they were thinking, they were taking it all in.

I shared my scrapbook and talked about my birding adventures the year I took part in a Big Year competition. I told them about riding horseback in the Rocky Mountains of Colorado to finds birds, climbing the walls of a rock quarry in Vermont to observe a nesting pair of peregrine falcons and my adventure riding an airboat through the Florida Everglades. They were all paying attention and seemed excited to look at the pictures of all the different looking birds I saw. I asked them if they had noticed how many of the birds in the Everglades had very long legs, did anyone know why that might be? One young student quickly raised his hand and says, "To get away from the alligators!" Well, that was a good answer and just might be one reason. I explained to the students that the tall birds are called Wading Birds, and that they need to be tall to walk through the swampy waters in search of food like small fish and frogs. They all agreed with that explanation.

Then I played a little game with them, I played different bird songs on my Nook and asked if anyone knew, which bird was singing. I kept it simple and showed them a page of my book with birds on it and told them the song was one of the birds on the page. They enjoyed hearing all the bird songs and really seemed awed by the very different songs. They had some difficulty matching which bird was singing to a picture but heck it's not easy, many birders have trouble identifying bird songs.

Then I asked them if there were any birds they would like to hear the songs of. Hands were raised quickly, and I played a variety of bird song for the students, they were all enjoying the bird songs. One student asked if he could hear the song of the eagle. I explained that the bald eagle doesn't really sing like other birds. That his call may not be what they would expect. When I played the call of the bald eagle and the students heard that loud screech, they all looked wide-eyed and shocked. I explained the bald eagle is the king of the sky, he doesn't sing a pretty song, his call is meant to let all the other birds know, I am king! Beware!

The students were all well behaved and polite I enjoyed talking with them about birds. The best part was when their teacher says, "Class, do we have a cheer for our guest to thank her." Then the class calls out what they call their "looking-good cheer" as they all clap to thank me. Sure made me smile for the rest of the day. A cheer for me!

What's Better Than Birding?

April 2018

Last week, I spoke to another kindergarten class about birding. This has been the third class I was asked to speak to, so I guess the teachers and students enjoyed my previous talk and word has gotten out around the school about the birding lunch lady. I kept my presentation pretty much the same as the other classes I did, shared my scrapbook about my birding adventures with the students and played a game of "What bird is that singing?" I play bird songs on my Nook and show the students a page with different birds on it and ask if anyone can pick out which bird it is that's singing. They got a few right. They all had fun listening to the songs, it's not just about getting the identity right, and it's about listening to the many different sounds birds make.

The students were very interested in the mockingbird and the many different sounds it could mimic. We talked about the birds that mimic, and I played them the sound of a blue jay mimicking a red-tailed hawk, and we talked about why they do that. I explained that the blue jay knows that if he mimics the hawk that all the little birds on the feeder will scatter for cover and that leaves the feeder all to the blue jay to enjoy by himself. They found it very interesting how smart the bird was to do that. I was very impressed by the knowledge of two young boys about the osprey and bald eagle, I sure think we have two future birders there. All the students were excited to talk about birds and each had their own story of the "bird" they saw in their yard or the school yard.

The best part for me was a couple of days later, the class comes into the lunch room carrying a large rolled up banner which they presented to me! The students stood on each end of the large paper banner and held an end to unwind it open for my viewing. It was sooo cute! My eyes were tearing up with joy. Each student had colored a bird and added it to the background they drew. And they wrote across the banner in big letters "*Thank you* for teaching us about birds!"

So the question is, "What's better than time spent birding?" Well...time spent sharing my enjoyment and knowledge of birding with the next generation, that's what!

Colorado Adventures

Rocky Mountain National Forest.

This chapter is about birding adventures with family and friends in the amazingly beautiful state of Colorado. I went to places I never would have thought to visit in this state if it weren't for my quest to find new birds! The Rocky Mountains were scary and breathe taking beautiful at the same time. This old lady got on a horse to explore the canyons in search of birds, not something I would have ever imagine doing. I overcame fears and anxiety to experience new adventures. Believe me it was worth it!

Horseback Birding

June 2012

On our first sisters' trip to Colorado, my daughter Jeanine arranged a western adventure for us! She took us to Sylvan Dale Guest Ranch for a horseback riding tour. What a beautiful area the ranch was located in. My oldest sister Sissy had never ridden on a horse before and just wasn't ready to try it out. She stayed behind but still had an enjoyable day exploring around the ranch and sitting in the shade by the stream.

So our wrangler saddled us each up on a horse and gave us a quick lesson on steering the horse. Then Chris, Becky, Jeanine, and myself headed out following the wrangler along the trail. It surely was typical western landscape, open fields with rustic wooden fences and more horses grazing or gathered in the shade under a tree. Then we crossed into a more open area with cactus. Ouch, you sure *do not* want to fall off around there!

We rode across the plains then descended into a hidden ravine. It was instantly cooler and greener with birds flitting about and singing. I asked the wrangler what bird was singing and if anyone could see it. The wrangler stopped and rode back to me and helped me locate the bird we heard singing. It was a spotted towhee, a life lister for me!

We continued on and climbed out of the ravine back onto the plateau. I was amazed at how well the horse carried me up the rocky trail out of the ravine back onto the flat open plateau. We could see numerous bank swallows flying in and out of their burrows high above us in the sandstone cliffs. As we rode on, our wrangler pointed out historic Indian caves in the high cliffs and told us stories from the past what life was like on the ranch. Very interesting history.

Alas, after a wonderful ride out on the range it was time to return to the corral. When we got back, as a test of our new found cowboy skills the wrangler told us to lead our horses across some open water and past the watering tank, without letting them drink until we dismounted in the corral. Sissy was there waiting for us, she told us about her relaxing afternoon and about all the barn swallows she had been watching. She took us to the barn where she saw them, and we watched in awe as dozens of the brilliant-colored barn swallows zoomed in and out of the rafters of the barn like little fighter jets.

Yeehaw, it was a great day! Never did I imagine I would be taking part in horseback birding on a ranch in Colorado! A wonderful experience.

Rocky Mountain High

A Great Horned Owl in its nest with young.

May 2014

I recently returned from a fantastic trip to Colorado; if any of you have considered a visit to the area, I highly recommend it. We went out for Jeanine's Graduate Ceremony from Colorado State University, she has now earned her master's degree, we are very proud of her. Because of his work schedule, it was going to be difficult for John to make the trip. Luckily Becky agreed to join me, and we were able to add a few extra days so we could really enjoy the area.

The day we arrived, we met up with Jeanine for dinner, it was nice to relax, talk and unwind from our travels and begin to adjust to the time change and high altitude. Jeanine had made a delicious chicken pot pie and a yummy peach pie for dessert. While enjoying pie I scored a new bird! Right there on the patio bird feeder was a cassin's finch, very similar to our house finch but lives at high altitudes and has a raspberry crest. I had only been in the state a few hours and I already scored a new bird. Rocky Mountain High! (Because of the high altitude, my birders' happy dance was a bit subdued but no less enthusiastic.)

The last time my sisters and I had been to Colorado, Jeanine had wanted to take us to Poudre Canyon but because of the wildfires we weren't able to go there. So this time, Jeanine made plans for a picnic lunch in the canyon. A friend of hers, Libby, met us there, we enjoyed the surroundings and talked. There were broad-tailed hummingbirds buzzing all around us, we had seen these when we were here before, but this time, we got a better view. Becky scored a good sighting, three lazuli buntings in full plumage. This is the bird Chris, Beth, and I traveled to Cape Cod to see but that bird didn't belong there and was in dull juvenile plumage, why it was there has never been answered. But these buntings were in full color, a vibrant blue, cinnamon, and cream.

Our picnic table was near the rushing river and the canyon was a known location of the American dipper, a little bird I had been hoping to see. While we were eating Jeanine spotted a pair flying low over the water, needless to say I was heading for the edge of the river ASAP! Now this little bird (about eight inches) is not colorful it's a dull gray and has a stubby little tail, but it is how it feeds and where it lives that makes it so rare. The American dipper lives in high altitudes and must be near clear fast running mountain streams with rapids. They feed on insects from the bottom of the river. They dive into the rapids and walk along the bottom searching for food. They aren't ducks, they don't have webbed feet, they actually run along the bottom of the stream with their wings half open.

I was standing on the shore of the river for a bit when suddenly I see the American dipper jump out of the water and onto a rock. Then I watch as the dipper jumps across a couple of rocks and feeds the larvae in its mouth to a baby dipper sitting flapping its wings waiting for lunch! I watched as the parent bird again jumped into the water, this time I tried to hold my breath while it was under water, but I couldn't. What an interesting comical little bird. Score a rare bird! Rocky Mountain High!

On Sunday, we packed up a picnic lunch and headed to Rocky Mountain National Park for the day. The weather was mild and sunny, but as we got higher into the mountains it got very windy, I mean the strong kind of wind that can blow something unattended right out the car window! And the mountains were covered in snow, which made the strong wind have an icy touch to it. To say the views were stunning still can't begin to describe the beauty of the landscape.

Because there was still so much snow in the mountains, the elk were staying low in the meadows; we saw dozens of elk. Some even closer than I expected! We saw mule deer and even a quick glance at a pair of big horn sheep on the rocky cliffs. At the gate, we had asked the ranger if there were any interesting bird sightings reported in the park. He told us of a great horned owl that had a nest just off the road a few miles up. Oh boy, could it be possible, was I finally going to get to see the owl I have been chasing for years now?

Success! I finally got to see the great horned owl that Katie risked her life and limb to help me find! Not only did I get to see a fantastic sighting of the owl but as a bonus it was sitting on a nest with two young owlets. Such a grand bird to see, but I have to admit her babies were the ugliest balls of fluff I've ever seen. Becky described them right, that they looked like baby Wookies. Score an elusive bird! Rocky Mountain High!

After a day in the park, we had a tasty BBQ dinner at a local restaurant in Estes Park. Jeanine suggested that we take a light hike along Lumpy Ridge, this was a place she had climbed before. Lumpy Ridge is so named because it is an area of rocky out croppings and tall cliffs with rock formations and balancing boulders. It looked like sculptures put out by Mother Nature. From Estes Park you can look up at the ridge and see the most prominent rock feature, called twin owls. How could I not want to go there?

Even though we had now been in Colorado for four days, I found myself huffing and puffing as we climbed the trail up Lumpy

Ridge. A combination of old knees and thin air made my head spin. Jeanine bounded up the trail like a mountain goat. Becky held her own and climbed ahead of me. The views from the top were again unbelievable. I really need a new word to describe the views but there really isn't any word good enough to convey what we were seeing before us.

Thanks to Jeanine's suggestion I scored another new bird! The mountain chickadee! As usual, I heard them first, and it took a bit to chase down their location. When I finally spotted one, I knew it wasn't just a mirage brought on by my lack of oxygen. For there, sitting on a rock and flitting about a juniper tree was a small flock of five Mountain chickadees! I swear the one sitting on the rock tilted its head and looked at me as if to say, "What are you looking at?" I wanted to explain to the little bird how happy I was to see him. Score another high-altitude bird! Rocky Mountain High!

I had a wonderful time visiting with Jeanine. Along with the birds mentioned above, some other new birds I saw were the Brewer's blackbird, dusky flycatcher, and black swift all life list birds for me. We saw plenty of my sisters Chris favorite black-billed magpies too, made me think of our earlier Sisters trip each time I saw one we visited a really interesting outdoor sculpture garden in Loveland, Jeanine's dog Flick kept trying to give a bronze statue of a lady his stick for her to throw. So cute!

It made me very proud when at the reception before the graduation ceremony the dean of her college and one of her professors both introduced themselves to us and had such nice things to say about Jeanine. We had fun partying with her friends, don't worry when they broke out the tequila shots we made our appropriate exit. I made special memories (prairie dogs, bunnies, birds, and windy days) with my little sister that makes me smile each time I remember them. What a great travel companion!

Rocky Mountain high!

Week of Gluttony

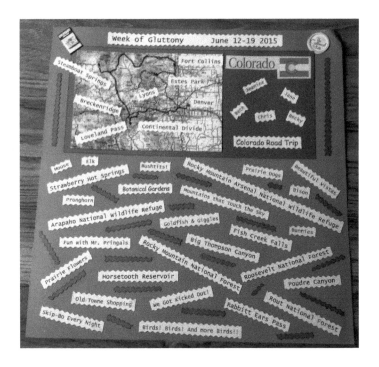

Our ladies' trip to Colorado in 2015 was an *epic* adventure to top all! My sister Becky called it our "Week of Gluttony" vacation, we enjoyed a road trip across Colorado, exploring and experiencing the many wonders of the state. It wasn't just about birding but every place we went did bring us new sightings. We all share the love of the outdoors and enjoy exploring new places. This epic trip together brought us all even closer. Many, many joyous memories for us all.

Bushtits, Hummers, Dippers, and More

Yellow-headed Blackbird in Arapaho National Wildlife Refuge.

June 2015

Chris, Becky, Beth, and I recently returned from a trip to Colorado to visit with Jeanine. I'm still on a vacation hangover. Did I really see that? Did I really do that? Was I really there? We had quite an adventure that's for sure! I'm still processing it all. Most of our adventures would be best shared around the campfire at family reunion but here is a short wrap up of our trip.

Friday and Saturday were spent in Denver, the plan was to try and acclimate to the high altitude before climbing higher into the mountains. Saturday Jeanine joined us, and we had her birthday picnic lunch at Rocky Mt. National Arsenal Wildlife Refuge. The vibrant orange Bullock's oriole and pale purple Cassin's finch serenaded us from the treetops above us. Later in the day we went to the beautiful Botanical Gardens to enjoy the landscaped grounds. It was there that we had an exciting sighting, the bushtit! For the rest of the trip the mere mention of bushtits put Becky in a fit of giggles.

Sunday was spent climbing higher into the Rocky Mts. A four-hour drive higher and higher until we made it over the Continental Divide at Loveland Pass. At nearly twelve thousand feet, it was windy and there was still snow on the ground! Looking over the edge Jeanine explains that this is where she drops over the edge on her skis and skis in the deep snow to the base of the mountain. No ski lift, no trails, no crowds. Oh, and as if to make me feel better about the danger she is putting herself in she tells me, "Don't worry, Mom, I wear an avalanche beacon." Honestly, I barely remember being there, the high altitude was kicking my butt all I could think about was "GET ME DOWN." On the plus side, Chris spotted the mountain chickadee in Breckenridge when we stopped for a great meatloaf panni lunch at a local eatery.

Monday was spent in Steamboat Springs where we really packed a lot into one day. We hiked out to the magnificent Fish Creek Falls. Along the trail, we saw the rare green-tailed towhee and the colorful western tanager. The waterfall was spectacular! Even a picture doesn't do the beauty justice; you just had to be there to feel the power of the falls, and the ground was shaking. As we sat to enjoy our picnic lunch, we could hear the broad-tailed hummingbird buzzing around us. But then we noticed a second hummer that wasn't making the buzzing sound and seemed smaller. Jeanine saw it land in a pine tree and went to investigate.

Amazing! What she sees is a rufous hummingbird sitting on a nest! She scares the bird away accidentally, and notices two baby hummers in the nest. The momma bird soon returns and was not happy about Jeanine being so close to her brood. The hummer buzzed her and Jeanine made a quick exit from the tree, she said she could feel the breeze from the bird's wings as it hovered above her head.

Later on Monday, Jeanine took us to Strawberry Hot Springs in the hills above Steamboat Springs. The water bubbles out of the ground steaming. There are terraced pools along the edge of the river, and they divert the steaming water into each pool. They mix the steaming spring water with the cold river water at different levels in each pool so you're bound to find one at the temperature that suits you. It was a relaxing afternoon after our hike to the falls. As we lounged in the warm mineral waters, we spotted the American dipper waking along the stone walls. This is a very interesting little bird that walks along the bottom of the river under water in search of bugs.

Tuesday, we began the trek over the Rockies and back to Fort Collins. But before leaving the high plains Jeanine brought us to Arapaho National Wildlife Refuge. What an amazing place! So unexpected to see a green oasis in the middle of the high-altitude scrub plains. The amount of birds and wildlife was incredible. I admit I was a bit nervous at first when we left the tarred road and set out along the bumpy dirt road into the wild plains. There were no people no buildings for as far as the eye could see. We did pass one ranger who was out patrolling the roads I felt I little more secure about that. It was as if we had stepped back in time, it gave you a sense of what our forefathers experienced as they crossed the plains in search of a better life. We added several new birds to our list, including the yellow-headed blackbird, cinnamon teal, red-necked phalarope, and more. Another of those surprising sights was watching as a northern harrier got to close to a red-winged blackbirds nest and as the harrier was chased away the blackbird jumped onto its back and held on with its claws and rode the raptor as it took off! Incredible sight!

Wednesday, Jeanine had to go back to work so we ladies were on our own. We needed a day to relax and soak in all Jeanine had just guided us through. We spent time in Old Towne Fort Collins enjoyed lunch and did some shopping. Hey a girl needs a little retail therapy now and then. Later in the afternoon we went out to Mountain Sky Ranch where Jeanine was working. Now that was an interesting drive, Jeanine said it was out in the middle of nowhere, and she meant it. GPS did what it could but the roads just ended, turned to thin rutted dirt paths. Cell coverage was spotty at best, we finally just pulled over and waited for Jeanine to come find us. Once at the ranch we got a brief tour and were able to hold a baby alpaca, it was only days old and so very, very soft.

Wednesday, after Jeanine got out of work, she took us to Horsetooth Reservoir high in the hills above Fort Collins for an evening to enjoy the stars and play some Skip-bo. We were going to have to say goodbye to Jeanine as we would be making our way back to Denver tomorrow. The last time we had been there two years ago was during the terrible wild fires, the whole area across the reservoir was in flames, we watched as helicopters scooped up water from the reservoir to douse the flames. It was so sad, we were glad to see the area had now recovered, everything was green and the houses destroyed were all rebuilt. We were enjoying gold fish crackers and giggles around the picnic table lit by Jeanine's make shift lantern. She used her water bottle full of water and attached her headlamp to the bottle thus illuminating the water with a soft glow to play cards by. Beth spotted a new bird: the spotted towhee, and there were nighthawks circling above our heads, calling and catching the evening bugs. We were having a grand time, until the ranger busted us! We were unaware the park closes at dusk. Yup, we got kicked out!

Thursday was our last day of adventure in Colorado. Becky had researched and planned a really fun day for us all. ATV rides into the Rocky Mountain National Forest, unguided, on our own for a three-hour ride! I kept thinking come on is this for real? They are just gonna give us helmets, set us up with an ATV hand us a map and say, "Have fun." Yup, that's what they did! These trails were rough too, it was quite a ride. Something I never would have thought to do but so glad Becky did, it was a blast! I drove a side-by-side UTV, with Beth as my passenger. I had a few chances to open it up and got airborne over a few bumps at 24 mph! What a rush! Did I just do that?

Friday, we boarded the plane to head home to New Hampshire. On the flight, my mind was racing with thoughts, replaying the past week of adventures. Of wild Bison rolling in tall grass, Pronghorn bounding across the open plains, elk grazing in high altitude meadows, and Moose enjoying tender greenery along the river. I thought of the tight narrow canyons, plains that went on forever and mountains that touched the sky. I thought about gold fish and giggles, playing Skip-bo every night, fun at Rabbit Ears motel and drawing names to see who got the big bed. Did I really see that? Did I really do that? Was I really there? Yes!

Colorado Bird Count

Western Kingbird.

2015

    Canada goose
    American widgeon
    Mallard
    Blue-winged teal
    Cinnamon teal
    Northern shoveler
    Redhead
    Double-crested comorant
    Great blue heron
    Cattle egret
    Turkey vulture

Bald eagle
Northern harrier
Swainson's hawk
Red-tailed hawk
Prairie falcon
Sora
American coot
Killdeer
American avocet
Red-necked phalarope
California gull
Eurasian collared-dove
White pelican
Mourning dove
Common nighthawk
Broad-tailed hummingbird
Rufous hummingbird
Northern flicker
Willow flycatcher
Western kingbird
Black-billed magpie
American crow
Common raven
Tree swallow
Northern rough-winged swallow
Bank swallow
Cliff swallow
Barn swallow
Mountain chickadee
Rock wren
American dipper
Swainson's thrush
American robin
Sage thrasher
European starling

Yellow warbler
Townsends warbler
Spotted towhee
Green-tailed towhee
Brewer's sparrow
Lark sparrow
Lark bunting
Song sparrow
Gray-headed junco
Western tanager
Bobolink
Red-winged blackbird
Yellow-headed blackbird
Western meadow lark
Common grackle
Bullock's oriole
House sparrow
Bushtit
Cassin finch
American goldfinch

Grand total: 66

Parking Lot Birds

I just returned from a trip to Colorado to visit with Jeanine. Chris, Becky, and Beth joined me on our Wild West adventure. Jeanine had suggested that this trip we should rent a cabin in the Rockies instead of staying in a hotel. It was a great idea that worked out well, we each had a private space and there was plenty of room for hanging out and playing Skip-Bo. We rented Aspen Creek cabin in the mountain town of Nathrop, the cabin was flanked on both sides by the high canyon walls of Chalk Creek Canyon.

Jeanine sure did her research, and she had mapped out a number of good birding spots for us to explore. I was a little bit concerned about my ability to hike the trails in search of new birds. With the recent diagnosis of severe arthritis in my knees, I was worried I might not be able to keep up to the others. But most of the areas Jeanine mapped out were easy walking paths, though the high altitude still gave me problems. But it didn't matter because our best sightings were parking lot birds!

We spent a day exploring Colorado Springs; we went to an area called Garden of the Gods. It is an area of red rocks that have been shaped by the forces of nature into all different shapes, the area looks like a giant sculpture garden. Unfortunately, shortly after we arrived, a strong thunderstorm blew in with heavy rain and fierce winds. We retreated to the safety of the gift shop to wait out the storm. When the clouds cleared, Becky and I went out onto the gift shop porch to sit and enjoy the cool rain-soaked air. Just as I sat down movement in the trees along the parking lot catches my eyes. I quickly grab my binoculars and scan the trees, and there he is a western scrub jay! Yay, a new bird for me!

I ran back into the gift shop looking for Chris and Beth to alert them to my great sighting but by the time they came out onto the porch the western scrub jay was gone. We tried to locate the bird again but to no avail, he had left the area, as Becky reminds us often "birds fly." But that sighting was just the first of other even better parking lot birds we would see.

We spent a day exploring the small town of Salida, they were holding an arts festival with a parade of the Mud People, which was quite interesting. Jeanine brought us to a great restaurant along the river, we sat and watched as rafters and kayakers sped by trying to navigate the rapids. They all made it no one fell in, but it did confirm to me that white water rafting was not something I wanted to try.

Before we got into town, we stopped at a small park Jeanine had found along the river to look for birds. I pulled the car into the parking space, and before I even turned it off, we get a sighting! There in front of us on the lower branches of a tree is a brilliant orange Bullock's oriole! Not only do we get a great bird sighting, but we get quite a show as the bird is dive bombing a squirrel and flying about the branches chattering loudly. That oriole did not like that squirrel. Another great parking lot bird sighting!

On another day, we stopped for a picnic lunch in Buena Vista at a park. I pulled the car into a parking space and directly in front of us is a table under large willow trees next to the river. We settle down to eat. Suddenly I see a bird fly onto the tree trunk, it looks familiar but different. We pull out the bird guides and study the markings and confirm it is a pygmy nuthatch. Yet another parking lot bird!

We traveled to the high-altitude town of Leadville to take a train ride up into the mountains, at 10,151 feet it was the highest town we visited. The train ride was fantastic! Boy did we climb higher and higher, at times the train seemed to be clinging to the side of the mountain I wondered how it stayed on the tracks. But the views were remarkable. Before we got on the train, we stopped for a picnic lunch at Turquoise Lake, a beautiful high-altitude lake surrounded by snow-topped mountains. I pull the car into the parking spot; we unload our picnic gear and head for a table by the water. Then Beth catches sight of a dark bird landing on the side of a tree. We pull out the bird guides and confirm we just saw a Williamson's sapsucker! Super cool sighting, yet again a parking lot bird!

We saw a total of thirty-six different species of birds in Colorado. I saw seven new birds to add to my life list, which now totals 307 species. We saw a number of birds just hanging around the cabin sitting on the deck, I added the black-headed grosbeak, western wood peewee, and the gray flycatcher to my list. Beth also added the green-tailed towhee and mountain blue bird to her list. I was so worried about rather I was going to be able to keep up and explore the area for birds, but it didn't matter, we saw great sightings sitting on the deck, riding in the car and the best sightings of all were the parking lot birds!

We enjoyed beautiful scenery, soaking in hot springs, shopping in interesting shops, eating together around the big table, playing Skip-Bo and just relaxing together. Deer wandered through the cabin yard and as we sat on the deck with our morning coffee, we were buzzed by broad-tailed hummingbirds. And we had multiple great parking lot bird sightings!

Birds We Saw in Colorado

Black-billed Magpie.

June 2017

Pygmy nuthatch
Western scrub jay
Western wood pewee
Mountain bluebird
Violet-green swallow
Black-headed grosbeak
Williamson's sapsucker
Gray flycatcher
Green-tailed towhee
Spotted towhee
Rough-winged swallow

Tree swallow
Bank swallow
Cliff swallow
House wren
Turkey vulture
Western meadowlark
Mallard
Broad-tailed hummingbird
Canada goose
House sparrow
Northern flicker, red-shafted
Rock pigeon
American pelican
Black-billed magpie
Mourning dove
Common raven
American crow
Ruby-crowned kinglet
Common goldeneye
Yellow warbler
Red-winged blackbird
American robin
Bullock's oriole
American coot
Black-capped chickadee

Total count: 36 species

Colorado High

June 2019

I just returned from another trip to Colorado. But this time, I went by myself. As I was unpacking, my mind was flooded with thoughts of all the birds I saw and the adventures I had. The main reason for the trip west was to see Jeanine and Charley's new house, and spend time visiting with them. They were great hosts! I love their new house and its location, the view from the back patio was fantastic. With the Rocky Mountains in the distance and open marsh land in the foreground filled with bird activity, I enjoyed morning coffee sitting out on the patio listening to all the birds, in the evening it was relaxing watching the fiery sunset and refreshing to sit out there with the cool breeze and listen to the distant freight train blow its horn as it passed through town. So happy for them they worked hard and searched for a while but definitely found that perfect first house, don't we all remember that special milestone in life.

Of course, it's no secret that my hobby is birding, and they had planned three days of sightseeing around possible bird sightings for me. On Saturday, we met up with Charley's mom, Carla, and the four of us headed to the Rocky Mountain National Park. We enjoyed a picnic lunch at the base of the mountains and Carla spotted the first bird of the day, the brilliant blue Steller's jay! Okay, I understand the rules of the park state: "Do not feed wildlife," but I just happened to drop a few of my cheese curls, and the jay scooped them up before I could. Sorry, LOL. I also watched a rock wren sitting on a log singing his heart out serenading all the picnickers enjoying the area. Broad-tailed hummingbirds were buzzing back and forth enjoying all the wildflowers. All this bird activity only minutes after we passed through the gate into the park! I sure felt confident more sightings were to come.

After lunch, we began the ascent to the top of the mountains. The climb to the top is very steep! And there are no guardrails on the sides of the road. I was confident in Charley's driving but still gasped with fear when I looked down, out the window! I have to apologize to Charley for grabbing his arm in anxiety. Now Jeanine knows very well that I am not a fan of heights and that the high altitude bothers me, she was thoughtful enough to buy me an oxygen bottle to carry with me. Geez who ever would have thought I would be grateful someone paid for a disposable can of air at the convenience store for me? Believe me it worked for me!

When we got to Rainbow Curve, which is the pull off area, we sisters had turned around at when we visited and is the beginning of the climb above the tree line I told them, "Okay, I'm fine, beautiful view, lets head back down." But then Jeanine tells me, "Come on, Mom, the summit is only around the next curve and then you can get a chance to see the Clarks nutcracker and the elk herds." So I took a snort of air from my oxygen can and agreed, one more curve.

Three curves later the summit was still not in sight? There were snow banks taller than the car! Everywhere you looked was snow, rocks and sky. Did not expect to see snow in mid-June. My heart was racing, I took another puff of air. I asked Jeanine, "How much farther is the summit?"

She answers, "Just around the next curve, you can do it, Mom." I felt embarrassed, gee what kind of impression was I making on Carla and Charley? I had to pull it together, and just when I doubted my ability to control my anxiety, as we came around the next curve, we spotted the elk herd! It is amazing to see these majestic animals in their native habitat. There were little baby elks running alongside their parents. There were about a dozen elks running along the high ridge. I tell myself okay, Jane take another puff of air! Enjoying what you are seeing.

A few curves later, we finally came up to the summit! There it was the summit lodge sitting atop the rocks. We sisters sure missed out on a great gift shop and snack bar when we turned around to soon. The views were beyond amazing, we were looking down on the clouds. At 11,796 feet, it certainly was the highest land I'd ever, ever stood on! Jeanine spoke to the park ranger asking about any interesting bird sightings he could suggest. He shows her on the map where to stop on the way down to see the Clark's nutcracker. This high-altitude bird would be a very special life list bird for me, if we could find one.

So we begin the long drive down, which is still scary. Take another puff of air Jane! We stop at Rainbow Curve where the ranger said to look. And sure enough, we barely get out of the car and Jeanine yells, "There they are, Mom!" Over the edge on the tops of the pine trees sit three Clark's nutcrackers! Score a new life list bird for me, yippee!

Sure, Jeanine tricked me to get me to the top of the mountains, but it was worth it. I can't guarantee I'd be any less anxious doing it again, but I do feel confident that with a can of air in my hand and a bird guide in my backpack I can handle getting Colorado high!

Those Doofus Juveniles

Boy, Jeanine and Charley's yard had a *lot* of bird drama! Sitting on the back patio was like watching a soap opera called All My Children, a series set in a quiet neighborhood in Fort Collins Colorado. The story of the trials and tribulations of an American robin family and of a young red-tailed hawk. The villain of the story is Monty the three-legged cat. The hero and heroine are homeowners Charley and Jeanine, always ready to spring into action to help save their avian neighbors.

In the world of birds fledgling season is the most dangerous time in their lives. In human terms, think of it as those teenage years, time for the young to begin to test their wings, explore the world and set out on their own to make their mark in this world. For bird parents it's double/triple the work. When they are babies and cuddled up in the nest safe and sound, the parents always know where they are. Dinner time is one stop at the nest, regurgitate equal portions to all, and settle down in the nest to keep everyone safe and warm. Good night.

But during fledgling season daily life changes dramatically for both the parents and the young. The young are encouraged to get up out of bed! To sit on the edge of the nest and stretch their wings, to step off the edge onto the surrounding branches and test the strength of their talons, flap their wings and hold on. To stay put until it is determined they are ready to fly away. Wait for Mom and Dad to bring home dinner. When the parents feel they are ready, they will sit in a tree close by the nest and loudly call and call for the young to follow them. The parents will fly off with the young following and show them the way of the world outside the nest. Well, that's the parents plan but of course every nest has that one rebellious fledgling that has to test the limits.

That's where Monty the three-legged villain comes into the picture. Since his traumatic accident that caused Monty to need to have his back leg amputated, he has been mainly an indoor cat. Jeanine does let him outside now, and then, she has a neat tracking device attached to his collar, and she can watch his movements on her phone. But a cat will be a cat, never underestimate an amputee! It seems one of the robin fledglings left the nest too early and fell to the ground unable to fly back up out of the grass. It was left sitting there on the ground calling and calling for help from its parents. Monty found him first!

We were sitting on the back patio when we heard the commotion, the robin parents were going crazy squawking and flying about. Jeanine jumps up and yells, "Where's Monty!?" She runs into the house gets her phone and checks on his location; she runs out the door to the front yard. Monty has the baby robin pinned to the ground. OH NO! She grabs Monty and brings him back into the house. Then she goes back out to check on the baby robin, it appears to be okay. She carefully tries to direct the little robin toward the bushes where it can seek some shelter. She can see the parents are still watching.

Over the three days, I was there this scenario played out more than once. At one point, while I was sitting on the patio and Monty was walking around in the grass I watched as both robin parents dive bombed him, and he ran like heck up onto the patio and hid under the table. I guess Monty learned a lesson there, leave that baby bird alone! The final outcome of that doofus juvenile robin is still uncertain. Hopefully it smartened up and flew away with his siblings and parents.

More birdy drama happened soon enough! Charley was on the side of the house fixing the hose when he suddenly comes around the corner to the patio and yells, "Hey, Jeanine, what's that big bird sitting on the front lawn doing?!" Jeanine jumps up yelling, "Where's Monty?!" and she runs around the house to the front yard. There she finds a large hawk sitting on the ground. It doesn't appear to be injured but lets her walk right up to him. That's unusual. The hawk flaps his wings and tries to fly up to sit on the fence but falls down to the ground. He was huge! I pull up my bird app and try to figure out what kind of hawk it is. I swear its feet were bigger than mine! Its beak was quite the weapon. By its molted coloring, I figured it to be a juvenile red-tailed hawk. The tables were turned this bird was a threat to little Monty, who only weighs eight pounds, it could have grabbed him for a dinner. The hawk tried a few more times to jump up onto the fence, and then it shakes his wings tilts his head and gives us that "What are you looking at?" look and then walks away across the road into a neighbor's yard. Strange behavior.

Jeanine was concerned about the hawk's safety and called the Raptor Rescue Center in town. The man she spoke to tells her it's fledgling season in Fort Collins and that they had received multiple calls about "Those doofus juvenile red-tailed hawks roaming around the neighborhoods!" He said as long as the hawk didn't seem injured that the best course of action was to leave it alone and watch your pets. Jeanine decided Monty was under house arrest until fledgling season was over for his own safety and the safety of those doofus juveniles roaming about. The last update was that she saw an adult red-tailed hawk calling and flying overhead and heard a response call from the wetlands behind the house. Every fledgling season, it never fails that at least one baby bird leaves the nest too soon. But who knows, maybe it's the birds siblings playing a hoax on them and sent them out on a snipe hunt. After all, one less mouth begging for food meant more for the others.

Unethical Birder

June 2019

Before leaving on my solo trip to Colorado to visit with Jeanine and Charley, I did do some research to see just what birds I might get to see. Surprisingly I came upon some very interesting news, a *new* species of scrub jay was spotted in Lory State Park, Fort Collins Colorado! Right where I was going to be! The bird was thought to be a western scrub jay, which is common in Colorado but ornithologist found it had a different song and didn't look quite the same as the western. DNA testing confirmed it was *not* a western scrub jay. It was named after the ornithologist that found it, woodhouse scrub jay. No question about it I had to get out to Lory State Park ASAP!

Jeanine and Charley agreed to get me there. We arrived at the park and stopped at the first picnic area, like most jays it was most likely if the Woodhouse's was around, it would seek out people, that equals food. We got out of the car and immediately I heard *chee… chee…chee…jreet*, typical jay kind of call! The call was coming from inside some dense scrub brush along the edge of the picnic area. I quickly returned the call *chee…chee…chee…jreet*! I had my staple snack crackers in a baggie, which I began to shake as I called to the bird hiding hoping to leer it out into view. Nothing. I asked Charley to find some small rocks and throw them into the brush to try and flush the bird out. He obliged but yet again, *nothing*. Jeanine ventured through the scrub brush to get closer to the spot, when suddenly from behind her a black-billed magpie flew into the bushes! "Mom!" she yells. Looks like it's likely just a fledgling magpie hiding in there. We need to leave it alone. Well, as we had learned it is fledgling season in Fort Collins.

Okay, so I admit I was partaking in unethical birding, teasing the bird by mimicking a call, tempting it with unhealthy snacks, and throwing rocks into the bushes to scare it out. I apologize to fellow birders and to Jeanine and Charley for roping them into unethical birding. But come on! I had a chance to see a new species of bird that isn't even listed in bird guides yet! I remember the experience when I was visiting Sissy, Keith and Kris, and we got to see the endangered Florida scrub jay on Merritt Island. I remember at the trail head all the signs stating Do Not Feed Wildlife and even signs saying, "It Is Illegal to Feed the Scrub Jays, Violators Will Be Prosecuted." But the awe and excitement as I called in the jays, and they landed in our hands to eat the snacks we had for them was worth breaking the law. Rest assured I do respect the laws, and I do volunteer to help protect Mother Nature and God's Creatures. But yet again I took part in unethical birding!

We did return to the park again another day but never did see the woodhouses' scrub jay. We stopped at the ranger station and asked about any resent sightings, and he tells us there have not been any resent sightings of the woodhouses' scrub jay since June 18, I was there on the twenty-eighth. Even though I never did see that new bird, I did have a great time birding with family and exploring beautiful Lory State Park. Fun memories for all!

Though I am beginning to wonder was it all just a snipe hunt to fool all us tourists?

Green with Envy

On my last full day in Colorado, we went back to Lory State Park for the day. It's a lovely area just outside of Fort Collins by Horsetooth Reservoir. It is typical western landscape with wide open fields and rocky outcroppings of red sand stone and rolling hills of scrub brush. We packed a picnic lunch and headed out. I was looking forward to getting another chance at finding the woodhouses' scrub jay.

When we got there, Jeanine had a particular site in mind, an area by the water under the trees for shade. Perfect! Though I will admit after we parked that the walk along the dirt path across the open prairie in the hot sun seemed longer than it was. I grabbed Flick's leash and the little dog helped pull me along, the water was in sight almost there! Along the path, there were numerous flowering cactus to enjoy, certainly not something I get to see in New Hampshire. Gee, I was complaining about the long hot walk and all I had to carry was my backpack! Jeanine and Charley both had their paddleboards strapped to their backs, Charley was also carrying our picnic cooler and Jeanine was also carrying a folding chair for my comfort, with Revi on leash as the excited dog raced toward the water. Oh, to be young again!

We made it to the perfect spot next to the water under the tall Cottonwood trees and there was now a cool breeze coming through the canyon across the lake. I played fetch with Flick for a while, throwing sticks into the water for him, believe me I gave up throwing sticks before he gave up fetching them. Boy, that little dog loves to play fetch! Jeanine and Charley set off into the lake on their paddleboards with both dogs along for the ride. I was happy to sit in the shade under the trees munching on my sandwich while listening to the birds. It was kind of magical; as the breeze came through the cottonwood trees, they dropped their puffs of cotton, sort of like dande-lions from a tree. The fluffy white puffs floated around me and birds were singing like crazy! Was this real or was I in a Disney movie?

I saw a total of sixteen different bird species just while sitting there under the trees! A bullocks oriole sat on a low branch and ser-enaded me. A western tanager flew low overhead and landed in the bushes behind me giving me an up-close look at this beautiful bird. As I was sitting, munching on my sandwich of all things, suddenly a Cordilleran flycatcher lands on a branch barely arm's length away! This was a new life list bird for me Yippee! But all the while I sat there one bird was singing loudly from way atop the trees. It was so high in the tree I couldn't get a good look at it other than its silhou-ette against the blue sky. It was the size and shape of a vireo, sang a long complex song like a vireo, but what kind could it be? I checked the Birds of Lory State Park pamphlet I got at the park ranger station that did list the plumbeous vireo and the warbling vireo as being seen in the park. I had limited cell service so I couldn't play my bird songs app to compare the songs to what I was hearing. So I listened intently trying to memorize the song so I could look it up later.

When we got back to the house while relaxing on the patio, I lis-tened to the bird songs on my birding app. But neither the plumbeous nor warbling vireo song sounded right. What bird did I see!? Oh well, that's how birding goes sometimes, confusion. Then the next day, I get a Rare Bird Alert on my phone! I have the American Birding Association Rare Bird Alert app. Which sends out alerts when a rare bird is sighted, giving you the location, time, etc. Of all sightings guess what was seen. A very rare yellow-green vireo from Mexico was spotted in the Front Range area of Colorado! Fort Collins is in the Front Range area. Could it be possible that was the bird I saw?! I'll never know. When I did listen to the recordings of this rare Mexican bird, I couldn't remember the song I had heard. I just wasn't confident enough to count that super rare bird on my life list. I have to wonder just *who* are these Colorado birders seeing these super rare birds? I was green with envy of them that's for sure. Are they real?

Or just jokers sending us tourists out on a snipe hunt for laughs?

The Great Snipe Hunt

Okay, so I saved the best story of my 2019 adventures in Colorado for the last. Now have you noticed my reference to a snipe hunt in the last couple of stories? How many of you Googled snipe hunt to figure out what it is all about? Well, for those inquiring minds a snipe hunt is known as a joke/right of passage played on adolescents coming of age. Where the older boys would send the youngest out on a mission to find a snipe and catch it, and they would be given a burlap bag to carry it back in as proof. Yet to each group the snipe was a mythical creature, each group had their own description of what a snipe looked like and sounded like. And the older kids would often hide in the bushes and make noises pretending to be a snipe to fool the hunter. Then all those in the hunting party would all insist that they just saw one and excitingly point in the sky but of course the hunter saw nothing because nothing was there! So a snipe hunt is a wild goose chase joke!

A couple of days after Jeanine moved into her new house, she called to tell me that there was a bird calling out in the marsh behind the house that she didn't recognize, she wondered if I could give her any idea what it might be. She tried to describe the sound she was hearing, she asks me, "Can you hear it? It's calling now!" She tells me she is out on the patio and has her phone on speaker. But I heard nothing! I suggest that she look up birds that would live in the habitat behind the house and try to listen to some of the bird calls to try and identify the bird. I wish her Good Luck. A few days later she calls again to tell me that she saw the bird while walking the dogs out on the path that goes around the marshland, she tells me it's a *snipe*! Wow, cool, I say, that would be a new life list bird for me. I tell her I'm anxious to arrive for my visit and get to see the snipe for myself!

The first morning I was there we were sitting out on the patio enjoying morning coffee and Jeanine suddenly says, "Mom, listen, the snipe is calling!" Ummm, I didn't hear anything unusual? I heard red-winged blackbirds and Robins but that's all. Jeanine and Charley both had to work so I had the day to myself that was the plan I was fine with that. Gave me a chance to acclimate to the high altitude and time change. I spent the morning enjoying looking around and relaxing. I walked around the yard and into the marshland a bit, but not being familiar with the area I didn't want to venture to far from the house alone. The only birds I saw or heard on my walk were red-winged blackbirds, robins, brewers blackbirds and the common yellow-throat but no snipe! Was Jeanine just playing a trick or me?

Did this snipe she keeps talking about really exist?

Jeanine only worked a half day, and when she got home, she suggested we take a walk along the trails into the marshland to look for this allusive snipe. Sure enough, we didn't get far when she stops and says, "Mom, listen there it is!" as she is pointing across the marsh to the other side. Yup, I heard it! Or I heard something but couldn't see anything. The sound was coming from across the small stream almost seemed like it was in the backyard of one of the houses on the opposite side of the marsh. I considered trying to jump across the stream to get to the other side but nixed that idea soon as the reality was pretty unlikely that I would make it without falling into the water! Jeanine grabs my arm and tells me, "We could drive over to that side, I'm sure those neighbors won't mind if we walk through their yard to try and find the snipe."

I answer, "Ummmm, no, thank you, we can try again later."

Jeanine and Charley were just great hosts! They planned fun adventures for me every day, they put up with my whinny anxiety as we drove to the top of the Rockies. I hope I didn't bruise Charley's arm as I grabbed him in fear on the drive up to the mountain tops. I enjoyed our day in Rocky Mountain National Park and in Lory State Park, Colorado is indeed a beautiful state. I especially enjoyed spending time with the two of them, relaxing on the patio, dinner on the grill, and we even watched the movie The Big Year together, to give Charley an introduction to the crazy world of birding. *And yes!* I did finally hear the snipe right off the patio winnowing in the marsh! But even though some birders agree it is legal to count a bird on your life list even if you only heard it, I personally think it unethical, and I will only count a bird I *see*.

On the last day of my vacation after supper, Jeanine suggested we go out on a final snipe hunt. She suggests we should ride bikes along the path, that we can go farther and faster giving me a better chance at finding the snipe. Well, it sounded like a good idea, but it's been years since I was on a bike, in fact the last time I was on a bike was there in Fort Collins on our first sisters' trip in 2012 to visit Jeanine in college. But Charley was so kind, he got out one of their extra bikes and lowered the seat to fit me better, and he explains that I can just leave the bike in the gear he set, not to worry about shifting.

Still, with my arthritic knees, it was difficult to swing my leg up and over the bar, but Charley showed me a trick to lower the bike down sideways and step over the bar then slowly raise the bike under me.

I was shaky, but we headed out together on bikes for our snipe hunt!

Like a flash Jeanine and Charley set off on the trail with Revy and Flick running along beside them! They kept looking back to check on me, I was slower but still upright. Jeanine was right we sure could cover a lot more territory and soon stopped to scan the marsh. There in front of us was a large flock of red-winged blackbirds all sitting in the tall reeds noisily chattering. Jeanine got off her bike and was walking in the tall grass toward the noisy flock with the dog's right behind her. She turns back toward me and yells as she is pointing, "Mom, there's the snipe, in the reeds in the stream!"

I quickly get off my bike and head toward where she is pointing. But the dogs assume she is talking to them, and they both excitingly run off barking in the direction she is pointing. Of course, we all know what happens next! The dogs flush the large flock of birds out of the tall reeds, and they all scatter to our right away from us into the distance. Jeanine yells, "Mom, look, the snipe is flying away with that flock!" Well, I did see one bird a different size and color than all the red-winged blackbirds, but was it really the snipe?

The three of us stood watching as the large flock settled back down in the tall grass and reeds far across the marsh. They asked me, "Okay, did you see the snipe, can you count it now?" I tell them, well sort of, yes, I heard it. Yes, I saw a brown bird flying among all the blackbirds, but still not a really good sighting. I thank them for their effort. Jeanine and Charley are huddled together taking.

I start getting ready to get back on the bike to leave when Jeanine says, "Mom, wait, we have an idea!" She tells me Charley has offered to ride his bike back along the trail cross onto the street and come up to the distant end of the marsh where he can come back onto the trail from the opposite side and see if he can flush the flock up again and toward us. Wow! Could this possibly work? Okay, let's try! Charley takes off on his bike at full speed; soon, we can't see him. Minutes later he suddenly comes bursting out of the bushes on his bike into the marsh heading straight for the stream. The flock of blackbirds noisily burst out of the reeds and fly straight at Jeanine and I! Charley is waving and pointing as the flock races toward us. BINGO! There among the blackbirds is the medium-sized brown snipe! It flies straight at me, passes feet away from me. It turns as it passes me giving me a perfect view of his belly and wings and his long-curved beak! No binoculars needed. Thanks to Charley I got to see my first Wilsons snipe to add to my life list! The great snipe hunt was a success!

Colorado Bird Sightings
June 2019

Bullocks Oriole.

Canada goose	Mallard ducks
Turkey vulture	American crow
Red-tailed hawk	Prairie falcon
Mourning dove	White-throated swift
Broad-tailed hummingbird	Red-shafted northern flicker
Eastern kingbird	Western kingbird
Blue jay	Steller's jay
Black-billed magpie	Cliff swallow
Rock wren	American robin

European starling	Common yellow-throat
Western tanager	Lazuli bunting
Chipping sparrow	Red-winged blackbird
Brewer's blackbird	Bullocks oriole
House finch	House sparrow

Life List New Birds

Cordilleran flycather	Clark's nutcracker	Wilson's snipe

Florida Adventures

Pic of Natural Florida area.

This chapter is about my many adventures and discoveries in the state of Florida. Thanks to the generous hospitality of my family members who gave me a bed to sleep in, food to fill my belly and drove me around to explore so many natural sites. If it weren't for birding there sure were a lot of beautiful places I might not have ever been to. Believe me the state of Florida is more than just amusement parks and beautiful relaxing beaches. The less frequented natural areas are a definite go-to place to put on your things to-do list.

Go Back!

February 2014

I have just returned from a fantastic vacation to Florida. I have to thank my wonderful hosts, Sissy and Bill, if it weren't for their hospitality and chauffeur service, I wouldn't be able to take such a great trip south each February. This has been an especially cold and snowy winter here in New England, and it was so nice to step off that plane and see greenery and feel the warm sun.

Sissy and Bill are always so thoughtful, they had researched a new place for me to visit, Corkscrew Swamp Sanctuary. This is a protected five-hundred-year-old bald cypress forest in Naples Florida. The trees rise nearly one hundred feet above the red maple and strangler figs among the swampy forest floor. They have a two-and-a-half mile boardwalk that winds through the swamp. Reports were that a very unusual bird, the painted bunting, had made the sanctuary his home. Of course, this piqued my interest so off we went in search of this rare little bird.

Upon arrival we ask at the ranger station if there were any recent sightings of the painted bunting. We are told it makes regular visits to the bird feeders hanging in the courtyard, but that it hadn't been seen since early that morning. We sit and enjoy our lunch watching the feeders all the time but to no avail. We decide to head out into the swamp to see what we can find. It is a beautiful place, the boardwalk is wide and has railings, which I later understand is to keep the alligators from climbing up onto the boardwalk.

We see plenty of birds, delicate jeweled butterflies, pastel orchids growing in the forks of trees, but no painted bunting. Along the boardwalk, there are areas with covered benches where you can sit to enjoy the beautiful surroundings and get out of the weather if need be. Every now and then, there are short side trails you can take to a point of interest or special view. Park rangers patrol the board-walk and place index cards along the railings indicating an interest-ing sighting or point of interest of the day. We can hear a musical call high in the trees and wonder if it may be the painted bunting. We ask a ranger if he has seen a painted bunting, he tells us to go back a bit to a side trail, that they have put up a feeder in the woods and the bunting often visits. So we turn around and head back; there were some colorful butterflies flitting about but no painted bunting. We walk onward.

We are getting deeper into the swamp now, and we start to see many pretty interesting flowering plants and small alligators resting. We see yellow-rumped warblers, black and white warblers, and palm warblers but no painted bunting. We walk on. We meet a man with fancy camera equipment and ask him if he has seen the painted bun-ting. He tells us to go back to the courtyard of the ranger station, that he got a good picture of one on the bird feeder. We walk on.

Next, we meet a ranger and ask if there are any interesting sight-ings, he tells us that up head there is a roosting barred owl just off the boardwalk. He tells us to watch for an index card on the railing with *owl* and an arrow pointing the direction to look written on it. Sissy is very interested! She has heard the barred owl many times while in Pittsburg but never seen one. I ask him if he has seen the painted bunting, he tells me to go back to the courtyard and watch for the bird at the feeders. We walk on scanning the railing in search of the index card.

It seemed like we walked for an awful long time and never did see that index card so the next ranger we came upon we asked about the owl sighting. The ranger tells us, "Oh, dear, go back! You missed it!" Ugg…so we turned around once again and headed back; it was quite a ways back/ I still don't know how we missed it. But sure enough, there was the barred owl sitting peacefully in a tree just watching us watch him. Sissy was very happy. In fact, I do believe she broke out in a little birders' happy dance. We walk on a short distance when Sissy decides that she would like to take a picture of the owl, so she goes back to snap a few pictures. Then we walk on in search of the painted bunting.

We come to Lettuce Lake, which is just what you would expect a bowl of water with bits of lettuce floating across the top to look like. We see many herons, an anhinga, and a red-shouldered hawk; but the main draw are the alligators. There is one of the biggest alligators I've ever seen sunning himself along the shore. I overhear a woman asking the ranger if it is safe to be so close to the alligators, and he tells her that's why they have the railing on the boardwalk. It's not to keep the people in but the alligators out that they can't climb up and over the edge. I don't know about that, some of those smaller alligators looked like they would fit between the rails. I ask the ranger about the painted bunting, and again I'm told, "Go back to the ranger station." I give up. We decide to walk faster and get back to try and see the bird.

But is seems Sissy dropped her sweatshirt somewhere along the way. I was in shorts and T-shirt and sweating but Sissy was concerned that it would be chilly so she had draped her sweatshirt over the strap of her binoculars in case she needed it. Yup, turn around and go back yet again. Luckily, she didn't have to go far; a ranger had found it and returned it to her. By this time, we had gone back so many times I think we added at least an extra mile to the walk. We finally get back to the ranger station and go straight to the bird feeders set up in the courtyard hoping to see the painted bunting. Nope, it's not there. We did get to see the cutest little birds, common ground doves, they look like mourning doves but are twice as small. We talk to other birders there while watching the feeders. I met a man who was from Massachusetts. He tells me about a time he was on Plum Island during the eagle festival weekend and saw the snowy owl in the field on the farm equipment just before the bridge, just like I did that same day with Chris and Beth. How strange to think we had been there at the same time and then to meet in Florida.

Then it happens! From out of nowhere there sitting on the feeder in front of me is the painted bunting! I can't even speak; I grab Sissy's arm and mumble something unintelligible. Finally, we get to see the bird we had been searching for all day. He is beautiful, in shades of blue, red, green and yellow. Everyone crowds around the window, camera's snapping, enjoying this small vibrant bird. I run out side onto the dinning deck and get to take couple of pictures. Success! Birders' happy dance time!

I had a great day in a wonderful, serene, mystical place. And I can definitely say this is some place that I must go back too soon.

Operation Pink Bird

February 2014

I have been taking a vacation to Florida for the past five years now and one of my goals has been to see the roseate spoonbills. The first year I was there I got a brief peek at a couple through the scrub brush on Sanibel Island, but I wanted a better view. It has been reported that the oil spill of a couple of years ago damaged the spoonbills nesting habitat and that was why there has been fewer birds in recent years. So each trip I make to Florida, Sissy and Bill try to find the roseate spoonbill for me.

This year I extended my stay so that I could spend some time with my nephew Keith and his wife Kris. They used to live in Texas and recently moved to Florida, much to Sissy's delight. While in Texas they were able to see flocks of these beautiful pink shore birds when they visited Galveston Island. I was so envious. I enjoyed their pictures but wanted to see some for myself.

Since Keith and Kris moved to Florida, they have been able to explore their surroundings, and it seemed like everywhere they went they saw spoonbills. Come on, they even saw some in a drainage ditch at their local CVS store! So Keith appointed himself commander of Operation Pink Bird. He and Kris were determined to help me find the elusive roseate spoonbill.

On Saturday, we arranged to meet at a state park that they had seen spoonbills at often, Myakka River State Park. With Keith in the lead, we headed out on our quest. He knew all the locations of the perfect habitat areas, some off the beaten path I never would have noticed. We scanned every wet land spot with our binoculars. We saw plenty of herons, white ibis, a few glossy ibis, and a red-shoul-dered hawk. There were many alligators in the water and sunning themselves on shore, but sadly no roseate spoonbills.

It looked like Operation Pink Bird was going to be a failure. But it really didn't matter, I was enjoying spending time with them looking at the birds. Sharing my hobby with them. It has been at least ten years since I had seen Keith and Kris, yet in seemed like only yesterday. I was having a great day just being in the outdoors enjoying their company.

Since it seemed like we weren't going to see any spoonbills, I had to let them in on a secret. I didn't want Keith to feel like he let me down. I told them about a river boat ride Sissy and I took the day before up the Peace River estuary to a Wood Stork rookery. Sharing the rookery with the Storks was a small group of roseate spoonbills. Finally after five years, I was able to get a good look at them. So no worries; I spotted my roseates. Keith can keep his title as commander of Operation Pink Bird, for I will be back...

Fine Dining

A Crested Caracara.

February 2014

Fine dining, just what is the definition of fine dining? Is it the food, the surroundings, or the presentation? I guess it all depends on whom you ask. My philosophy is simple, fill the belly and move on. With my diabetes and food allergies, I'm just not into experimenting or trying new things with food. Makes you think about the way of nature, what do birds and animals consider fine dining?

When Bill, Sissy, and I were heading to visit with Keith and Kris at Myakka River State Park, we traveled through Florida cattle country. This is one of the few areas that the unusual Crested Caracara lives. Bill and Sissy had seen one once before while traveling in this area so Bill was on the lookout for one for me. Sure enough, he spotted one on the side of the road, I didn't see it, but he turned around and went back for me. There sitting on a fence post was the odd-looking crested caracara!

The bird is from Mexico and considered a threatened/endangered species in Florida so this was a very good sighting for me. They are large birds with huge yellow chicken like feet, and he looks like he is wearing a black toupee. They are like vultures and eat road kill or other dead carrion they can find. The bird sat patiently on the fence post for a few pictures only because he was guarding a recent road kill that he didn't want me to eat. Yuck, umm, fine dining? I think not!

When we were looking for the roseate spoonbills in Myakka River State Park with Keith and Kris, we stopped along a bridge to scan the wetlands. There were a few people there fishing and of course the alligators as well. There were a couple of good-sized ones there, and I watched one rolling and splashing in the water and wondered what he might be eating. There are signs posted everywhere warning people to not feed the alligators. I wondered if a more appropriate sign would have been warning people of "No Swimming" allowed. But perhaps the bridge is a fine dining spot for the gators. To each his own.

Keith took us off the beaten path to a back wetlands area that he had seen roseate spoonbills at before. We could see a large flock of vultures, and as we got closer, we could see why they were all hanging around. They were crowded around a dead animal; some were sitting on top of it. It was hard to even tell what the animal was there were so many vultures surrounding it, and they were making this awful grunting sound. The vultures were pecking and pulling at the animal, Keith said he could make out a snout and figured it was a wild hog. I watched as the vultures pulled at its hind quarter causing the animals leg to jerk skyward. I considered going back to the car for my camera but I'm not sure if it was the heat, low blood sugar or the grotesque scene before me, but I was feeling woozy. It was time to move on. Fine dining? I don't know, that's a long stretch in my opinion.

After an enjoyable day of birding at Mayakka River State Park, we all decided to head to Venice Beach Jetty for a picnic dinner. After a quick stop at the deli for sandwiches, we were on our way. The jetty is one of Sissy and Bills favorite picnic places, and I can sure see why. The water is beautiful and at times we have been there and watched as a dolphin or two would glide past. It was crowded but Bill found a nice parking space along the end of the jetty with a picnic table free. Unfortunately, the weather had taken on a cold chill, well Floridian cold the temp was in the sixties, and the wind had picked up. But that wasn't going to stop us, we still sat outside and enjoyed our sandwiches and watched the goings on of the birds, boats and people. It was a nice end to a nice day. Fine dining? Well, yes, it was!

Here in New England, it seems like old man winter is never going to loosen his grip on us, but we know spring will be here sooner or later. But as I sit at my kitchen table and eat my dinner looking at the snow-covered ground and barren trees it seems very far away indeed. But I can look at the picture of the beautiful sunset we enjoyed along Sanibel Causeway while eating our picnic dinner, close my eyes and imagine I am in paradise. I have to again thank Bill and Sissy for their hospitality, if it wasn't for their opening arms, I wouldn't be able to enjoy a vacation in Florida each February. And it was an added bonus to get to spend time with Keith and Kris. I look forward to making my reservation for the same time same place next year for more fine dining!

Big Day

February 2015

Thanks to my Florida family, I had a fantastic break from the cold and snow of our New England winter. I wouldn't have been able to enjoy the warmth and see so many beautiful birds without their generosity. I left Boston at breakfast time with an icy mix falling. We had to sit on the tarmac while the plane was de-iced before taking off, but it was only a slight delay. By lunchtime, I was standing in the warm waters of the Gulf of Mexico along Sanibel causeway!

On Monday, Keith and Kris picked up Sissy and I, and we all headed to Corkscrew Swamp Sanctuary in Naples for a day of birding. We had a splendid day walking the boardwalk through the swamp. We saw a total of seventeen different species, not the highest days total, but we saw real quality birds. Like the delicate blue-gray gnatcatcher, the vibrant colorful painted bunting and the always impressive pileated woodpecker, the largest woodpecker in North America.

Although I did my best cat calling I couldn't get the gray catbird to show itself for Keith and Kris. He was there I saw him, and he was answering my calls, but they just didn't get a chance to see him. Last year when I visited, we met at Myakka River State Park for some birding, and I heard the catbird then too, but we couldn't spot him. I tried so hard to get that darn bird to show himself to no avail. Sorry, Keith and Kris, I guess we will have to try again next year.

Bill out did himself this trip, he planned a trip for us to Merritt Island on the Atlantic Coast. We drove from one side of the state to the other to explore the Cocoa Beach area. Merritt Island National Wildlife Refuge was a whole different habitat than any other places I have visited before. Bill took us along the Black Point Wildlife Drive, which is a seven-mile one way drive across the vast estuary. The dirt road was just barely above sea level, we were driving along a raised dike, it felt as if we were eye to eye with the wading birds we passed. We were a part of their environment.

We saw alligators cruising the shallows and the dike was lined with flowering thistle of pink and white with colorful butterflies floating about. And boy o boy did we see birds! We saw forty-four different species! We actually saw more than that, but we couldn't identify some. Bill was taking pictures of the birds in hopes that we could ID them later when we could study them closer on the laptop.

I was able to add new birds to my life list. I got to see the unique American Avocet, actually I saw a dozen or so of these graceful long billed shore birds. I got to see the colorful purple gallinule, Sissy and I watched as a pair was fearsomely fighting and causing a ruckus in the marsh. The most unexpected sighting was when we came across a small flock of roseate spoonbills feeding in the shallows. Previous years these birds eluded me no matter how hard we tried to find them yet this year we stumble upon a flock. Isn't that the way it goes. But what a beautiful way to end our day on Merritt Island.

My grand total of bird sightings for my six days in Florida was seventy-three. But defiantly my all-time best Big Day total was our day on Merritt Island! Thank you, Bill! Thank you, Keith and Kris, for a great day in the swamp. Thank you to my dear sister, Sissy, for a very memorable trip I miss you already. Till next year.

Bird Sightings in Florida February 2015

A Painted Bunting and Roseate Spoonbill.

Corkscrew Swamp Sanctuary

Anhinga	Great blue heron	Great egret
Little blue heron	Black-crowned night heron	White ibis
Red-shouldered hawk	Eurasian collared dove	Red-bellied woodpecker
Pileated woodpecker	Acadian flycatcher	Blue-gray gnatcatcher
Carolina wren	Gray catbird	Painted bunting
Snowy egret	Ground dove	

Merritt Island National Wildlife Refuge

Mottled duck	Blue-winged teal	Northern shoveler
Hooded merganser	Pied-billed grebe	Wood stork
Double-crested cormorant	Great cormorant	Anhinga
American white pelican	Great blue heron	Great egret
Snowy egret	Little blue heron	Tricolored heron
Reddish egret	Cattle egret	Green heron
White ibis	Roseate spoonbills	Black vulture
Turkey vulture	Bald eagle	Purple gallinule
American coot	Black-bellied plover	Semipalmated plover
Piping plover	Killdeer	American avocet
Sanderlings	Dunlin	Rock pigeon
Eurasian collared dove	Mourning dove	Belted kingfisher
Gray catbird	Northern mockingbird	
Common yellow-throat		
Yellow-rumped warbler	Northern cardinal	Painted bunting
Red-winged blackbird	Common grackle	Boat-tailed grackle

Port Charlotte Area

Osprey	Brown pelican	Bonaparte gull
European starlings	Northern flicker	Palm warbler
Fish crow	Merlin	Sandhill crane
Long-billed dowitcher	Northern shrike	House Sparrow
Royal tern	Laughing gull	Ruddy turnstone
	Least tern	Caspian tern

Week of Firsts

A Florida Scrub Jay.

February 2016

I recently returned from my annual trip to Florida; I have been going to visit family each February since 2010. But this year was different, this year there were a lot of "firsts." Here is a synopsis of my roller coaster week. I flew in to Fort Myers late Friday night.

Saturday was all about "those eyes." Keith and Kris had never seen the burrowing owl, and Sissy remembered where we had seen them in Cape Coral a few years ago, so we headed out on a search. Keith and Kris seemed a little unsure when we pulled up to an abandoned empty lot in the middle of a residential neighborhood and told them to get out. I told them to quietly walk up to that mound of dirt and carefully look into the hole in the ground. They did as told, and sure enough, when they looked into the burrow, there, looking back at them, were the big yellow eyes of the tiny burrowing owl! A first for Keith and Kris!

Sunday, we left the Gulf Coast and headed to the East Coast for an overnight stay to visit Merritt Island National Wildlife Refuge. Along the way, we stopped for a break, and as we pulled off the highway, suddenly, we spotted a huge bald eagle's nest at the edge of the parking lot. We watched as the two parent eagles fed their downy young, tearing apart a freshly killed squirrel into pieces. Certainly an unexpected sighting! A first for all of us.

Sunday afternoon we arrived on the refuge ready to do some serious birding. On the first trail we took, we spotted the gray cat-bird! Finally, Keith and Kris get to see this noisy bird that we have been chasing for three years now. Meow! A first for them! As we were leaving that area, I spotted an armadillo foraging in the palm fronds on the ground. Cool! A first for me, I have never seen an Armadillo before, they are very cute.

Monday we were back on the refuge early, intent on finding the endangered Florida scrub jays. We hit the trail prepared, Sissy had a bag of peanuts, and I had a little baggie of granola. I walked a little ahead of the others holding the baggie of granola up in the air and shaking it to make noise to draw in the curious jays. It worked! Soon we had multiple scrub jays flying around us, and they landed on Sissy and Kris's hands to take the peanuts. The look on Kris's face was priceless as the jay landed in her hand and took the peanut. A first for Keith and Kris!

Later on Monday, we took a wildlife drive through the refuge along the water; we came across a huge alligator just laying across the dirt road. We also saw a river otter playing in the tall grass along the road. But the funniest sighing were huge flocks of coots "running" across the surface of the water. I mean they literally run across the top of the water. They don't take flight; they just seem to be having fun running across the water. It was the funniest thing ever, we all laughed. A first for all of us!

Tuesday was a day to pay my respects. Sissy and I headed to Sarasota National Veterans Cemetery to visit Bill's graveside. It was an emotional day but offered some closure. He so bravely fought cancer but his suffering is over now, and he is in God's hands. RIP to my dear brother-in-law. Later as we were driving home, a very large black bird came into sight coming toward us. It was flying low over the "poop factory," as Sissy called it. I could see it had a very distinctive forked tail. It was a magnificent frigatebird! A very unexpected surprising sighting, that brightened my mood. A first for me!

Wednesday was a whirlwind, well actually a tornado. Sissy and I were running errands, it was a rainy, windy, thunderstorm day. Little did we know what Mother Nature was about to throw our way. We were in the grocery store when suddenly all the lights started blinking off and on, there were loud thumps and bangs on the roof, power went out. The store employees were rushing around gathering all us customers and directing us to the back room. Then just as suddenly it got quiet. It was only after we got home and saw the news reports that we realized how lucky we were. An EF1 tornado touched down just a few streets away from the store we were in during the storm. The tornado turned over cars and ripped the roofs off some houses, but thankfully there were no serious injuries. That was the closest I ever care to be to a tornado that was a first I prefer to not repeat.

On Thursday, Sissy and I went on the Babcock Wilderness ninety-minute eco-tour across different ecosystems on the ninety-thousand-acre Crescent B Ranch. It was very interesting, we saw alligators in the cypress swamp, deer in the hardwood forest, wild turkeys on the prairie and lots of cows. The Crescent B Ranch is a working cattle ranch. Some cool sightings were the Florida panther, which lives on the ranch and the fox squirrel, which is the largest squirrel in North America, it measures more than two feet, not including the tail. The very best sighting was the endangered red-cockaded woodpecker I saw in the pine forest! That was three, first for both of us!

Friday was time to head back to New England. While sitting in the airport I was passing time by reviewing all the birds I had seen and listening to their songs on my iPad. I was trying to be respectful and had the volume low, but some passengers near me commented that they were enjoying listening to the bird songs. Then suddenly the fire alarm blares from the overhead speakers, the person sitting next to me says, "Was that you?" Then the voice on the loudspeaker says, "Attention, attention, a fire has been detected in an area near you, please prepare to evacuate." Everyone groans, they herd us off to the left and then herd us back to the right. After a few minutes, they announce that all passengers departing at gates D6 or D9 may board their planes for takeoff. Luckily, I was gate D6! Never saw any fire or smoke and my plane was on time. I arrived home safely. Another first for me that I prefer to not repeat.

It was a week of highs and lows of first-time experiences and bird and animal sightings. Yes, it was different without Bill there, I missed him. But none of us can turn back time, we have to accept the reality of the present and push forward into the future. I thank Sissy, Keith, and Kris for making my vacation special, and I look forward to many more firsts on my next visit!

Sammies and Sunsets in the Red Cafe

Pic of Burrowing Owls.

February 2017

On my annual February vacation to Florida, I left the snow and ice in New Hampshire in the morning and by that evening I was standing in the warmth on the jetty in Venice Florida watching the beautiful sunset over the Gulf of Mexico. As usual, the Florida crew (Sissy, Keith, and Kris) made my stay fantastic! If it weren't for their generosity hosting me, my vacation wouldn't be as great. I'm a simple person I'm not about hotels and restaurants, I prefer a picnic meal over an indoor dining meal any day! Years earlier Bill had come up with a nickname for his red SUV, he called it the Red Cafe, Sissy would ask him, "Where do you want to go for dinner?"

Bill would answer, "The Red Cafe." Sissy didn't understand the joke at first, and it became a joke Bill and I shared. I sure understood what he meant, that when Jane is visiting meals are sammies and sunsets in the SUV parked in places with beautiful views. It was sad that Bill passed away in 2015, he is greatly missed, but we had to smile with memories of all times enjoyed together in the Red Cafe.

Each morning began with coffee on the lanai with Sissy and then a quick microwave breakfast Sammie, and then we were off on our daily adventure. We had a great day of birding at Ding Darling Nature Refuge on Sanibel Island, Keith and Kris were able to join us for the day. We saw twenty-six different species of birds. Many of the regular residents of the island, American pelicans, snowy egrets, anhingas, double-crested cormorants, and many, many more Florida birds. We enjoyed sammies for lunch in the Red Cafe parked on the Causeway along the Gulf of Mexico watching dolphins swimming back and forth in front of us. We explored the beach collecting shells and wading in the warm waters of the Gulf. The day ended sitting on the lanai relaxing and watching the sun set over the lake in blazing colors!

The next day, Sissy and I packed up our picnic supplies in the Red Cafe and headed out to explore Pine Island. Found a great parking spot near the water in the shade of tall trees. Suddenly I noticed activity in the treetops; it was a large osprey nest! We watched as the two adult osprey took turns flying onto the nest with fish and fed their young. Enjoyed our sammies in the Red Cafe while watching the osprey grab a fish in the water in front of us and return to the nest listening to the young call out loudly. We walked along the wooden pier out into the ocean. Saw numerous brown pelicans swimming around waiting for some of the fishermen to drop their fish. Watched as a reddish egret strolled along the rocky shoreline in search of food. Bonaparte's gulls were sitting on the pilings of the pier. When we got to the end of the pier, we watched as two dolphins were circling around and breaching out of the water. Another great day enjoying nature!

Ending with watching fiery sunsets over the ocean in the Red Cafe.

The next few days were casual relaxing adventures. Every day started the same, out on the lanai relaxing watching the activity on the lake. Then pack up the Red Cafe for a day visiting local parks around Port Charlotte Harbor, Sissy knows all the perfect parking spots with the best views! Seemed like everywhere we stopped there were dozens of little Ruddy Turnstones scurrying along the shoreline. Every day was sammies in the Red Cafe and ended with beautiful sunsets over the water.

On my last full day in Florida, Sissy and I headed to Cape Coral to visit with Keith and Kris. Cape Coral is well known for the burrowing owl colonies that are across the area. The city protects their colonies from damage and works to preserve their habitats. There was no way I was going to visit Cape Coral and Not visit the burrowing owls. Now that Keith and Kris live in Cape Coral they were more familiar with the resident burrowing owl locations and took me there. We enjoyed, from appropriate distance watching the cute little owls sitting by their burrows or popping in and out and kicking dirt up into the air. No matter how many times I see these adorable owls I will never get tired of it! We headed back to Keith and Kris place for a pizza dinner and played a rousing game of Bird Opoly. This is a game my daughter gave me that is styled after Monopoly but is all based on birds. It is described as "a high-flying game of feathery fun." What a fun night; though, I couldn't tell you who won the game as we called it quits after about three hours of fun; though Sissy was in the lead at the time.

Yet again another wonderful happy visit with family in Florida exploring and sharing nature's beauty while enjoying sammies and sunsets in the Red Cafe.

Circle B Hacienda

February 2018

Well, this year's annual escape to South Florida was different. Added two new members to the Florida Crew, Becky and Christopher. A few months earlier, they moved from New Hampshire to Cape Coral. My youngest sister never was a fan of the cold harsh New England winters and their jobs gave them the option to move to Florida. I was very sad when she moved away, and I missed her so much. So this trip I split my time between my oldest sister Sissy, in Port Charlotte, and my youngest sister Becky, in Cape Coral, occupying their guest rooms. How lucky I am to have two such graciously welcoming sisters! Again, if I had to pay for hotel rooms and meals, I would not be able to enjoy my escape from New Hampshire to Florida every February.

As sad as I was that Becky moved away from New Hampshire, when I arrived at their new home I was in awe! Their new home is amazing! Seeing how happy they were in their new home how could I feel sad? So not a New England-style place, the architect was very Southern Florida style. The floor plan was so different than any house I'd been in, the interior design was beautiful. I felt like I was staying in a five-star hotel. They have a large lot of land, beautiful flowering gardens and even a small fruit grove where we could pick fruit to enjoy at breakfast. Add to all that a good size pool just off the lanai. Believe me my little sister and her husband are the ultimate party hosts! Every day, the rest of the Florida Crew would join us for a cookout, fun games and relaxing in the pool. I nicknamed their new place the Circle B Hacienda. Lots of laughter and memories!

On one of our Florida crew outings, Becky took us to a small rookery they had discovered in Venice. In the middle of a small pond was an island that was crowded with nests of different birds. There was an alligator that patrolled the waters around the island and the birds seemed to know that the alligators presence meant no land predators like a fox or raccoon could get to the island to raid their nest. Nature's creatures working together. There were great egrets, anhinga, great blue herons, black-crowned night herons, white ibis, wood storks, and cormorants nests all crowded together on the small island.

Becky had been there a few weeks earlier, and she said there was a lot of activity in the nests. That the adult birds were flying back and forth with food and the nests were alive with squawking young birds. It appeared that most of the young had fledged and there were only a few young birds left sitting on the branches waiting for food. Many of the adult birds were now flying onto the island carrying sticks to rebuild their nests. Looked like they were all getting ready for the next brood.

But on shore near us, I noticed some unusual behavior by a young cormorant. There was one large dead tree with an adult cormorant sitting on a high branch, just preening in the sun. At the base of the tree was a young cormorant that kept waddling toward the tree and jumping onto the trunk of the tree trying to hold on. The cormorant has the ability to grab onto branches to perch, but this young bird was actually trying to climb the tree! It kept jumping onto the tree trunk and scratching the bark to hold on all the while loudly squawking at the adult sitting above him. Meanwhile, the adult bird completely ignored the young bird and finally flew off. I don't think that was its parent.

I wasn't the only person witness to this climbing cormorant, others nearby were concerned and asking what they could do to help the young bird. There was an attendant at the park, and she came over and talked to some of the people worried about the young bird. I wasn't close enough to hear exactly what she was saying but those gathered around her all backed away from the climbing cormorant and the attendant was directing others away from the tree.

Soon the young cormorant gave up trying to climb the tree and waddled over to the edge of the water. Now the concern was that if the young bird got into the water to swim to the island that the alligator might snatch it up in its jaws! The young bird flapped its wings awkwardly splashing in the water, but he did it, he took to the air and flew low over the water to the island! Once he arrived at the island and landed on a low branch, he caused quite a commotion among all the other birds on the island. They all began to squawk and flap their wings, to them any arrival onto the island meant food was being delivered. There were plenty of cormorants on the island but for some reason the young cormorant was sitting on a branch begging for food from a great blue heron. The heron just sat there staring at him as if he was saying, "Go away, kid! Ahh this youngster had better get things straightened out, he is barking up the wrong tree!

We sat at a picnic table in the shade and enjoyed a picnic lunch. It was a nice park; we walked around a bit. Before leaving, we did see that the young cormorant was sitting next to another adult cormorant, so guess he found Mom. Now it was time to continue on to the Venice jetty. Saw brown pelicans, dozens of Ruddy Turnstones and dolphins jumping in and out of the water. Never a bad view off the jetty! Another great day with the Florida Crew now it was time to head back to the Circle B Hacienda for an evening cookout and fun and laughter.

Surprise!

Well, it seemed like surprise was the theme of my 2019 annual February trip to Florida. Again, this year I planned on splitting my time in Cape Coral and Port Charlotte with family. Since Becky had work on Monday, the plan was to stay at the Circle B Hacienda for Saturday and Sunday then stay with Sissy during the week, as she had the whole week off, and then head back to Becky's for the last weekend of my trip. Christopher was very kind to shuttle me back and forth to and from the airport. He picked me up at the airport and when we arrived at the Circle B Hacienda I walk in, and surprise! The whole Florida Crew was there to greet me! Becky planned a Welcome to Florida cookout party for me. I started my day in New Hampshire having to clean fresh snow off the truck in the freezing cold to make it to the airport. I ended my day in warm sunny Florida partying with my family and relaxing in the pool. I am so lucky to have such a great family!

On Sunday, we went to the Cape Coral Burrowing Owl Festival at Rotary Park. This was an event I had wanted to attend previous visits but just never got a chance to. So I was looking forward to this outing. Keith was so thoughtful, he got us an Uber driver with a vehicle big enough for us all so we could ride together to the event rather than have to drive multiple cars and find parking spots. I was surprised about that plan but what a great idea, as when we arrived it was indeed a crowded event. It was very interesting to stroll about and see all the exhibits set up in a large tent. They even had a guided tour ride in a special van to take people to see the burrowing owl colonies around town. Kudos to the city of Cape Coral for hosting such an event to educate people on the burrowing owls and measures to protect them.

Of course, we ended the day back at the Circle B Hacienda for a family cookout and relaxing in the pool. As it got later and was beginning to get dark, I asked Sissy when she was leaving for the drive back to Port Charlotte. Surprise! She tells me she is also staying at Becky's, in one of the other guest rooms. Becky smiles and says, "That's why we bought this big house so we would have lots of room for family and friends to visit and stay overnight." Actually, that was no big surprise, my youngest sister has always been the ultimate hostess and fun event planner in the family. It sure has been years since I could say I slept under the same roof with my oldest and youngest sisters. Becky enjoys crafts, and she got a cute craft kit of small stained glass style birds for us to make. I started my day looking into the eyes of cute burrowing owls, I ended my day sitting across the table with two of my sisters laughing and looking into their eyes. What an evening of great memories of time spent with my two sisters. I am so blessed to have such a great family.

Monday morning after breakfast together, Sissy and I packed up and headed to Port Charlotte in the Red Cafe. Of course, we packed a picnic lunch and meandered our way back to Sissy's. We stopped at Bay Shore Live Oak Park and enjoyed our picnic lunch in the Red Cafe with a great view of the harbor, watching passing fishing boats with gulls and pelicans chasing them hoping for scraps. After our picnic lunch, we continued on to Stump Pass Beach State Park to check it out for my grand "surprise" that I was anxiously waiting for. It was a surprise phone call from my daughter Jeanine a few days before I left for Florida. She told me that she and Charley were able to take off a couple days from work and were coming from Colorado to Florida to visit while I was there! Totally unexpected! Jeanine tells me it was a trip she had been in the planning process with Aunt Becky for a while, who had invited them to visit and told them they were welcome to stay with them, and Christopher even offered them his car to use. Yet again the welcoming doors of the Circle B Hacienda are wide open for family!

She tells me that originally Aunt Becky had wanted to make the visit a complete surprise for me, for them to arrive while I was there and make a grand surprise entrance. Jeanine tells me she thought it was a wonderful idea but that she felt bad expecting my sisters to keep a secret from me. Jeanine said she was looking forward to visiting some of the many places I have told her about, and she knew sharing the news with me and planning together was all part of the fun of the surprise visit. Yes, that made sense, it was fun to plan with my sisters, ideas of things to do, places to go with Jeanine and Charley. I asked Jeanine if they had any specific things they wanted to see and do. She tells me the top of the list things were to paddleboard in the ocean, see some of the Florida birds and wildlife I have told her about, and enjoy their escape from cold snowy Colorado to warm and sunny Florida. Oh, I sure could relate to that, leave the snow and cold behind.

They flew in on a red-eye flight, and Christopher picked them up at the airport and brought them home to the Circle B Hacienda. I knew I wouldn't see them right away. The plan was to let them catch up on sleep, adjust to the time change, and enjoy the day and the beautiful surroundings at Aunt Becky's, relaxing in the pool. The Florida crew all met up at a sort of half way point between Becky's and Sissy's, an outdoor seating restaurant along the water at Fisherman's Village. It was so great to see Jeanine and Charley and get to hug them, it had been nearly a year since I had seen them. The weather was beautiful, and there were numerous gulls and pelicans flying low across the water, all typical Florida. We enjoyed dinner and discussing plans for some of the adventures we had planned for them.

The next morning, they drove over to Sissy's for breakfast then afterward we packed up the Red Cafe for our day of fun. Jeanine says, "Oh, so this is the Red Cafe I've heard so much about. Now I finally get to enjoy a picnic in it." We headed to Myakka River State Park first, hoping to get a sighting of the roseate spoonbill, and they wanted to launch their paddleboards into the lake or canals to explore. The first stop in the park was the canopy walk, this is a series of wooden walkways suspended high in the trees through the forest. And it leads to a tall tower you can climb and get a magnificent view of the lake and whole forest of the park. Can't visit the park without enjoying this spot. Then on to find them a good area to launch their paddleboards. The first launch area we stopped at we barely got out of the car when SURPRISE! There in the water is a large alligator looking right at us! There were signs posted to "Beware of alligators, indeed they were right. After multiple sightings of alligators at each launch area, we stopped at and then talking to the Park Ranger Jeanine and Charley decided maybe Myakka wasn't the best place to go stand up paddleboarding (SUP). Good decision, Jeanine and Charley. We enjoyed lunch by the lake watching as alligators swam back and forth. That was more alligator activity there than I had ever seen before. Jeanine and Charley wanted to see some Florida wildlife, and they sure did.

Now it was time to move on to the next spot; we took them to Venice Beach Jetty to see if they could get out into the ocean. When they had loaded up their gear at Sissy's, I did ask Jeanine, "Where are your paddleboards how did you get them here from Colorado?" She pointed to a large gym bag with wheels that Charley was lifting into the SUV and says, "That's them, they are inflatable." What? Really how safe are these things? When we got to the jetty, they quickly removed the rolled up SUPs from the gym bag, and it was interesting to watch them inflate them. Others at the jetty walking by were also interested in "What's those? What are you guys doing?" Jeanine and Charley were entertaining people as they walked by them as they inflated their paddleboards. Didn't take them long, and they put on their life vests and headed for the end of the jetty. They couldn't wait to get into the Gulf of Mexico! I wasn't so sure if launching off the jetty rocks was the best idea as they were scampering across the rocks with the little Ruddy Turnstones hopping about. But they did it and were soon just a speck on the horizon!

I was getting a bit nervous as they paddled farther and farther into the distance. I wasn't the only one, as others on the jetty were also watching them and pointing. I headed over to the crowd thinking maybe they weren't watching Jeanine and Charley maybe they see a bird. Then SURPRISE! One of the onlookers yells, "Wow, I just saw a bolt of lightning!" Another man yells, "Yes, I see the clouds are getting darker, maybe we better call marine patrol to help those people out!"

I quickly tell them all, "That's my family!" I had my binoculars and zoom in on them and instantly I could tell they were headed back to shore! The onlookers all agreed and clapped as Jeanine and Charley got closer to shore. I knew they were very experienced outdoors people, and yes, they knew what they were doing and followed all the safety rules of SUP in the ocean. They enjoyed their adventure and the gathering storm clouds only intensified the colors of the sunset. Another great day enjoying nature's beauty with family.

On my last full day of vacation, I headed back to Cape Coral. Becky was able to take the day off work and took Jeanine, Charley, and I out to explore some local parks. Becky had a few spots in mind that she thought Jeanine and Charley could launch their paddleboards. The first place we tried there was yellow caution tape strung across the launch area by the water. No surprise, that tells us stay away alligators! After searching a few more places, without alligators, to go paddleboarding Becky suggested we head over to Cape Coral Beach. When we arrived and as Jeanine and Charley were inflating their paddleboards, we could hear a constant chattering of birds. We couldn't see the birds, sounded like it was coming from high up in the palm tree grove. As soon as Jeanine and Charley were out on the water paddling away, Becky and I headed for the palm tree grove.

It is a beautiful beach area with picnic tables and all the amenities to spend a comfortable day at the beach. Becky suggested we grab an empty picnic table with a great view of the ocean and the palm grove. She told me to sit down that she would be right back. The bird sounds had stopped, but I sure was enjoying the tropical weather and serene view. Then surprise! Becky comes back carrying two ice cream sundaes! Yummy sure has been a long time since I've enjoyed a strawberry sundae while sitting on the beach with my little sister. Then suddenly Becky says, "Jane quick turnaround look up" while she is pointing into the palm grove. We spotted a large flock of monk parakeets! What a great sighting, we saw multiple nests with the parents flying in and out of the crown of the palm trees to feed their young. Now all the noise made sense, if we hadn't seen the parents fly into the nests wouldn't have known they were there. It was very, very noisy with parakeets everywhere!

We enjoyed another great day together then headed back to the Circle B Hacienda. Met up with the rest of the Florida crew and had a goodbye cookout party. I may have said it a million times but can never say it enough. Thank you, thank you, to my Florida family for a wonderful visit. See you all next year!

I am indeed so blessed to have such a loving family.

Butter Butt

February 2020

I was so anxious to get to Florida for my annual February vacation. Not just to escape the cold and snow of New Hampshire but to finally get to see and hug my youngest sister Becky. Unfortunately, a couple months after my visit last year Becky became very ill, was even in a coma for weeks. The final diagnosis was the fear of us all, cancer. But Becky fought hard! She battled through radiation, chemo, multiple hospital stays all the while staying positive of a good outcome and end to her struggle. I couldn't wait for my plane to land in Florida so I could get out and hug my sister. I tell you to exit the plane and walk up the corridor at the airport to see Becky standing there to greet me was the best arrival ever! I swear as I hugged her with tears in my eyes it felt like a Disney moment, hearts flying about, glitter sparkling around us and the sound of horns blowing! Or maybe it was just my low blood sugar? Who knows who cares? But it was a happy moment I had dreamed of to finally get to see and hug my little sister! Thank God.

Christopher loaded up my bags, and we headed to Cape Coral. We made a quick stop at the local Publix to pick up a few supplies for a cookout dinner. It felt like a game show as Becky quickly navigated the cart up and down the isles as I threw items into the cart. Sure, she looked different, no surprise considering what she had been through, but it was reassuring that she seemed the same Becky as last year. So proud of how well she handled her challenges. After settling in at the Circle B Hacienda, I joined Becky out on the lanai to relax and take in the beauty of her tropical surroundings. Ahhhh, Florida! I sure didn't miss the snow and cold I woke up to that morning, as now I was sitting with my dear smiling sister surrounded by rustling palm fronds, sunny blue skies and chirping bird sounds all around us.

There were multiple little birds flitting about the trees, they were Becky's favorite little brown birds as she calls them! Last year, when I visited, I never could get a good look at the little brown birds that seemed to be everywhere, could only get a quick glimpse as they flitted about the trees. So this year, I was determined to get a close up look and identify them! Becky has two bird baths set up in the yard with fresh water, one even bubbles like a mini fountain. Offering birds fresh water can bring them into your yard even more than feeders. Her yard offers birds so much of what nature can provide that the bird baths are very popular.

As I was outside walking around the yard, it happened. A little brown bird landed on the bird bath! I stood still behind a tree quietly and watched. Finally, it was out in the open, sitting still drinking water, I was able to watch it for quite a while. As it then jumped into the deeper part of the bird bath and splashed about, I finally saw the telltale markings and immediately knew it was a butter butt! Or as the world of ornithology calls them yellow-rumped warbler. Remembering birds' names can be challenging but nicknames for them can be easier to recall. This little brown bird is called a butter butt because it looks like it sat in a bowl of butter, as it's behind and a small patch under its shoulders is all bright yellow. It is hard to see the yellow as they flit about, and then they are just called little brown birds.

Call them whatever name you want, to me they will always be Becky's little butter butts. A reminder of our time together chatting, laughing and enjoying watching the birds in her tropical paradise. Be thankful, remember even the little things in life can give you the biggest smile.

Keith's Poop!

February 2020

Sunday my second day in Florida was *packed* with family, laughter, kitties, strange sounds and mystery poop! I started the day sitting on the lanai with Becky, in our jammies enjoying morning coffee while being greeted by the kitties Teddy and Cricket for their morning pats. Later in the morning Sissy came by to take me to visit Keith and Kris at their new place. Becky stayed home to prepare for a Welcome to Florida get together she had planned for me later in the day. Keith and Kris's new place is great! What a nice place—so, so much nicer than the old third floor apartment they had. They work hard they deserve a house of their own. The best part was the lanai and pool! They have a small yard, but it is very private with lots of greenery and trees. The kitties were certainly enjoying being able to lounge out by the pool sniffing the fresh air, enjoying the sights and sounds of nature yet still protected by the screened in lanai.

After getting the full tour of the house, we all sat out in the lanai enjoying the surroundings and catching up. Keith asked me if I could help him figure out a strange sound he had heard the last couple of nights in the yard. He explained in detail what he heard, loud, duck/frog like, squeaky dog toy like, definitely in the trees, moving fast across the yard. Okay, I pulled up my bird app and began playing sounds of some of the possible night time singers I thought it might be. Nothing! None of the bird sounds I played for him sounded right. So the mystery continues.

I decided to walk around outside to investigate the trees and see if I could find any signs of bird activity that might explain the weird sounds Keith was hearing. Sissy, Keith, and Kris sat in the lanai watching me as I walked around the yard. Then Keith calls out to me, "Hey, while you're out there maybe you can identify some strange poop I saw on the ground, tell me what kind of animal it is?!" I tell him, "Okay, sure, where is it?" He calls to me from the lanai, "Go to the left, back along the tree line." He directs me as I walk around the yard looking down at the grass.

Then he calls out, "Come forward a little bit!" I couldn't see any poop at first, Keith continues to direct me from the lanai, "You're almost there. Don't step in it!" I look down. Yup, there it was!

Honestly at first, I thought my nephew was just sending me on a wild goose chase, looking for sh——t, as the three of them sat in the lanai, laughing at me as I wandered around the yard looking for poop. As I lean over to investigate the "poop" better, Keith calls out to me, "Do you think it's a dog? Cat? Raccoon? Skunk? Opossum?"

Ummm, well, actually not sure who it belongs to. I tell Keith, "Not a dog to small, not a cat not the right shape, not a raccoon to big, not a skunk the wrong consistency." As I was poking at the "poop" with a stick, I thought Sissy was going to fall out of her chair laughing at me. Heck the Citizen Scientist in me came out full force! I took two sticks and used them like chop sticks and held the "poop" up to smell it. Didn't smell like sh——t. I had a feeling Sissy wasn't going to let me back in the car to go back to Becky's so I put the "poop" back down on the ground. I began to break it open, saw small bits of fuzz, noticed the outside surface was like a shell. Then I knew what it was! It wasn't *poop*; it was an owl pellet!

All this time the three of them are sitting on the lanai laughing at me, yet also excited to hear my commentary as I dissected the pellet! But as I dissected the pellet it became more obvious something important was missing...bones. Owls can't digest the bones, fur, and tail of a rodent they eat. Instead, they "throw up" the pieces they can't process through their system. The pellet they spit out is held together by fur and saliva. I saw no remains of a rodent? What was this pile of crap I was poking through?

I joined the others on the lanai (after scrubbing my hands) and pull up my birding app and start to look through the pictures of owl pellets. Ummm, and so the poop mystery continues. The size and color was wrong for any possible owl pellets. I shared the pictures with Keith as he was the only other one there who had looked at the "poop." When suddenly from the left side yard, a medium-sized brown bird streaks by like lighting! It lands on the top of the fence just outside the lanai, sits proudly, turns and looks right at us! It was a merlin! We all got a good look at this beautiful bird. The merlin belongs to the falcon family, and it is a raptor, is about fourteen-inches long, he feeds on small birds. The merlin also expels the indigestible parts in a pellet. Bingo! Keith's poop matched the description and size of the pictures of merlins pellets! That explains why there was no tail or leg bones in the pellet. The fuzz was likely downy feathers from the small birds they eat. What a lucky find that pile of Keith's Poop was!

Okay, enough about Keith's poop! Time to head back to the Circle B Hacienda to party! Nobody throws a better party than Christopher and Becky, they are the best hosts ever. I was looking forward to seeing Shelby and Shawn and the newest addition to our family, Sophia! As Becky reminded me, Sophia is the first Florida native born into our family. I really appreciated that Shelby and Shawn came over to visit me, gee Sophia wasn't even a week old yet. What a beautiful little girl they have. Talk about Disney moments… to look at Shelby and Shawn sitting together in the love seat holding their little bundle of joy, you could see the love radiating around them like a cloud of sparkling hearts. And as Christopher held his little granddaughter, again the magical sparkling hearts floated around them. Awe. And as Becky sat with Sophia in her lap gazing down at her the Disney moment kicked into high gear! Little blue birds flitted about singing as the sparkling hearts radiated around them. Maybe it was just my dramatic imagination but there surely was no denying the amount of love and joy surrounding us all!

So I started my day focused on poop, but it sure ended in love, joy, and family.

Beautifully Ugly

A Muscovy Duck.

February 2020

Sunday was a whirl wind day of fun and family, so I was looking forward to a chill kinda Monday spending time alone with Becky. Started the day off my favorite way! Sitting out on the lanai with Becky in our jammies enjoying our morning coffee, watching the kitties patrol the perimeter of the pool and enjoying the visiting butter butts and little bunny rabbits hopping about. A relaxing morning chilling with Becky.

Becky suggested we go out for a picnic lunch at a new local park she had found. I'll never say no to a sammie outside! We packed up our sammies and snacks then headed over to the new park, Sarasota

Lake Park. Yet again a nice little Florida park along the water's edge. We settled down at the perfect picnic table with a great view of the water. Becky quickly spotted a trio of ducks along the opposite shore. She says, "Yikes, look at those weird ugly ducks! Look at their heads they look sick, poor things maybe they went through chemo too!" She was kind of chuckling, I got it. I understood she felt very uncomfortable about losing all her hair due to her chemo treatments. I told her they were muscovy ducks and known to be beautifully ugly. I hugged her and told her she was beautiful with or without her long hair, it will grow back. That we were all so proud of her brave battle against cancer, and we were all here to support her and for her to stay positive. Muscovy ducks are actually domestic escapees that cross breed with other duck species. That produces a large-sized strange miss mash this and that kinda duck. But that strange look is what tells you they are muscovy ducks. The one feature that they all exhibit is a turkey looking head with raised red bumps. They are indeed beautifully ugly creatures!

Unfortunately, the weather was not cooperating. A "cold front" was passing through, gee poor Florida, temps were in the mid-sixties with strong winds. Believe me I was *still* warmer than I would have been back in New England. But fighting the wind made enjoying our picnic lunch tricky. Each time a gust of wind came up we had to hang on to our sammies, baggie of chips, and napkins. The wind even blew over my water bottle, luckily the cap was on. The worst was the sudden gust of wind that lifted our mini peppermint patties right off the table, and they cart wheeled away! I jumped up and chased them as they tumbled across the grass. I ain't gonna let candy get away! The best part was listening to Becky laugh out loud while watching me chasing our dessert.

The cold wind cut our picnic short but that's okay. A day filled with beautifully ugly ducks, chilly windy weather and chasing flying peppermint patties created a fun memory picnic with Becky to look back on and smile.

Eric's Cranes!

Well, Tuesday I did something in Florida I hadn't done before! Since Becky planned on putting in some work hours the next couple of days, the plan was for Sissy to pick me up in Cape Coral, and I was going to stay with her in Port Charlotte. Unfortunately, Sissy had some car issues and ended up without transportation. So I rented a car (well, was supposed to be an economy car, but I ended up with a Dodge caravan) and I headed to Port Charlotte on my own. Of all the years, since 2010, that I've been going to Florida over February vacation I have never actually needed to drive due to the graciousness of my Florida Family. Now it was my turn to pay back for all the times I was chauffeured around!

I picked up Sissy and took her out to take care of a few errands she needed to do. I was happy to be able to pay her back by helping her out while she was without a car. As we were crossing the bridge in the harbor, she says to me, "When Eric was here, he told me to remind you to keep your binoculars handy to see the big cranes along the waterfront!" My youngest brother Eric had been there, visiting family a couple weeks before I was. He also lives in New Hampshire not too far from me, he is very aware of my hobby of birding; though, we have never gone birding together. I was excited to see what these big cranes that he saw were! As we get to the end of the bridge, Sissy tells me, "There they are!" But as I was the one driving, I had to keep my eyes on the road and couldn't look for Eric's Cranes. I asked Sissy to describe them to me, what color are they? How big are they? Do you know what kind they are? She laughs and tells me I've got to find them myself. She tells me she will take me to the park that they were at when Eric saw them.

I will admit navigating the big Dodge through the snowbird crowded streets of Punta Gorta was a new experience. Heck to the locals I sure stood out as a snowbird myself since the rental had Kentucky plates and was big and black, not the typical Florida vehicle. But Sissy sure knew the secrets of avoiding the congestion. She directed me to a good parking spot for the van, and we walked to Gilcrest Park to grab an ice cream along the waterfront. The moment we sat down out on the deck overlooking the harbor I saw them. Eric's cranes! My younger brother is indeed the joker in the family. Sissy was laughing. What was there along the shore were large metal construction cranes, there was a new complex being built on the harbor. Yup, they weren't bird cranes but yes Eric they are cranes. They will from now on be known to me as Eric's great gray-legged Florida cranes. Thanks, Eric, for a new sighting to add to my list—hahahahaha...

After laughing with Sissy and enjoying ice cream, we continued on to Ponce De Leon Park for an early bird picnic dinner. Every February trip, we stop at Ponce at least once, though I've never actually swam in the ocean there, it is a nice park. We walked along the boardwalk through the mangroves. There is a bird rescue shelter there, but I don't count any of the birds I see at the shelter since it's against the birding rules to count a captive bird on your life list. We sat on a bench along the water watching a little blue heron hanging out by the boat launch. He was sitting on a sign that said "No Fishing"; guess he can't read. As he kept jumping off the sign into the water grabbing a little fish then settling back onto the sign to eat it, he was great entertainment! As we headed back to the Dodge, we saw two little Bunnies hopping about and munching on the grass. Bunnies seem to be a theme this year's vacation. There were bunnies at Becky's each morning, bunnies each morning at Sissy's, Bunnies at Ponce De Leon Park. Ummm, guess I need to see a bunny at Keith and Kris's before I leave for New England.

Ended another great day back at Sissy's out on the lanai just as a tropical storm blew in! Strong winds blowing the rain sideways, palm fronds tumbling across the yard. Even sitting undercover on the lanai, we were getting wet! We retreated indoors and watched a movie in our jammies. Perfect relaxing end to a great day.

Pelicans vs. Dolphins!

February 2020

Here it was, Wednesday, already halfway through my Florida visit; time sure passes fast. I started the day my favorite way, enjoying coffee out on the lanai with my sister Sissy planning our day's adventures. After relaxing for a bit, we gathered up our picnic supplies and headed out for the day. I took Sissy to a couple places she needed to get this and that done, I was glad to be able to help her out since her car was still at the garage. We meandered our way to Venice Jetty for a picnic. Arrived at the Jetty to the usual crowd, I was a little worried about navigating the big Dodge van in the tight parking area at the Jetty. But luck was shining on us today! Right up front by the ocean was a wide spot open. I pulled in with a sigh of relief.

We sat in the van and enjoyed our lunch while watching the wind whipped waves crash over the rocks right in front of us. Some of the sea spray even hit the front of the van, and I had to turn on the windshield wipers to clear the windshield so we could see out. After eating, we walked along the Jetty, there were multiple brown pelicans bobbing on the waves, waiting patiently for some of the fishermen along the Jetty to share some of their catch with them. Little Rudy Turnstones scurried about the rocks at the water's edge. These are one of my favorite little shore birds. They are fun to watch as they scurry among the rocks in search of food.

We got to the end of the Jetty and there was a pod of three or four dolphins feeding! There must have been a school of fish just off the Jetty, we watched as they circled and dove in and out of the water. None of them actually breached, but they waved their tails and fins as they came up out of the water then dove back down. I've seen dolphins here before but not so many at once. We were enjoying watching them, and then suddenly, a group of four brown pelicans came flying in overhead and dove into the water right where the dolphins were. It was obvious that there was a large school of fish out there as the dolphins and pelicans began to battle for the fish. The water was swirling with activity as the dolphins dove in and out of the water and the pelicans dove in grabbed a fish and flew away. It was quite a show! But it looked like everyone got a belly full.

We headed back to Port Charlotte after watching the fiery sunset. I was heading back to Cape Coral in the morning. I was excited about Thursday! Again, this year, Jeanine and Charley flew in to join me in Florida while I was there. They took the red-eye from Colorado to Florida and arrived very early Wednesday morning, Christopher was very gracious to pick them up at the airport. Jeanine had told me ahead of time that they were coming but to not expect to see them till Thursday. She said they wanted to hang out and chill at her Aunt Becky's all-day Wednesday, which I certainly understood.

Exploring Sanibel Island

February 2020

So Thursday morning, I packed my stuff into the van, left Port Charlotte and headed to Cape Coral alone. Sissy had an appointment at the dealership to work on getting her car issues settled. On our way back from Venice, Jetty Wednesday I dropped her off at the mechanics to pick up her car so she was mobile again. I was disappointed she couldn't join us today, but she had to do what she had to do. When I arrived at the Circle B Hacienda, I felt like a teenager trying to sneak into the house after curfew. I knew both Christopher and Becky were working, and Becky's home office is right inside the front door so I was trying to be very quiet as I dragged my suitcase, etc., passed her office door, so as not to disturb her. Becky was sitting at her desk in front of her computer with her headphones on working, she looked up at me, I gave her a wave as I walked by. I put my belongings away in my assigned guest room. Gave Christopher a wave as I passed his office on my way to the lanai to greet Jeanine and Charley.

Got my hugs from Jeanine and Charley then we loaded into the van and set off on our adventure for the day to Sanibel Island! They were considering trying kite-boarding on the island. Unfortunately, yet again it was a Florida "cold" day and very windy. As we crossed over the causeway to the island, we went by a launch area. Just as I pulled in, we saw a wind gust catch a kite-boarders kite and lift it up off the surface of the water and slammed it back down into the water! A second kite-boarder also got blown over sideways and slammed into the water. Ummm, okay, kids, maybe today isn't the best time to try this new sport for the first time. We moved on.

We headed to Ding Darling National Wildlife Preserve to do some birding. Jeanine sure has heard enough stories about my birding trips there, I was anxious to show them one of my favorite Florida spots. I was hoping going on a weekday would mean less crowds. Nope! I couldn't even find a parking spot for the big van at the visitor center that was the first time I'd seen it so crowded there. We continued on along Wildlife Drive, though at a slower pace due to the crowd. There were rare bird reports of an African great white pelican being seen on the island; I'm sure that explained the crowd.

We stopped at the Mangrove pull off and walked along the boardwalk, it certainly was a very different environment to Jeanine and Charley than Colorado. I was hoping to see the roseate spoonbills or the African great white pelican in the lagoon at the clearing at the end of the trail. But all we saw were dozens of tree crabs and spiders! They were quite the attraction as a man pointed them out to us and others were taking close up pictures of the spiders sitting in their intricate webs. Interesting but not my cup of tea! Time to *move on*!

I was disappointed that Jeanine and Charley didn't get to experience Ding Darling at its best as the cold windy weather was keeping many of the birds in hiding and the crowded roadway made it tuff to stop at all the pull offs to explore. But they did get to experience the craziness of birding! It wasn't a total loss we saw twenty-four different species of birds. Jeanine got to see a Wood Stork to add to her life list. I got to enjoy watching one of my favorites, a purple gallinule as it plodded through the marsh with its big "snow shoe" yellow feet. On the shell mound trail, Charley was the first to locate the red-bellied woodpecker—good eyes, guy! And I was the one with the binoculars, but I couldn't find it. The three of us stood staring into the dense bushes trying to locate a songster flitting about the branches singing loudly. Found him! It was a blue-gray gnatcatcher.

Next, we stopped along the Causeway as we headed off the island. I just had to show them my favorite picnic spot. We found a picnic table in the shade and sat enjoying our picnic lunch and the beautiful ocean views. We walked along the water's edge collecting a few shells. Charley even found a star fish! That was a first! I've never found a star fish there before. We watched a group of brown pelicans diving into the water after fish. Gee those birds hit the water so hard and so fast you gotta wonder how they don't break their necks! Jeanine and Charley were enjoying strolling along the beach. We relaxed and hung out for a while, I enjoyed sharing one of my favorite spots with them, and they agreed. Now it was time to head back to the Circle B Hacienda.

Ended the day having fun with Becky doing a craft project she had bought. It was a craft kit intended for ages six and above, ummmm, but it wasn't super easy, or maybe it's just because it's been years since I've played with clay, LOL. Each of us had a plastic snow globe to design as we pleased. There were cute little plastic figures, a mermaid, seahorse or octopus and clay to shape into whatever else you wanted to add to the snow globe. And of course, lots of sparkling glitter to add to give the snow effect! It was indeed fun, sitting around the kitchen table with Becky, Jeanine, and Charley playing with clay, laughing and talking. Best way to end another great day with family!

Alligators! Alligators! Alligators!

February 2020

Okay, so now it's time for Friday's grand adventure! I had to leave tomorrow to return to New Hampshire, Friday was my last full day in Florida. The Florida crew all had to work, we had plans to meet up at the end of the day. So Jeanine, Charley, and I drove down into the Everglades for a day of adventure. Jeanine and Charley wanted to go on an airboat ride through the Everglades and Christopher had recommended a fun place he had tried out. It is defiantly one of those things you just gotta do when visiting Florida. The Everglades are a very special place. So we loaded the van with our picnic supplies, topped off the gas tank, and headed into the real Florida wilderness. It's a nice drive just under two hours from Cape Coral.

It's like night and day when you leave the highway and start the long straight cruise into the Everglades. Both sides of the road are mangrove swamps as far as the eye can see. Mixed with high spots here and there with scrub brush and palm trees. There are drainage ditches all along the side of the road separating the paved road from the wilderness. I told Jeanine and Charley to keep their eyes open! To watch for pink! As we were in the prime habitat for roseate spoonbills and flamingos, suddenly Charley says, "There's a pink bird flying overhead!" SCORE! A roseate spoonbill glided passed us. Good eyes, Charley! Then seconds later Jeanine calls out, "Look there's a swallow-tailed kite!" Believe me two sets of young eyes on the road were a birding bonus!

We arrived at Wootens Airboat Tours. Oh, I wasn't shy, as soon as the captain said to us all. Come on board, I headed right to the front and grabbed the front row seats on the large airboat! I wanted to make sure we got the best seats on the airboat so Jeanine and Charley got the full experience of an airboat ride. I have been on an airboat before, a few years earlier Bill took Sissy and I on a great adventure. But that airboat only sat five this one here sat almost a dozen, bigger boat, bigger engine, faster speed. Yeehaw! The captain gave us all the whole safety drill and told us all to put on the headphones provided, he warned us that this airboat had a big engine and that the ride was going to be noisy. Yippee! Sure sounds like we are about to have some fun!

As we were pulling away from the dock, the captain is apologizing to us all. He says, "Folks, sorry the weather is a bit below normal and it's windy today. I'll try not to get ya all too wet. Raise your hand if you don't want to get wet." I turned around, and yup, a couple of people did raise their hand, whimps. LOL. I will admit never thought I'd be in the Florida Everglades wearing long pants and a sweatshirt wishing I had gloves on. We raced through the swamp, zigzagging through the canals through the mangroves! The captain was doing circles in the wide-open areas and bouncing over dry land from canal to canal. Water splashing us! It was loud! It was windy! What a fun ride! It was exhilarating!

Boy did we see alligators! A good dozen or so. As the captain was telling us, that due to the cooler weather the alligators were spending more time out in the open lazing in the sun. That sure was to our advantage! Then the captain took the airboat through the grass lands area. He tells us to be prepared to see flocks of birds flying up as the Airboat flushes them out in the open. It was beautiful as a flock of snowy egrets is flushed up from the deep grasses and flies frantically in front of us! So glad we had the front row seats, it was so great watching the birds fly just feet away from us. I highly recommend if you're in the Everglades take this airboat tour.

On the drive back to Cape Coral, there were even more alligators everywhere, sunning themselves in the grassy areas along the side of the road. They weren't there on our way down but sure were on our way out. Alligators, alligators, alligators everywhere! Ended the day back at the Circle B Hacienda relaxing on the lanai with the rest of the Florida Crew enjoying a Farewell cookout. Tomorrow it was back to reality for me, as I had to board the plane and fly back into winter in New Hampshire. None of my winter escapes would be possible without my Florida family! I am so blessed and grateful for the generosity and hospitality from Sissy, Keith and Kris, Christopher and Becky. And thank you to Jeanine and Charley for taking time out of their busy work schedules to fly from Colorado to visit! Thank you to Shelby and Shawn for coming by an introducing me to our newest family member, Sophia! Thank you, thank you, thank you all! I so look forward to seeing everyone again at Family Reunion in August. Then it can be my turn to be the hostess and entertain you all.

Becky's Bluebirds

I was only home from my Florida February visit a couple weeks when I got an unexpected phone call from my sister Becky. She called to tell me that her follow-up posttreatment scan showed that the tumor in her lungs was still there! Additional testing revealed that the cancer had spread to other organs in her body. So shocking! We had all been praying for her recovery and were hopeful she had won her battle against this evil disease. She tells me she has an appointment with the doctor to discuss the next steps to take. I tell her how proud I am of how well she has handled this challenge she has had to face, that she has my love and support, and she is in my daily prayers.

To try and be a little bit upbeat we change the subject to birds. Becky tells me that she has continued to see the butter butts at the bird bath and that she thinks of me each time, she sees them. I thank her again for a wonderful visit. We talk about the fun times of doing crafts together, I tell her my favorite craft was the stained glass painted blue bird she made. I tell her I will send her a picture of the cute hummingbird I made that night and now have hung in my window and think of her each time I see it. She tells me, "I like hummingbirds but blue birds are my favorite. That's the reason I bought that craft kit." We laugh a little, and she tells me she will try and get another craft kit for my next visit and maybe she can find one that has a butter butt ornament.

I tell her I am praying for her complete recovery and looking forward to my annual February escape to Florida. She tells me that she is looking forward to putting an end to this hell and that she can't wait to fly back to New Hampshire for family reunion to relax at the cabin and see everybody. We end our conversation on this positive note. After I hang up the phone, I cry and pray to God to protect my dear sister Becky.

A few weeks passed, Becky did all she could but the situation spiraled down into darkness beyond anyone's control. The phone call from Christopher was the call no one ever wants to hear. Our dear sweet youngest sister Rebecca had passed away, peacefully at home surrounded by her immediate family. The grief and emotional pain was overwhelming. I understood she was in God's hands now, that her pain and suffering were over. I knew that Mommy and Daddy and Bill would be there at the gates of heaven to greet her. But life would never be the same without our Becky.

The next few weeks were very difficult for us all; the grief was overwhelming. The current pandemic travel restrictions made it impossible for family to travel to gather and say goodbye to our dear sister. The memorial plans Christopher had planned kept having to be put on hold, or canceled. The final plan was to bring Becky's remains back to her hometown in New Hampshire to place her remains in the family plot next to our Mother and Father. Christopher's grief was intensified by conditions completely out of his control. He had our support, and we all were praying conditions would improve soon.

As I would sit and say my daily prayers, I would ask God, "When will things be better? When will travel restrictions end, and we can bring Becky home to rest in peace?" When will our family's grief ease? I had faith that things would work out, I trusted God. Then it happened, a blue bird flew in and landed on the railing of the deck just outside the window I was sitting at! I instantly knew it was a sign from Becky in heaven! That she would be flying home to New Hampshire soon. I said out loud, "Becky, is that you?" The blue bird actually looked at me and cocked his head. It reminded me of my story, Stink Eye that the blue birds in Becky's yard used to give her. Brought back memories of time spent with Becky when she lived here in New Hampshire, sitting at her kitchen table watching the blue birds in her yard. My sister was indeed the queen of the blue birds.

To see this blue bird in my yard was unusual as I don't have the normal habitat that they live in. I began to question my sanity; did I really see that blue bird? Yes, I did it was real! Every day, I saw blue birds in the yard, ended up with a small flock of six, was that one blue bird to represent each sibling? I named them Sissy, Dougie, Jane, Christina, Eric, and Becky. Each time I took my daily walk I would see one or more of the blue birds in the trees along the driveway. Every morning, I would hear them singing just outside my window and sure enough one would land on the deck railing and look at me.

The final confirmation that I wasn't crazy, that these really were Becky's blue birds sent from heaven as a message of hope was unexpected. I drove to our old home town about an hour from my home to pay my respects to my parents at their grave site. As I was standing by their gravesite, saying a prayer and talking to them, telling them the plan to bring Becky home to New Hampshire and place her remains there in the family plot. The silence is broken by a singing blue bird in the tree above my head! I'm shocked and my eyes tear up.

Never ever have I heard or seen a blue bird here before. Becky's blue bird is defiantly here! And she will be here soon as well.

Looking back at all the fun memories shared with Becky on our birding adventures brings smiles to my broken heart. I cherish each memory. That is something we all need to remember, to enjoy time spent with loved ones, to cherish the everyday moments. Have faith in God. Be hopeful everything will be all right, be grateful for every moment of life. Get outside and enjoy nature. Look for Becky's blue birds! Stay positive.

As the old saying goes, the blue bird of happiness is present, as is hope.

About the Author

Since Jane Neskey was a child, she has enjoyed being outside exploring nature. She has worked to share and encourage her children and others to appreciate and protect nature. She has volunteered her time to various organizations, served on her town and states organizations to protect the environment and its creatures. Birding became her main hobby and brought so many great adventures and experiences to her life.